A PLUME B

I SAID YES TO EV

Praise for *I Said Yes to Everything*

"The elegant theater and screen actress bares all of her insecurities and regrets. . . . But there's also an intimacy and directness in how she shares— including numerous dishy, behind-the-glam anecdotes. . . . Grant has lived a long, full life. While she may prefer to be coy about precisely how long it's lasted so far, *I Said Yes to Everything* serves as evidence that it's been long enough to give her a meaty, multifaceted, and compelling story to tell."

—Jen Chaney, *The Washington Post*

"Lee Grant's blacklist memoir is deliciously indiscreet. She has written the definitive tell-all about life on the blacklist, and no one who cares at all about those dark days can afford not to read it."

—Victor S. Navasky, author of National Book Award–winning *Naming Names*

"Lee Grant came to know herself as a child, as an actress, as a woman, and as a thinker. I have come to know her intimately in reading her book, and am so grateful for the experience."

—Vanessa Redgrave

"Having had the privilege to work with Lee Grant on the motion picture screen was truly a delight. Now, out of nowhere, she has written a most wonderful book about her family and herself. It's warm, it's touching, and it's a book that speaks of the human experience—the wonders of it, the magic of it, the difficulties of it, the history of a life's unfolding, beautifully and brilliantly, with purpose and with guts."

—Sidney Poitier

"Read this book—every juicy page! Lee has lived her life and practiced her craft with reckless abandon, bravery, honesty, and ultimately brutal clarity. You will want to be her friend, lover, child, or student, and you will finish the final pages her ardent admirer. A ferocious and fragile woman who unapologetically states: 'For better or for worse, I'm right here!'"

—Frank Langella

"If there is any adventure, from love to politics, that you feel you've missed in life, Lee Grant has had it for you—and describes it here with wit, honesty, and all five senses. No one, but no one, has better explained, say, the difference between the theater and Hollywood, between love and romance, or between families born and chosen. Go ahead, live a little. Say yes to Lee Grant."

—Gloria Steinem

"Lee Grant's *I Said Yes to Everything* is heart-stopping. More than just a show-business memoir or chronicle of the Hollywood blacklist era, it is a terrifying account of a gifted artist's tumultuous journey—both personal and professional. You will feel every jolt of terror that Grant endured, wondering if you would have been as brave. Her triumph becomes our own. Readers of this gripping book will surely reach the final page shouting a victorious 'Yes!' to everything that is Lee Grant."

—Marlo Thomas

"Lee Grant—I have worked with her—is a great actress. Lee Grant is also my friend—a great conversationalist. I never knew about her writing talent. She has written a wonderful book. It made me laugh, it made me cry. Read it!"

—Kirk Douglas

"Lee knows how to tell a good story with passion, honesty, and a good sense of humor."

—Michael Douglas

"It's so easy to say 'Yes!' I loved Lee Grant's memoir—everything about it! She is direct, honest, witty, and compelling!"

—Dyan Cannon

"The minute I looked at the new memoir [by] actress Lee Grant, I knew I wouldn't be able to resist *I Said Yes to Everything*. . . . I'm afraid I pretty much abandoned everything else until I read it. Lee Grant is one of America's greatest actors, most heroic survivors, a contradictory enigma one minute, a sympathetic victim the next . . . who keeps turning it all around into triumph."

—Liz Smith

"Lee Grant's *I Said Yes to Everything* is a fantastic read. Beautifully written and brutally honest, she takes us through the highs and lows of her brilliant career and incredibly interesting personal life. I loved every page of it."

—Joy Behar

"No-holds-barred . . . Grant doesn't make us read between the lines here; it's all right there, on the page. When she was jubilant after winning an Oscar for her supporting role in *Shampoo*, we know it; when she was disgusted, as when a television network canceled her series without telling her, we know it, too; and, of course, when she was dismayed and bewildered and depressed when she couldn't find work during her twelve-year blacklisting, we know it for sure. . . . An excellent show-business autobiography."

—*Booklist* (starred review)

"In this wonderful memoir, actor Grant charts her life from a childhood in New York City through her performance in *Shampoo* and beyond. . . . Whether recalling the traumas of her first marriage to screenwriter Arnold Manoff or sharing entertaining memories of her famous friends, Grant does so with a lively, approachable tone. Though famous for her achievements as a multi-award-winning actor, director, and documentarian, Grant reveals herself to be a woman unafraid of continual self-reinvention. These pages tell a gripping story full of drama, humor, and hardship, offering an intimate look into the singular life of one indefatigable protagonist."

—*Publishers Weekly*

"The resilience of [Lee Grant's] career outlasted the twelve-year period when she was blacklisted by HUAC for her political affiliations. . . . She became one of the most respected actresses of her generation. . . . Rife with appearances from some of Hollywood's biggest names, including an unsuccessful date with Marlon Brando, Grant's career proves that the elusive and oft-sought-after second chance can not only be had, it can be triumphantly redeeming. An insightful, sharp Hollywood memoir that will appeal to fans and newcomers alike."

—*Kirkus Reviews*

i said yes to everything

| A MEMOIR |

LEE GRANT

A PLUME BOOK

PLUME
An imprint of Penguin Random House LLC
375 Hudson Street
New York, New York 10014
penguin.com

First published in the United States of America by Blue Rider Press,
an imprint of Penguin Random House LLC, 2014
First Plume Printing 2015

THE LIBRARY OF CONGRESS HAS CATALOGED THE BLUE RIDER PRESS EDITION AS FOLLOWS:

Grant, Lee, date.
I said yes to everything : a memoir / Lee Grant.
p.   cm.
Includes index.
ISBN 978-0-399-16930-4 (hc.)
ISBN 978-0-14-751628-2 (pbk.)
1. Grant, Lee, date.   2. Actors—United States—Biography.
3. Motion picture producers and directors—Biography.   I. Title.
PN2287.G6753A3   2014   2014011916
791.4302'8092—dc23
[B]

Printed in the United States of America
10 9 8 7 6 5 4 3 2

Original hardcover design by Amanda Dewey

I dedicate this book to

Joey,

to Dinah and Belinda and their families,

Phyllis,

and

to my mother, father, and Aunt Fremo.

CONTENTS

*i said yes
to everything*

OVERTURE

Once, when I was little, I dreamed that I could fly. I dreamed that when I breathed in, I flew upward, weightless, above the heads of all the children in the granite playground. When I breathed in I went up, up, up; when I breathed out I could swoop down and touch the tops of their heads. I swirled gracefully in the air, in my brown winter coat with the velvet collar from De Pinna's. I woke up so excited that I threw off my blanket and ran from my bed to the window in my bedroom. I threw the window open and climbed onto the radiator cover. The birds were flying outside. I would join them. I spread my arms, and from the seventh floor I saw the sparrows swooping toward the concrete below. Suddenly I saw myself smashing beside them. It shocked me, and I was afraid of myself and how easily I could fool myself into disaster.

I climbed down from the radiator. My mother opened the door. "Who opened the window?" she said. "It's cold in here."

I've experienced that sense of exaltation and intensity in my life many times: in adolescence, when the boys made my heart pound; in acting, when I jumped without a net, and flew, and turned, and *believed for those few hours that I inhabited another's life, and experienced new joy and pain. I've felt safe in flight, in love, in sex, and with those who flew with me.*

I've also jumped and died, not once, but many times, unwisely and impetuously. I flew into fame as a very young Broadway actress, then jumped (through my first husband) into the Communist Party, only to find myself blacklisted for twelve years. I've reinvented myself many times over, picked up my broken wings and flapped till I could hop around again.

I'm flying again now, in my bedroom, writing, looking out my window. I had no idea, until I began putting pen to paper, that so many memories were inside me waiting to be rediscovered. I'm very lucky. I may even come to know myself.

My Family

My mother's job was to mold me into her American Dream. Didn't young Witia from Odessa expose the child in her belly to every art museum in New York City, every day that she could carry me on her long legs? The magic of transformation was real in her young life. The Jewish child hunted in her cellar by goyim on horseback was transplanted to a new land where anything was possible, if you made it happen. And she wanted to make it happen for her daughter.

Witia was determined to plunge her hands into my baby fat and model me into a superior, beautiful being, who would either marry rich or rise above all others in the arts: ballet, theater.

There was no question about it.

My father was born in the Bronx, the youngest son of Polish Orthodox Jewish immigrants. His brother and sisters were ambitious. His brother, Aaron, and sister Anne were show business lawyers.

My father, Abraham, was the good son, the good man. He graduated from Columbia, where he had studied economics with John

Dewey and was on the wrestling team. He kept a neat, tight, muscular body all his life. He bent his head over the radio every Saturday afternoon to listen to the Metropolitan Opera. He loved coloraturas. My father was the director of the Young Men's and Young Women's Hebrew Association of the Bronx. It was a position of great responsibility, great dignity. He was the moral compass of the family.

My grandfather went to shul every day. His tiny wife, Ida, kept an Orthodox home. They lived in a clean, old apartment on College Avenue in the Bronx. Their children must have supported them, because my grandfather never left the shul for his hardware store. But they and America raised smart, goal-oriented children.

The story goes that my mother went to the Bronx Y to get a job giving classes in dance. She had just graduated from college, where she majored in movement in the Isadora Duncan tradition. I have pictures of her from school. She was beautiful—five feet seven, straight back, long shining dark hair, hazel eyes. When she smiled, her top and bottom teeth glistened like a Spanish dancer's.

She sat in the chair in my father's office, reciting her qualifications for the job. She was rocking in the chair, nonchalant, when she did one rock too many. The chair tipped over and she landed on the floor. My father came from behind his desk, laughing, and helped up my flustered, embarrassed mother. And that. Was that.

My mother's name was Witia Haskell, Americanized from Vitya Haskelovich. Her mother, Dora, had five children—three boys, Joseph, Raymond, and Jack, and two girls, Witia and Fremo. I never knew my grandfather Leon, for whom I was named. He was a clothing designer and a committed Zionist who left for Palestine with several other Zionist men before I was born. He must have done well, because he bought the brownstone on 148th and Riverside Drive before he returned to Palestine to establish a Jewish state.

They all died of malaria while fighting for their cause. There is a plaque in Rishon LeZion with his name on it. In Russian *Leon* is *Lyov*, as in Lyov Tolstoy, Leo Tolstoy. My name is Lyova. There is no such name in Russian. Try being a Lyova in a world of Bettys and Judys and Emilys and Janes.

Position your tongue for an *L*, then say *yaw*, then *vah*. In high school I changed the *V* to an *R* and Lyora, pronounced *Leora*, was born. Hence Lee.

From the time I can remember remembering, I was my mother's beloved thing, little girl, petted, brushed, combed, bathed, fed, beautiful, lived through. Her life. Her lovely sweet breath. The light in her hazel eyes.

I woke up this morning dreaming about my childhood on 148th Street. I'd learned early on from my mother that some of the women in my father's family had made my mother's life so miserable, had criticized her and picked on her so much, that she didn't know where to turn. And her husband, my father, refused to take sides or defend her. The mean women in my father's family, the Rosenthals of Poland, thrived on attack, thrived on gossip. My mother didn't have a chance. There was no mean bitch in her Russian genes. She took me to my grandmother's brownstone on 148th Street to live. I must have been three or even younger when she and my father separated.

We lived at 620 West 148th Street between Riverside Drive and Broadway until I was six. My mother and I slept on the bird's-eye maple beds in the big bedroom on the second floor, with an ornate white potty underneath. There was no bathroom on the second floor. On the ground floor was the Haskell Nursery School that my mother and her younger sister, Fremo, ran.

In summer the Haskell Nursery School was a busy, humming place. All the attention wasn't on me. Fifteen or so little children from the neighborhood arrived every morning. One morning, as I opened the door, one of them asked me, "Does everyone call you Lovey because they love you so much?" A lurch went through me. Is this what love is? A new word, a new concept.

In warm weather there were games in my grandmother's house with children, painting with Fremo, and being wild and free in the backyard. In winter the children didn't come and I was pushed alone into an empty, cold yard in my ugly orange and brown snowsuit, the first snowsuit on the block, my mother told me. I was bored much of the time. Bored and lonely. I had two ratty baby dolls with cloth bodies that I felt really close to. Their eyes, blue of course, opened and closed.

I fell inside myself as an only child. Other children were the holy grail—I longed for little girls to play with. My Aunt Fremo was a girlfriend. She was a grown child, delightful, peculiar.

Mostly I was coddled, and bored, and observant. I was participant and audience. I was steered into dance, given books, which I read and read. I listened. To Mother and Fremo. I was sleeping awake, doing what I was told.

In winter I climbed up to the window and pressed my forehead to the cold pane. I could see our cement yard with its one big tree in the middle.

Our house was full. Uncles Joe, who became a lawyer in Great Neck, and Raymond, who worked for the post office, and Jack lived there, Fremo, Grandma, Mother, and me. I was four. My uncles, especially Joe, teased me and played jokes on me. After my bath, when I was naked. They teased me about my behind when I clutched the towel in front of me. When I covered my behind they teased me about my front. They laughed deep men's laughs, especially Uncle Joe.

My childhood was a waiting period, cocoon-like and plump. I don't remember any strong feelings. I was a not-unwilling lump, but watching carefully.

I was not allowed to play on the streets with the exciting and exotically normal children. Right next door was the mysterious huge white apartment building 706 Riverside Drive, which contained all the children I longed for. It also contained Mrs. McCarthy and her handsome twenty-year-old son, John.

My mother allowed me to visit Mrs. McCarthy in her apartment by myself. I would sit on the footstool, looking up at her. She sat in the armchair opposite me. There, with the shades half-drawn, she would pour out her fears and concerns for her son. John was a drinker. Her pale face was crumpled in sadness and worry. Her sad, limp fingers played with a hankie, and she poured her heart out to me. I loved it. I loved Mrs. McCarthy. I loved her for raising me out of the oatmeal plainness of my days. Her stories were moving and thrilling. John was the center, the hero, the villain, the love of her life, lost to her now. Once, the front door opened. "That's him," she said, tightening her hand on my arm. It was midafternoon. A tall, dark-haired young man entered, a little off balance. I remember his head coming down to mine, the gray eyes crinkling, the white smile and pink cheeks. He must have said "Hello there" and gone off to his room. Mrs. McCarthy's hand was tight on mine. I understood everything.

Her John reminded me of my Uncle Jack, who lived on the top floor. Jack was younger than John, but also handsome and funny, and he teased me and made me laugh as if I were tickled. I wasn't allowed to enter Uncle Jack's room because he had TB, but I would climb to the top of the stairs and run down again. It was our game—he sitting in bed on his white sheets cross-legged, me running up to his open door and down the staircase. Jack died when he was twenty-one. I'm crying as I write this, thinking of his lonely spirit trapped on the fourth floor. Mother said he was in the sky with the stars. She took me to the window and pointed at the purple sunset. It made no sense to me.

Mrs. McCarthy gave me a book. It had caricatures and illustrations of human foibles acted out by wonderful, outrageous cats. Men cats in camel-hair coats, lady cats dripping with pearls in compromising positions. I got it. The cat book disappeared one day. My mother must have opened the pages. I wasn't allowed to visit Mrs. McCarthy anymore.

I missed Mrs. McCarthy. She trusted me. She didn't treat me like a five-year-old but saw the person I could be. I worried about her for a long time. Maybe it was she who opened me to the fear and pain of others. Maybe it was my Uncle Jack.

My heart aches for us all. The lonely only child; the beautiful immigrant mother responsible in her heart for everyone in our house. Her dreams for me, and her protectiveness, would result in an explosion of rebellion from her only child that almost destroyed her.

The Met

I was four years old crossing the walkway high above the stage at the old Metropolitan Opera House on my way to ballet class. The sound of the song rising from the tenor on the big stage below was so powerful, I almost fainted. I hung on with both hands to the rope on the sides.

"Move!" they were hissing behind me.

We had to be quiet. I couldn't move. I was waiting for the thick buzz in my head to clear. I was literally drowning in the passion the unknown singer had thrown up to the old Metropolitan eaves. Someone, maybe an older girl thinking I was frightened, unhooked my hands from the rope railing and led me to the door of our ballet class. I later learned it was an aria from *La Bohème*.

The big elevator had broken down again, so our class, like little Madelines, had the rare privilege of crossing the great stage on our way to the opera house's elevator, which would take us out on that catwalk crossing the top of the theater.

That morning Giulio Gatti-Casazza, the Met's manager, pointed at me.

"You," he said. "You."

He needed a Chinese prince, a child, who is kidnapped in San Francisco by Antonio Scotti, the great baritone, in a short opera called *L'Oracolo*. It was to be Scotti's farewell performance, and he had to be able to carry the "prince" across the big stage and into the wings. The more Gatti-Casazza screamed "Relax!" the more I stiffened in Scotti's arms, until I lay across them like a board. I finally collapsed and he carried me across the stage. I got the part.

I'm on the big stage at the Met. I'm Hu-Cî, a Chinese prince. Antonio Scotti rolls an orange to me and I roll it back. Then he races to the wings carrying me. I love the big, big stage. I can't even see the edges. The lights are pink and blue and white and reflect off the dark wooden floor. The orchestra is in front, in a huge dark place, and beyond in the dark, a sea of people stretch to the back walls and to the ceiling in tiers. People, loving the music, the singing, and me. Loving me. I love the world onstage. I am swept away, surrounded by the boom of the music, the glory of all the voices, especially the soprano of Lucrezia Bori, the violins, the brass, and the big thumping drum.

I shared a dressing room with Gladys Swarthout, who sang in *Cavalleria Rusticana*, on a double bill with *L'Oracolo*, but my dressing room rights were taken away after I warned the tenor onstage that Mr. Scotti was sneaking up on him with a big knife to stab him in the back.

It was my Uncle Joe who had convinced me to save the tenor's life.

"You ought to do it," he said. "You see the bad man with that big knife? The tenor's back is turned to him. Only you can save him. Everyone would be so proud of you."

"How?"

"You pull the tenor's sleeve. Say, 'He's coming, he's coming. Turn around.' Yell it at him. Surprise him. Surprise your mother. She'll be so proud."

And so that night, as Mr. Scotti raised his big knife and the tenor was singing his heart out to Miss Bori, looking down from her balcony, I whispered, "He's going to kill you. Please, please turn around, he's coming behind you—"

The music was loud, his voice was loud and frantic. I started to yell above the music and pull at his arm. He pushed me away, his eyes flash at me in terror.

"Turn around," I insisted.

He turned just in time to see the knife raised to kill him, then turned back quickly to resume his aria to Lucrezia on the balcony. Come to think of it, why didn't she ever warn him? She could see the whole thing, too.

The audience burst into laughter as the knife plunged into the tenor's back, and into applause for me as I joined the finale, making up my own song with its own language, joining the opera stars singing theirs in Italian. Even the serious prompter in his box facing the stage was smiling and winking at me.

When my distraught mother confronted him, my Uncle Joe said he never really meant for me to actually do it. Gatti-Casazza was so angry that I was banned from Miss Swarthout's dressing room. I was no longer visible when the tenor was stabbed. A replica of a sidewalk cellar shed was created onstage, and I was stored there from the time I was kidnapped until the finale. I wasn't bored. I could see everybody's feet and the parades upstage and hear the music.

And *The New York Times* said, "Little Lyova Haskell Rosenthal is precocious."

I thought at the time it meant "precious," and at that time in my grandmother's house, I really was.

. . .

Abner Rasumoff lay stretched out on a string hammock in the backyard of the brownstone. I sat on a tree stump. His brown-blond hair dipped in a wave over his forehead. He swung in the hammock. We were very conscious of each other. I found it difficult to breathe and make conversation. Two lines appeared between his eyebrows, as if he were concentrating on something important, manly.

"Don't frown," I said, echoing my mother's constant warnings. "You'll get wrinkles."

"If I don't will you marry me?"

My heart lurched. I could feel the air go out of me. I waited until I could talk.

"Yes," I said with certainty.

There was a minute of hesitation. Something more should follow. Should I lie on the hammock, too? The yard still looked the same.

"Let's tell our mothers," I said.

He was still looking ahead, not at me. I was afraid the moment would pass. He rose up from the hammock and held out his hand. It was dry and warm. We walked across the yard, up the wooden steps to the porch, and into the kitchen.

"Abner and I are getting married," I said.

Oh, the cries from our mothers, the cakes, the tea that was pressed on us, the celebration. His mother, Musea Rasumoff, of the white, white skin and red hair, my mother, Witia, and my grandmother, with her rough fingers in my hair. Abner and I accepted the music of our mothers, basked in their warmth and our own importance. I was five years old. Abner was nine.

To celebrate, Musea, clapping her hands, danced to the upright piano used for the nursery school. A hand at her heart. Her eyes matched her blue eyelids. She sang in Russian, swaying, carried away by her own passion. Overcome by longing, she pulled at the low neckline of her dress, sang and pulled until a whole breast appeared. She ignored it and finished on a husky high note. My mother clapped her hands.

"Musea, your breast, your breast is exquisite," my mother exclaimed, gesturing toward it. "You've had two boys. How do you manage to keep your breasts like that?"

Musea pulled down her dress to reveal the matching one, and my mother gasped.

"Oh Musea!"

"Witia," said Musea, "when I have breakfast in the morning, I say to my orange juice—go-o-o to the right breast." She pantomimed a sip. "Go-o-o to the left breast . . ."

I looked over at Abner. He was eating his fruitcake, drinking tea, his eyes fixed on the table, his ears and cheeks pink. I wanted to move over to him, but I knew he didn't want me to.

That whole winter, I would steal glances at my mother during breakfast. With each sip of juice or cider vinegar she would close her eyes, tilt her head to the side of her body she was addressing, and mouth the words silently and prayerfully.

I entered the office with my mother. She said that maybe I could be in a movie, with a great songwriter. There, sitting at the edge of the desk, her long legs crossed in front of her, was a beautiful lady with an orange face. She was turning over pages with orange hands. We were greeted by Gus Edwards, an older man, short and square, with a wide smile. His forehead and hands were also orange, but mixed with tan. Edwards had cowritten "School days, school days, dear old golden rule days, readin' and writin' and 'rithmetic, taught to the tune of a hickory stick," and was now starring in and directing a short movie set in a classroom.

He was set to sing the song to a classroom full of children seated at their desks while their mothers milled around before filming began. The lady with the orange face was the teacher. My mother flashed her shining smile at Gus, showing both rows of teeth.

I was placed at a desk in the back of the class, with a pencil and a notebook. A cute boy with brown hair and an Irish face turned to me and looked into my eyes when Gus sang, "You were my queen in calico, I was your bashful, barefoot beau."

When Gus sang "I love you, Joe," I held up my notebook to show the boy; it was written on the page. The camera was on me, looking at him so seriously, a big white bow in my hair.

I saw it once, I don't know where, and felt the jolt of recognition. Somewhere in that five-year-old girl was a presence, a mystery, the me to come, hiding behind the eyes.

Paris

I would visit my father some weekends, on College Avenue in the Bronx, where he lived with his parents. The walk-up apartment smelled of stewing chicken and spices.

My grandparents' small, neat, white bedroom looked out onto a courtyard that was pure theater. Fire escape upon fire escape full of families popping in and out of windows. The duvet on the bed was a marvel, a two-foot-high cloud of soft feathered down, which they let me dive into.

Aunt Anne, who lived in the front room overlooking the street, invited a friend over, a lady with a big red mouth who kept laughing and touching my father. She leaned on him, laughing. Sitting on the chair watching, I felt a clutch at my heart. I was jealous. I ran to my father and pushed her away. They pointed at me and laughed, but I didn't. I hated her.

Not long after, I was asleep in my bed when my mother woke me. She was radiant and smiling. She wore a dress the color of cream of tomato soup, crepe, with a V-neck edged in a white organdy collar that stood up in waves and framed her beautiful face.

"Daddy and I are getting back together."

She squeezed me and hugged me, imprinting me with the scent of Shalimar, then held me away so she could see my reaction.

"Lyova, we'll all be together . . ." I was sleepy. It was a good dream.

The condition my father agreed to in order for our family to be together again was to grant my mother's wish to spend a year in Paris with Fremo and me.

No wonder she was so excited. A year in Paris!

Fremo left for France weeks before us because I had a fever. So my mother and I sailed together on the *Île de France*. As I reached the top of the gangplank and followed the curve of the ship, heady with excitement, a young man reached out and pulled my hair. I turned. He was sitting on the railing, laughing, the sun behind him giving his tweed jacket and his black hair an aureole. I leaned against my mother's legs and looked up at his shining face, his shining teeth, his teasing eyes. I fell in love.

Looking up at my mother, I felt she had, too. Her face was glowing from his attention. He was a young doctor, I remember. Days later, they went to the ship's masquerade together. She had made a costume for me, a gypsy girl, I think. I had never been so excited before. I wanted to show my costume to him, to dazzle him, but the night of the masquerade my mother told me I couldn't go. Children weren't allowed.

Plead, plead, plead.

"No!" She stood her ground.

"Why?" I yowled, the unfairness of life closing in on me, yet another life lesson.

The magic of attraction, the unfairness of my competition: my mother.

Then one morning, in the belly of the big boat, a family of beautiful blond-haired children ran past me, like a shimmering stream of white goldfish. The girl's hair was long. She was about ten, her brothers younger. I turned and started to run after them when the youngest boy, maybe six, turned suddenly and punched me hard in the belly. I was so startled by the pain that I stood still, in the middle of the big ship's hallway, feeling circle after circle of pain rise and ebb inside me, holding my breath till I could breathe again. I stood there a long time afterward.

On deck the next day I saw the girl without her brothers talking to a bursar. It was sunny and breezy. Her white-yellow hair flew behind her, her arms were tan, and on her head was a blue satin ribbon that said ÎLE DE FRANCE. I went up to her.

"Where did you get your ribbon?"

"Jews aren't allowed to wear these," she snapped, then turned and ran.

"What's a Jew?" I asked my mother in the stateroom.

"Why?" she asked. I told her.

That evening she brought me three ribbons that said ÎLE DE FRANCE on them. But I didn't care.

Paris was spring dresses, a pale green one with a collar that crossed and buttoned. I prayed when I put it on, "God, please let Fremo say changing to this dress was wise."

The door opened. Fremo came in.

"Lovey," she said. "How wise of you."

Yes!

We stayed with a French uncle and aunt, my cousin Charlotte, and her brother. The French girls my age were delicious scamps. Charlotte and I walked back from the bakery with fresh baguettes, smelling the tops of the hot bread, then eating it, while the girl downstairs stuck her tongue out at me. I was like a sheltered puppy out on a leash for the first time. The children didn't love me, as they had in the Haskell

Nursery School. They were wild and beautiful, and I loved them, not they me.

The Luxembourg Gardens, the puppet shows, the sounds and smells of spring, the boys whipping their wheels, learning table French at my cousins' table—"*Donnez-moi le pain et le beurre, s'il vous plaît*"—all were enchanting. Fremo and I wandering the back streets together, coming on a wedding and climbing the little church steps to sit in the back and watch.

In autumn we left my cousins and found grim rooms for the three of us. My eyelids stuck together in the morning. My mother bathed them in warm boric acid till I could open them. It frightened me. Mother was having gas pains and staying in bed. We stuck out three months of our year in Paris and steamed home on the *Paris*.

And so, for the first time in my memory, we were to be a family, a traditional American family. Mother, Daddy, and me. Before my sixth birthday I'd discovered I had a low tolerance for boredom, a high tolerance for physical pain, fell hopelessly in love, found an ally in God, and discovered I was a Jew.

Reunited, we moved to 706 Riverside Drive, the big beautiful white apartment building next to my grandmother's brownstone. One entrance led out to 148th Street; the other, grander entrance was on the Drive. There was a bus stop in front of it. In those years all the buses were double-deckers, and the life seen through other people's windows—other children looking back at me or playing in their rooms, grown-ups setting tables—became my fascination. I spent a lot of time on that bus from the age of four till nine. Those were the early years, when my mother's lofty dream was that I be a great ballerina in the Met's corps de ballet. Twice a week in coldest winter we traveled down to the old Met on Broadway and 37th Street for my ballet lesson with Miss Curtis, the children's ballet mistress. In snow, in wind, we rode downtown and back again on the number 5 bus. It seemed an interminable ride. In those days, girls wore neither pants nor tights. All winter long I wore a warm English wool coat with a velvet collar and kneesocks. The space where my socks ended and my white cotton panties began was open to the fierce, bitter cold wind of the Drive. I always had chapped thighs in the winter. Once, when it had snowed for days and an icy wind was blowing, I went out the entrance on the Drive. The snow was thigh-high. A cat with gray fur was frozen. Standing on its back feet, its claws out to fight the wind, its mouth wide open, its teeth bared, yellow eyes opened wide in rage. Facing the river.

Our seventh-floor living room had a big window that covered almost the whole wall. We had a view of the Hudson all the way up to the George Washington Bridge. My mother built a long window seat fitted with a long pillow. It was a wonderful place to sit and read after school when it was too cold to go outside. In the warmer months, in spring and fall, all the girls from 706 would tumble out onto the street, breathless with freedom from school, from parents, from piano lessons or, in my case, ballet.

My mother had charmed George Balanchine into inviting me to join the newly formed School of American Ballet, along with another child from Miss Curtis's class at the Met, Anne Marie Conradi. Anne Marie was a marvel. We were only eight or nine, but already she had a dancer's body, long and lithe—and remarkable, almost mathematical technique. We were the only children in Pierre Vladimiroff's classes. Anne Marie could keep up with all the great dancers in the class. It was clear to everyone but my mother that I could not. I was obedient but unhappy. Anne Marie was absent for a couple of weeks. We learned she had tuberculosis of the hip and could not dance anymore. The sense I had of my own lack of talent and of Anne Marie, a real star being brought down, was vivid and haunting. I spoke to my father about it. He had no notion of my dancing ability. All he heard was tuberculosis, and he informed my mother at dinner that night that there would be no more dangerous ballet for me. It was an edict. My mother regretfully accepted it, and we moved on to the other arts. I was free (of ballet). No more buses in winter, cold legs, no more peering into other people's windows and lives.

Life Lessons

I was raised in a house where no one ever suggested I read a newspaper. The outside world had no meaning for me whatsoever. If my mother opened the paper she went straight to the sales at Bendel's. Or Bergdorf's. She knew the salesladies intimately, and went to the final sales. My father was an intellectual, but his job was where he discussed the world, not his home. Our home seemed to be built around me. Like Gigi's guardians, my mother and Aunt Fremo had very grandiose ideas, which they drank up from the American movies, and I was the recipient of all their passionate attention. Now I would be groomed to be a great painter, a great singer, then actor, and if all else failed, I would marry a rich boy, then divorce him, get alimony, then marry another rich boy. Oh, Colette! Oh, Gigi!

I started public school in third grade, at the age of seven, at PS 145 on 145th Street and Broadway. Up till then, my mother and Fremo had taught me at home.

Mrs. Cherry was my teacher. Straight-backed, red-haired, hard. My first week in school we had a spelling test for the entire school. Blackboard walls were slid away and all the different classes were revealed—one large auditorium holding first through eighth grades. Our class was in the middle of the last row. The teacher of another class sat at her desk behind me, facing her own class.

My mother had taught me to call pee *number one.*

In the middle of the spelling test I tiptoed up to Mrs. Cherry at her desk.

"I have to do number one."

"Get back to your seat, we're in the middle of a test," she hissed.

I hurried back to my little desk and tried to concentrate on spelling. Trying to hold everything in. I couldn't concentrate. I tiptoed up to Mrs. Cherry again.

"Mrs. Cherry, I really have to go," I pleaded.

"Back to your seat." She rose and pointed.

"Please?"

She pointed to my desk again.

I was wearing a short cotton dress with puffed sleeves. As I sat down again, the dam burst. My long wooden seat filled with warm, yellow liquid that spread and spread until my little bench filled. It spilled over the sides onto the floor. The boy at the next desk watched in disbelief. Looking at me, then at the seat, then at the floor.

The teacher at the desk behind me must have turned at the sound of liquid splashing. She grabbed my arm and guided me up the long rows of classes and out of the auditorium. She was young and kind. She took me to the bathroom, but I had no more use for it. My underpants were soaked, and the back of my dress and legs. I found the door to 145th Street and ran all the way home. My mother was furious with me. She changed my clothes and sent me back to school. I thought I would die of shame, but no one seemed to know what had happened. Not Mrs. Cherry, not even the boy.

The lasting memory I have of third grade is Mrs. Cherry and Foster. Foster was black. He was neatly dressed in a shirt and tie and was the tallest boy in class. He did something Mrs. Cherry didn't like. She punished him by having him walk from her desk, where she stood with a ruler, around the back of the class, back to her, then hold out his hands, which she hit hard with the ruler. At least ten times. The braver Foster was, the more I hated Mrs. Cherry; the harder she hit, the blanker his expression, the more I admired him.

One afternoon, I came home with a new friend from school. I remember how excited we were to find each other, running down 148th Street laughing. When I look at the face of my granddaughter Rachel, I see the face of that friend, so open, so dear, so beautiful, also black. After we played together in my room, and my new best girlfriend picked up her book bag to go, my mother swept into the dining room with a laundry bag of my old clothes, which she pushed on my friend with laughing generosity. "Take them, take them. Lyova can't wear them anymore!"

My new friend looked at me. I looked away. "She doesn't want them," I muttered. "She doesn't need them."

"Take them, take them," my mother insisted, pushing the full laundry bag into the little girl's arms.

I avoided her eyes. There was no arguing with my mother.

"All right," she said.

I was too ashamed to see her to the door. I was swallowing shame. "You ruin everything!" I cried, and ran to my room and wept. I knew, even then, how insulting an act of charity could be to a child, how demeaning, how "put in her place" my friend was. I never asked her home again.

Our new maid (housekeepers were called maids in those days), Rose, was a tall, thin, elderly black lady who had no teeth. She would hold her scarf or hand to her mouth when she spoke, covering it in a very genteel manner. Rose was kind. She would travel by trolley, accompanying me to my new school on 135th Street and Convent Avenue. I had entered a new school in the fourth grade. I was eight. I didn't know anybody in my class. They were a new breed. Wild. Reckless. I felt very outside.

I sat in the back of the class at first. The boy next to me leered at me and poked his yellow pencil up and down on the zipper of his pants. I looked away. He kept doing it. After the school day I told the teacher. The next day he was gone. *Hmm*, I thought to myself, *this teacher will like me if I keep telling her what is going on in class.* I didn't know what a snitch was. I soon found out.

One afternoon the teacher left the room. Two high-spirited athletic Irish girls started throwing the blackboard eraser to each other. Laughing and scrambling over the desks. Shards of chalk swam in the sunshine.

The teacher reentered. "Who did this?" she demanded, waving her hand to dispel the chalk and picking up the fallen eraser. "Who did this?" she demanded again.

I looked around the room and saw that no one was going to tell the teacher the truth but me, the new girl. I raised my hand high.

"Yes, Lyova?"

"It was those girls there. That one and that one that threw the erasers."

Silence. The girls I pointed out turned toward me, openmouthed, as did the whole fourth-grade class, even the teacher. Obviously, I thought, I impressed everyone with my honesty.

On the clanging iron stairs down to the courtyard after school, one of the Irish girls hissed in my ear, "I'm gonna get you for that. Just wait till we get outside . . ."

I can't believe this is happening. One shaking foot goes from one step to the next. I am becoming very afraid of what is going to happen to me. We empty out into the school courtyard, and the whole class forms a ring around me, my school bag, and my De Pinna dress. The two Irish girls are making boxing motions toward me, yelling, tough. The whole class is encouraging them. I am "it." I've never hit anyone. I don't know the protocol. I realize I am just going to have to take it when Rose, who just arrived to pick me up, breaks through the circle, grabs my arm, and pulls me out. I'm not scared. I'm confused. But the lesson was loud and clear: Don't Ever, Ever Turn Anyone In. Ever. That lesson was burned in my brain in the fourth grade. Thanks to two tough little Irish girls. The lesson served me well.

When Rose left, a peculiar little German lady replaced her. We were all scared of her. Sure enough, my mother found small shards of glass in the chicken soup. The German maid was trying to kill the Jews.

Then Carrie came. Carrie was the real deal. Competent. Smart. Relaxed. Ample. A lap comfortable to sit on, a bosom to rest my head on. She smelled of hot soapy water and fat.

I was sitting at the dining room table with my mother. She was babbling to me about the sales. De Pinna's was where she bought my clothes, all French labels or English imports. My winter wardrobe was bought in the summer sales, my summer wardrobe during the winter sales. On each item she'd proudly show us the sale tag: a ten-dollar skirt marked down from four hundred, a thirty-dollar dress down from whatever. And so it was that I was sent to public school in fancy dresses entirely inappropriate to the current fashion for skirt and sweater sets, which I longed for. I would rip the hems of these fussy dresses on the way to school, preferring that the ragged edge be stared at rather than show my pudgy thighs.

My mother was perusing the newspaper at lunch, talking in her high movie-star voice about the sales. We were eating aspic cubes held together with toothpicks. A toothpick broke and lodged in my throat.

I tried pushing it down with water, with bread. I excused myself and headed into the kitchen, where Carrie was washing dishes in soapy water.

"Carrie," I said, "I have a toothpick stuck in my throat."

She scooped up a cup of soapy water and walked me past my mother, up the hall, and into the bathroom. "Drink this."

I drank the water, threw up the toothpick, and went back to my seat. My mother had not stopped talking. I resumed lunch; she looked up from the paper. "Where were you?"

"I had a toothpick stuck in my throat. Carrie got it out."

Her face paled and she started to slip from her chair. "My brassiere, undo my brassiere." I did. "I almost lost you," she cried, wailing, now flat on the floor. "Call Fremo, Grandma." Fremo and my grandmother still lived next door in my grandmother's brownstone. They arrived. My mother was lifted onto the living room sofa, where she told the story of how she almost lost me again and again, begging me to play "Für Elise" on the piano, which I did.

I would never again tell my mother anything alarming about myself. Her fear that something would happen to her only child was matched only by her wonder at my genius. Jews in that period had lots of geniuses, virtuosos, in music, math, theater, films. All some proud mother's boy or girl.

The black-and-white films of glamorous women with glamorous lives were as real to her as food. Isadora Duncan, dancing the world over with all those lovers. The reality she chose to believe in was a magical reality. And that's what she imbued in me, her one child. "Look, Fremo, how she picks up the bread! Look how she spreads the butter! Look how she walks, talks, sings!" Omigod—sing!

I would sing "Embraceable You" to my mother and Fremo, seated on the couch, clutching each other.

"You and you alone bring out the gypsy in me!" I'd sing, pointing my finger at my mother.

"No, no, Lyova, don't!" she'd scream, so affected by my power was she.

"Lovey, please," Fremo would plead beside her, overcome.

How could I doubt my effect on the world when I had these two grown women hypnotized by my every move?

There were reasons I didn't tell my dear, silly, vulnerable, and theatrical mother anything that happened to me—except the things she could celebrate.

Carrie and I sat in front of the radio for hours, gossiping about all my programs. We went to the movies together. We saw Errol Flynn in *Captain Blood* and were both smitten. By his beauty, his smile, his dedication as a doctor, the sweat pouring down his wonderful face, the earnestness in his eyes. Carrie and I were bound together by Errol. We never called him Errol Flynn. Just Errol.

Carrie brought in the newspaper every day. The *Daily News*. Errol was being accused of doing something to a fifteen-year-old he wasn't supposed to.

Every day for a year, Carrie and I scoured the papers. Peggy something was her name. Hours of indignation: "Errol wouldn't do that," Carrie said. "She's just trash."

"Trash," I'd agree happily, "that's all she is." And we'd look at the picture in the paper again. In the morning I'd say, "What's happening with Errol?" and Carrie would shake out the day's paper. We'd read the story in shock, angry at anyone who was not on Errol's side. "Listen to this!" "Listen to this!" we'd say to each other. Carrie, the person in my house most in touch with reality. The one there for me in every emergency. Carrie was my closest friend and comfort.

Carrie left to have a baby. She called that poor little girl Lyova.

I must have been fourteen when my mother told me Carrie died.

I went by myself to the funeral home to say a private good-bye. The hard, unyielding body in the coffin didn't look like Carrie's. Nor did the face. Gray. The upper lip stuffed with something round and hard. I was shocked and shaken. My Carrie lives on, at 706 Riverside Drive, with her friend Lyova.

An odd postscript to our crush on Errol Flynn, Carrie's and mine. I read his autobiography many years ago. At the end of the book, a habitual drunk, but now a decidedly sober actor, he stands in front of his bathroom mirror on the boat he lived on. He examines the broken veins on his nose, the bags under his eyes, the folds on his neck, with triumph. He has managed to wreck his own beauty and free himself from its expectations. Many years later I bought an initialed belt buckle at an auction that once was worn around his waist. I wanted an object to remember him by. To remember Carrie by.

There was a very sick child who lived more than halfway up 148th Street in a brownstone with a big bay window. Her anxious, sweet-faced parents said she had a hole in her heart. They dressed in brownish dark colors and spoke in European accents. I always looked in the bay window when I passed their house. Sometimes they would hold up their frail blond-haired child and wave.

One day I was invited to a birthday party. Not on 148th Street, but another street on the other side of Broadway. I didn't know any of the children there. I was nine. Why was I invited? They were in a circle playing spin the bottle. When the bottle pointed at you, you left the circle, went into a closet with the boy who spun it, your lips pressed his, then you went back to the circle. It was strange, thrilling, but matter-of-fact. I don't remember a birthday cake at all.

Afterward, Lenny Black asked if he could walk me home. Tanned, dark-eyed, silky black hair. I was wearing the only dress I looked good in. Pale green silk, and saddle shoes. I kept looking at my saddle shoes, shyly walking beside him down the 148th Street hill, across the street from my building. It was spring. "Will you be my heartthrob?" he asked. There was a buzz in my ears as my heart sped, and my breath momentarily stopped. I kept looking at my saddle shoes, and in a conversational tone said, "Yes."

The week that followed was the most extraordinary in my life. Lenny Black came to 148th Street every afternoon. He brought leadership and adventure into the lives of all the girls on the block. When we played ring-a-levio, he always chose me to be on his team. I asked him to come with me to the back porch of my grandmother's brownstone. Fremo and my mother were lying in deck chairs. They shielded their eyes with their hands as they looked up at him. I was proud.

My status on the block shot up. I was no longer Lyova. I was Lenny's girl. The star of the block. When we played hide-and-go-seek, he pushed me to hide with him, not from him. We crowded together in alleyways, warm breath intermingling, warm arms and knees touching. We skated down unknown streets, climbed dangerous ladders, ran across tarred rooftops. It was thrilling. The games we girls played before Lenny—"What would you wear if you were a princess?" "Emerald crown, matching satin dress, golden shoes"—all gone. He was the gangster. I was his moll. We were all his molls.

One night my mother told me the little girl with the hole in her heart had died. "Tomorrow you'll get dressed, go up the hill, and pay your respects to her parents. It's very sad." The next morning, despite my begging and pleading, my mother insisted I wear the new wine-and-white-checked suit she'd just purchased from De Pinna's. The pleated skirt was up to my thighs; the jacket didn't close over my nine-year-old belly. The kneesocks emphasized my pudgy knees.

As I stepped out of my building on the 148th Street side, there was

Lenny, leaning against a car. I saw his eyes take me in. In an instant I knew it was over.

I crossed to the car and leaned against it, trying to hide everything he just saw. "I'm going up the hill to visit the little dead girl, want to come?"

"Nah!" He left the car and stood opposite me, unabashedly taking in the belly and the thighs, the whole thing. "Nah!" he said again, and put his hands in his pockets. I watched him turn the corner to Riverside Drive and knew I'd never see him again.

I went up the street to the brownstone where the parents were waiting for condolences. They had pulled a long white basket to the bay window, lined with white ruffles and pillows. On it lay a doll-like child of about two, as beautiful as any princess in a storybook. Golden curly hair, rosy lips and cheeks, her little white hands crossed on her chest, wearing a long white net dress and little white Mary Jane shoes. She seemed to be sleeping, like Snow White after she ate the poisoned apple, just waiting for a tiny prince to come and awaken her. "Look, look—how beautiful," her parents kept saying, wiping their wet faces. There was a smell of choking sweetness.

I left and walked heavily down the hill, past my grandmother's brownstone, to the entrance of my building. I opened the apartment door, went down the hall to my bedroom, and undressed. I put on my green silk dress and left the checkered skirt and jacket on the floor.

Not long after, I saw *Wuthering Heights* around the corner at the Dorset movie theater and met the love of my life, Heathcliff. The fierceness of that passion, the lover's rage, burned into my little heart, and it never left me. I walked out of the Dorset Theatre, around the corner, and down the hill dazed and stricken. I had given myself over to Heathcliff. I understood his need, his undying need for Cathy. I understood his revulsion at Geraldine Fitzgerald. I even understood poor Geraldine's hunger for his love. I stood in front of my bathroom mirror and wept for all of us.

Heathcliff burned himself forever into my brain chemistry. The angry orphan outsider, with more electricity in his little finger than all the landed gentry put together. The wild outsider, the moors, the wind. Heathcliff the outsider had set my taste in men for life.

Lenny Black had been replaced. I was free to worship a black-and-white star of the silver screen.

M y father owned a boys' camp, Pocono Camp Club. I was taken there every summer, from the first year of my life. Pictures show me, at eight months, perched on a nurse's white shoulders; at three, saluting the flag at the flag ceremony; and again barefoot, in a white petticoat, with someone's big sunglasses covering my face. I actually remember that picture being taken. The heat of the dry grass between my toes, the hot sun on my tan arms, and the person behind the camera saying, "Look here."

Snap.

My father wanted to raise and train boys with the same kind of dedication and religious ethic that he'd had in his education as a first-generation good Jewish American, moral and ambitious Columbia graduate, and responsible executive of a huge social machine like the YM and YWHA.

At seven, when my parents reunited, I was the only little girl in the boys' camp; I used to run after the ones my age as if I were a butterfly catcher. I would climb the hill overlooking the lake with my binoculars, lying flat so no counselor could see me, spying on the eight-year-old boys, leaping on one another, wet brown bodies with white backsides, naked, wild lemmings running toward the ice-cold water. Jumping off the pier, screaming with cold, shock, and joy.

I used to run after them. "Play with me, play with me!" I'd call.

The boys on the outer rim would turn their heads and look at me, alarmed, and keep on running.

One summer my cousin Genevieve Rosenthal showed up. Her younger brothers, Jack and Jerry, were campers.

We had each other. I was starving for a friend of my own. Genevieve was a leader. She'd bossed her two brothers and was up for anything.

Hiding behind the social hall, she and I were alternately singer and audience, did dying scenes with each other, and stole packs of cigarettes from the niche in the office where they were sold. Her idea. Bold. Wily.

I locked the hook on the small bathroom door in my parents' cabin and lit a cigarette. I blew smoke in the mirror, the way the movie stars of the thirties did. So glamorous, so sophisticated. As was I, eight-year-old Lyova, head back, hair swaying, eyes half closed under my eyelashes, a stream of smoke pouring out, the boy in the mirror under my spell.

"Lyova. Lyova." My mother's sharp voice. "What are you doing in there?" Knocking sharply on the wooden door, *rap rap*. "Open up this door." *Knock knock*.

I quickly threw the cigarette in the toilet, flushed it, opened the hook on the door, and faced my tall, angry mother. "What are you doing?"

"Nothing." My mouth opened, a gob of smoke escaped and hung between us. I started to cough. The rest escaped. She dragged me to the sink, then thought better of it, shook me, talking all the while. "No, the soap is too drying." I'd cunningly concluded that I'd escaped my mouth being washed out with soap when my mother grabbed her cold cream jar. "Open your mouth!" On my wail—"Noooo!"—she slapped in a handful of Pond's cold cream. I retched. "Cold cream is good for your skin," she said as she slammed out the screen door. I lay on the cot gagging and crying, trying to spit out the cold cream.

For a long time I couldn't even stand the smell of cigarettes.

But my cousin Genevieve taught me to be bold and lie, to be tricky and adventurous. Two against the parents and counselors. She was a great bad influence. Being bad was good.

The next summer I was alone, walking somewhere, it had to be August because the grass was parched. Stanley Baumschlag was standing watching me. I was nine; he was at least eleven. He stood barefoot, brown-bodied, thin, and muscular, in khaki shorts rolled up his thighs. He held a long stick of gum in his mouth between his teeth. His dark eyes watched me. He was the God of Mischief.

"Bite the other half of my gum off," he challenged.

"No, why should I?" Secretly thrilled.

"You'll see."

"Oh, all right." Acting bored, reluctant, I walked up to him, carefully putting my teeth around the stick of gum, biting, my lips brushing his. He jumped away, pointing at me. "Gotcha!" Running away barefoot, turning and calling "Gotcha!" again.

I stood, hands on hips, showing exasperation, like he'd really tricked me.

I wrote in my diary that night, *I am going to torment Baumschlag!* If. Only. My first kiss.

I had a very bad earache and my mother called the doctor. The doctor said I needed a mastoid operation. A lot of children did at the time; this was before antibiotics were common. I never hear about mastoids anymore. We were at camp. The summer was over. The boys had all gone home on buses. I remember lying on a cot in my mother and father's cabin. Looking up, I saw the doctor's white face, glasses, and gray suit, and my mother and two other strangers. The doctor held a large white gauze patch to my face. It had a terrible smell. It was chloroform. I was drowning in brown rushing water, reaching for the brambles on the side of the ravine, screaming for my mother to save me. "Mother, Mother. Save me, help me!"

I could hear my mother's voice. "Oh God," she cried, "let her go."

For a long time I was swept down the stream. And then I drowned.

There is life after death. The pavilion above the lake was turning slowly in the blue sky. I was on it, holding on to the sides. It landed softly. I looked out at the lake, the mountains. I was safe. Alive.

I wandered through the empty bunks. In one I found a book of poetry. The lines made me sit on a cot and read. *When I have fears that I may cease to be before my pen has glean'd my teeming brain.* Then, *Golden lads and girls all must, as chimney-sweepers, come to dust.* The inevitability of the inevitable. Pauline on the tracks—"Save me, save me"—with the train coming on.

I was gobbling books. Up the hill on Broadway was a small bookstore. It was there I discovered Tolstoy and Turgenev, and read them for hours on the window seat in the living room, eating apples.

My Uncle Raymond told me a joke as we walked up Riverside Drive. It was about the midget lady and the giant in the circus. On their wedding night, as they performed their conjugal duties, the giant said, "Is it in yet?"

She said, "No, not yet."

"Now?"

"No, not yet."

He pushed harder. "Now?"

"Yes," she garbled, lisping, her throat full. "It's in."

Something in that inappropriate joke stayed with me. Nobody had ever discussed sex with me. I knew where things went and what it was, but that was it. At nine I had found a hand-drawn picture of Hitler sticking his penis into Mae West. Shocked, I ran home and burst into the living room. "Do you and Daddy do this?"

My mother said gently, "Sweetheart, that's how babies are made."

Revulsion. "Like Mae West and Hitler? How could you!" Slam of bedroom door. Fury and shame, sobbing on a bed. That was pretty much it as far as technical information went.

Annie Kay and I had been best friends since we'd spied each other at our mothers' knees. Her red hair curled around her snowsuit hood, freckles sprawled across her nose. Annie Kay and I were inseparable. She lived on 150th Street, between the Drive and Broadway. She was there for me, sturdy, never leaving my side, when Mr. Forster, my fourth-grade history teacher, asked me to stay after school. Mr. Forster had a habit of touching my neck where my braids parted. A tall heavy-breather, he would stand by my desk during tests, whispering the answers to questions I couldn't answer. "Seventeen seventy-nine," he'd say. "The French and Indian War," or "John Adams." I'd feel a clutch of revulsion in my stomach, a temptation to get the questions wrong rather than write down his answers. So when he asked me, his big red face smiling, to discuss the problems I was having in history after class, I asked Annie Kay not to leave my side as he, hand on my neck, sought my averted eyes to discuss my lack of studiousness. Because my mother was prone to hysteria, I instinctively sought other allies to solve my problems. With Annie Kay by my side, Mr. Forster was blocked.

. . .

One day I walked up the hill on 148th Street and crossed Broadway on my way to the five-and-ten-cent store on 145th Street. On the way I saw a man stalking a woman. Like a snake ready to strike. They were off the sidewalk, in the street. A small circle of onlookers surrounded them. She, terrified, was moving within the circle, trying to get away from him. A bus pulled up. The doors opened. She tried to get on. When the driver saw the situation, he closed the doors and drove on. I looked at the faces of the onlookers. No one was moving to help her. How could that be? I looked around for a policeman. I ran about three blocks on Broadway before I found one and dragged him back to the place the woman had been. All gone. No more crowd, nobody left to tell but me. "He was going to hurt her. Find him, stop him."

"Oh, no, little lady, they're fine. They're probably sitting in a bar now around a table, talking about it."

"He's going to kill her."

"No, no, it's just a normal thing, don't worry your head about it."

Things happen in your life that leave an imprint. Injustice left the deepest imprint on mine.

While walking down Convent Avenue I discovered that the convents on the avenue had angry nuns who encouraged angry parochial school children to hate Jews. The nuns encouraged the children to throw nails at Annie Kay and me. "You nailed Jesus to the cross!" they yelled.

Outside of "I'm Jewish" and "I'm Amish," there is no comparable "ish" in describing a person's religion. No Protestant-ish, Catholic-ish, Muslim-ish. If someone asks me, "What's your religion?" I say, "Jewish." I don't say, "I'm a Jew!" unless I'm answering defiantly. As in,

"I'm a Jew, what are you going to do about it?" "I'm a Jew, so what!" "I'm a Jewess—a woman with powers to entrap a Christian man." I became scared about being Jewish when I was growing up. First there was the blond child on the *Île de France* who knew somehow that I was Jewish and believed I couldn't wear the ship's ribbon in my hair because of it, then the convent school girls on Convent Avenue being allowed or encouraged to throw nails at Annie Kay and me. How did they even know we were Jewish?

At Passover dinners, my father sat at the head of the table with his yarmulke on. He would read prayers in Hebrew, and my cousins would read the English translations, and the sense I got from reading about the plight of our people was that we were not a popular group. Ever. Thrown out of Egypt, wandering in a desert for forty years. Thrown out of country after country. Despised, forbidden to own land. And finally, six million of us exterminated. Gassed. Shot.

Someone had given me *Oliver Twist* as a present, and it suddenly disappeared in the middle of my fascinated reading of it. "Where, where, where did it go?" I demanded. No one ever said, but I'm sure my parents got rid of *Oliver Twist* because of Fagin, the Jewish villain of the book.

Except for the high holidays, when my parents went to temple, and of course in camp, where Jewish services were held every Saturday morning, there was no practice or discussion of religion in our family. No one discussed beliefs or God. My sense is that my father, who was raised in a deeply Orthodox home, and my mother, whose father was a Zionist, had a deep respect for their own history and an equal awareness of their great good fortune in their families' decisions to flee Poland and Russia and come to America. Also, that neither of them seemed to believe in the God of the Jewish bible. My mother believed in the possibilities, the promises; my father in morality and humanism.

I had a little Christmas envy when I walked along Riverside Drive, past windows through which I could see beautiful, brightly lit trees dangling with ornaments—the sense of surprises to come, of Santa Claus landing on rooftops, of a kind of United States of Christmas, to which I didn't belong. It was a country I wasn't a citizen of. I had that left-out feeling. The dreidel just didn't do it for me.

On Saturdays I studied for my confirmation, the Jewish girl's equivalent of the coming-of-age celebration of Jewish manhood. The other girls were thirteen, I was twelve—thanks to my mother's usual need to push me to the head of the line. Was it a month we prepared for the Bat Mitzvah? I don't know. There were about five girls, I think. Our assignment was to write a couple of pages, thanking our parents for giving us life and teaching us virtues and thanking God for making us Jewish women.

Just as I had in Hebrew class, I zonked out in Bat Mitzvah. Sitting with the other girls, all of them excited, I would sink into a vacant stupor. After *Thank you for giving me life*, I was done.

The youngish rabbi gave me kind, special attention. He sat me across his desk and asked questions meant to stimulate my mind, memory, and gratitude. I just didn't know how to say thank you in the form and with the dignity he wanted. "Thank you to Daddy for all the songs we've sung together." "Thank you, Mother, for thinking I'm brilliant, but as you can see, I'm not!" The young rabbi gave up on me and wrote out a standard form thank-you page for me to read in front of the confirmation audience. He gave it to me in his office and came around the big desk to hand it to me. Suddenly his hairy beard was on my bent neck, his arms around my body. I broke sharply away and looked at him. He moved forward. I ran to the front of the desk, opposite him. He moved. I moved. We both ran around the desk at least twice before he stopped. I said, "Thank you for writing my speech," and ran out the door.

I read his speech at the confirmation celebration, at Temple Ansche Chesed on 100th Street and West End Avenue. I never told my parents. I never told them anything, because my mother was a hysteric. My father was so moral, I was afraid he'd jeopardize himself to right a wrong. So I learned very early to take care of myself, to keep it to myself.

One day, a girlfriend and I went walking on the Drive, somewhere around 130th Street. There were more small buildings than big ones, and we began to ring doorbells, then run away, hiding, to see if anybody stuck their heads out. It was daring. My heart was beating like crazy. I rang a white button buzzer and looked around for my friend. Had she gone around the corner?

A hand reached out and clutched my shoulder. It grasped the blouse I wore and pulled me inside the door to a small apartment at street level. A small, intent, angry, middle-aged woman was screaming at me. "What do you think you're doing?" She shook me. "You're not on your own street, are you? You rang our doorbells. I saw you." She pushed me down onto a straight chair and went to a telephone. "I'm calling the police. They'll take you to jail!" She looked at me closely. "You're a Jew! Are you a Jew?" I nodded. "You're a Jew." She dialed. "Operator, get me the police. I have a Jew here who's ringing doorbells up and down the street. I caught her. Yes, I have her here." She hung up. The apartment seemed to be the super's apartment. She spoke with an accent. German? Polish? I was silent, terrified she would keep me prisoner. "I'm sorry," I whispered. "I'll never do it again." There was a moment of heavy air. I didn't breathe. "I knew it—Jewish!" She watched me. Then she opened the door and pushed me out into the street. "Don't come back here!"

I stood on the empty sidewalk, looking around me in shock. Then I walked home.

Boys

My parents added a girls camp. Pocono Camp Club was coed. I was falling in love with all the beautiful boys. Rough, pushy, ball-throwing, shoving, shining-in-the-lake-water boys.

The press of slow-dancing body against slow-dancing body, the rainy days, the pressing of tan cheek to tan cheek. The smell of fresh-cut mountain grass. Earth. Sun-warmed stone. The pine smell of the social hall. Lenny Buckner. Arny Roth. Mike Schimmel. Jerry Brown. Every summer these same children met again in July and said good-bye September first.

At eleven I was a nonperson, a non-girl. At twelve, to my great shock and rapidly beating heart, I emerged a hot girl—my dream come true.

I was in the arts and crafts bunk at the Pocono Camp Club, twining leather strips for a key chain, when I turned, and in the old foggy mirror between the windows I saw a beautiful girl. I stepped closer. Touched my face. Touched the mirror. It was a miracle. The beautiful girl was me!

I looked around for someone to show, but the bunk was empty. Where was everyone?

I ran down the hill to the dining hall. I knew my grandmother was in the kitchen.

"Grandma, Grandma, look at me! See my tan? It makes my eyes so blue, Grandma, doesn't it? Doesn't it? I'm pretty, aren't I? I'm so pretty."

My grandma became my mirror and nodded, caressing my hair.

Narcissus, gazing in the pool of water, falling in love with himself, and drowning in his own image—that was me.

My adolescence had begun. I'd morphed into Scarlett O'Hara. Pocono Camp Club was Tara, 148th Street the Old South. Completely delusional.

At Pocono Camp Club, from age twelve on, I slashed through all my competition, telling the senior girls to their shocked faces, "I can have any of your boyfriends I want." Boys, men, followed my Fabergé Woodhue perfume and my Flame-Glo lips. A spell was cast. I could not believe my sudden power. I developed whims, which changed weekly—for Lenny, then Marvin, then back to Jerry. But I could never have Mike Schimmel. Mike had contempt for me. I was the privileged daughter of the camp owners; you couldn't punish me. I couldn't be sent home. I fell into arrogance. I could do anything I wanted and it was all right, no one said no to me.

Mike Schimmel, who was the oldest boy and the camp conscience, bought a hundred tin clickers shaped like frogs. At lunch, the clicking started and seemed to spread. Conversation stopped. All was quiet except for the clicking sound. The boys swiveled, facing the girls' tables. At my place was a little tin frog facing me. Looking at me. I suddenly realized I was the target. I was being chastised and criticized for bad behavior, for hurting many feelings, boys' and girls'. I felt humiliated and helpless. I grabbed the little frog, ran through the girls' side of the dining hall to the screen door, and ran up the steep dirt steps, hurt and ashamed, holding one of the clicking frogs in my hand. I ran up the hill to my bunk. I threw myself on my cot and sobbed, clicking the little tin frog to further punish and humiliate myself.

A counselor came in and talked to me. I don't remember her words, but I knew I couldn't run away. I had no place to run. I had to take it.

I was very mean to the girls' head counselor that summer. I did caricatures of her in the camp newspaper. She was a tall, gangly Christian lady, very nice, but awkward. One day she called me in to her bunk, showed me a particularly devastating cartoon I'd done of her, and asked, quivering with hurt, "What have I ever done to you?"

My shock was total. Till that minute I had had no idea that children had the power to hurt adults. Caricaturing her had made me popular; any collateral damage was undreamed of. I was awkward and unprepared for her obvious pain. "I'm sorry," I said.

"Just go," she said.

Years later when I was on my way to the Neighborhood Playhouse, I ran into her on the subway. "I'm really sorry and ashamed to have . . ." She turned away from me.

Looking back, I think other children always taught me about boundaries. I never knew there were boundaries until I was slapped down; then I became shocked and aware. Like the little Irish girls in elementary school teaching me never to turn anyone in. Like Mike Schimmel. I always respected him for it and wanted desperately to be his friend. He wouldn't have it. The other girls couldn't stand up to me. I was the boss's daughter—a privilege I abused without realizing I had it.

I think going through puberty, coming out on the other side with sudden breasts and waist and cheekbones, made me fall in love with my new self, my new popularity, and the mirror. My new best friend, the mirror! Want me. Want me. Everyone.

The First High School
I Was Asked to Leave

I was a poor student in everything but English. In spite of that, my mother pushed me, and PS 145, so that I could graduate from elementary school at eleven. That left me too young to start at the High School of Music & Art, which had accepted me on the basis of my portfolio of drawings. While I waited to turn twelve, I attended the Art Students League, finally starting Music & Art in October 1939, a month after World War II began.

My first week there I was asked if I wanted to sing in a musical written by one of the music students. Of course I did. The art classes bored me. My artwork was sentimental, cliché. Any art I did at that age was entirely derivative of my Aunt Fremo's. Fremo, who attended the Art Students League every day of her adult life, was a second-rate artist except for one great painting of fat Suzy in a red hat, which is hanging in my house now. I painted large black women who looked like Carrie, with a baby at her knee.

It was some transition, from PS 145, De Pinna dresses, and Mary Janes to Music & Art, which seemed to have no rules at all. I went around the corner to the dress shop on Broadway and bought a blue silk dress with my allowance money. I skipped classes, climbed to the top of the metal doors in the girls' bathroom, eating my sandwich, and swung back and forth. I wandered the halls, peeking through the glass square on each door to wave to a friend. Mr. Rosenthal, my nice history teacher, looked at me with real regret in his eyes.

"You can do this work," he said. "Why aren't you doing it?"

My grandmother made me an evening dress out of green net to sing the song in the student musical. My song went like this: "I'm deep just like a chasm / I've no enthusiasm / I'm bored when I'm adored / I'm blasé!"

I was twelve, blasé, and had gone to high school heaven. At the end of the term I was called to the principal's office. I opened the door, and to my shock, my mother was sitting there, across from the principal, Miss Dvorak, looking anxious and small in her chair, shocked by my mascaraed lashes and red, red lips.

I was being thrown out of Music & Art for skipping classes and low grades. My heart thumped. Miss Dvorak was talking to me, but her words were a buzz. She leaned in close.

"You can't get through school on charm!"

Charm, me? I was charming? Really? Charming. I looked at my mother's anxious face. I had no idea what my punishment would be. I only wanted to hold on to this backhanded treasure of a compliment. What was it I had that I couldn't get through school on? Charm, that's what!

Punishment was my parents sending me to Walton High School in the Bronx. Walton was a run-down, third-rate institution. It would be a good place for me to finish out the half year. Next term I would enter George Washington High School in Washington Heights.

I had to be up very early in the morning to catch the subway at 145th Street for the half-hour ride to the Bronx. My parents were impressed by my lack of laziness in the morning. Orange juice and toast and I ran to the subway station. What they were unaware of was that I was the only girl on that subway, surrounded by twenty or thirty DeWitt Clinton boys on their way to their very high-achieving all-boys high school, also in the Bronx. They rode with me all the way there and got off one station ahead of mine.

"Java, Java," they'd call, since no one could pronounce Lyova, as they held the subway door open for me to run onto the train. The blue silk dress slid easily on my body, and the circular skirt swung. My heart fluttered under Russian blouses. Every morning, cute boys, funny boys, flirty boys, studious boys, were hanging on to the poles and overhead straps, bursting with boy stuff, and me. Java.

Once, I went to school without panties. In my circular skirt. I'd never been touched, my body had never been touched, by anybody but me. I wanted a secret, a daring secret to frighten myself with, to ride the train with. I was twelve and a half. Fearless.

I don't remember how we met. Maybe he was a friend of one of the boys on the subway. He was absolutely not Jewish—very proper, tan skin, blond hair, medium height, pleasantly Christian. He asked me to be his date for his high school graduation dinner and dance at the Waldorf Astoria's Grand Ballroom. Of course I said yes. I was at Walton by then. I was twelve and a half or thirteen. I know I wore the green net formal that my grandmother made for my song in the Music & Art musical.

Every date was a family affair, Grandmother Dora making my dresses, Fremo and Mother questioning the boy—was he rich? Living their romantic movie dreams through me. I was a kitten picked up by the back of the neck, helpless, that's me, examined until I meow, then put down.

I was nervous. The boy was a total stranger, and neither of us knew how to make conversation. Also it was a huge night—high school graduation, the Waldorf Astoria. We were seated at a big round table with five other couples. All the girls were blond and pretty. Everyone was smiling and glowing. They all knew one another from school. I was the only stranger. I wanted to go home. I wished I were home. We danced, stiffly. Everyone around us was loose—talking, doing dance moves, turning. In the middle of the dance floor a tall young college-age couple, she dressed casually in skirt and sweater, he in slacks, were moving together, as if no one else were in the ballroom. Just the two of them, slow dancing to the orchestra. It was so magical that it took me out of myself. They were so rich they didn't have to dress up, so sure of themselves. So involved and in love that they moved to their own beat. Long body to long body. Scent to scent, breathing each other in. Dropping into the ballroom from where? With high school formals and tuxedos bobbing all around them, pinks, blues, accentuating their offhand elegance.

The boy led me back to the table, where all the glowing strangers were seated. They started by introducing themselves to me. Each one focused on me, saying his or her name. Fear rose in me with each name. I was the Jew at the blond table. My heart was pounding. My turn. Low voice. "Lyora Rosehall."

My date turned to me with a smile. "I thought your name was Rosenthal. Didn't you say it was Rosenthal?"

I looked up, dizzy with shame. All the festive eyes were watching me, waiting. "No, no. It's Rosehall," I mumbled. Everyone leaned back in their seats. They began to talk to one another. My date and I sat there, not speaking.

The next year, my social life was soaring, bursting. I was fourteen. The older boys from camp were now in college, and their friends wanted to date me—boys from Harvard, Columbia.

Weekends were full of great New York places. Afternoon tea dances at the Pierre, evenings at the Plaza, fraternity parties at Columbia. Fremo and my mother were planning my future. Their Lyova was a popular party girl—convertibles, theater, opera. My grandmother had her sewing machine going on the old linoleum floor in her kitchen—she made me a blue velvet dress, a black satin dress, a beaver hat with a veil, a coat with beaver trim.

World War II was raging. One of the really handsome boys I knew from Harvard became a lieutenant. I met him and a naval cadet with his date at a huge restaurant in a hotel downtown. It was a warm night. They ordered Cuba Libres. "Is that okay?" they asked. "Sure . . ." I didn't know what a Cuba Libre was. I usually had ginger ale. I felt awkward, a little dazed by the white uniform and gold braid. They were a little old for me. The drinks came, tall, cold, with a straw. I was thirsty and drank it all down fast because I didn't like the taste.

Suddenly I was in a world by myself. I looked over the table at my date and there were two of him. I experimented with others at the table. I looked at his friend. Double. At his friend's date. Two of her smiled and nodded at me. If I moved my head too quickly, I had to hold on to the table to steady myself. My face was on fire. I told them I wanted to go to the ladies' room, but when I stood up, the black-and-white floor tilted, and I slid to the floor. The cadet's date held my arm while we crossed the slanting floor. When we reached the ladies' room, I looked in the mirror. I only remember seeing one of me, but I'd never seen that look before. My face was shimmering pink, my hair wet with perspiration, my eyes dilated and bright light blue, instead of blue-gray.

"When will this stop?" I begged the girl. "How do I stop this? I hate this feeling." She sat me down on a bench and tried to comfort me. I couldn't breathe. I stood up and begged her to get my date to take me home. I held on to the open window on the cab ride home. As soon as I stepped on the curb, the Cuba Libre vaulted out of me, a jet stream of six different kinds of rum. I took a deep breath of good summer air. That night I held on to my bed as I lay spread-eagle on my back, focusing on the ceiling as my bed tilted this way and back till the dark became light and I could safely close my eyes without sinking into a spinning vortex.

I hate being drunk. I hate the taste of rum, or any hard liquor but gin or vodka. I don't drink. I don't like those rides in the amusement park, either. A boy I used to like took me on one in the Jersey Palisades. I felt betrayed that he hadn't prepared me for how frightening it was. I walked away from the ride, away from him, went home, and never spoke to him again.

M y mother was now living her life through me, the dating she never had as a daughter of immigrants, caring for her younger brothers and sisters. I kept two diaries: One I hid for me, the other I hid for her to find and read in secret.

I was standing in our white kitchen on a weekend morning when my mother came through the swinging doors with an anxious face. "Lyova, could you come into the living room and stay with me when Sylvia comes?" Sylvia was Aaron's wife, my Uncle Aaron, Dad's brother. "I'm afraid of her," she said.

In that one instant our relationship changed, forever. I protected my mother. She was a charming bird of plumage, and Sylvia a pretty but deadly hawk; I became the kitchen cat. I realized for the first time that in the outside world my mother was vulnerable, helpless.

That morning, as my little, charming, but deadly aunt made light conversation, peppered with comments that shook my mother—"You really think those pants are becoming? They're so gaudy"—I broke in. "Sylvia, don't talk to my mother like that. It's mean."

Sylvia, unfazed, turned her pretty face to me. *Okay,* it seemed to say, *new game. I can't pick on Witia anymore.* Then she went on to tear someone else apart.

But something changed between my mother and me. She knew I would be there for her. And I discovered a grown-up strength. The instinct to defend the bullied and the unfairly treated coalesced into a new strength, even a talent.

Two of my best friends the last two years at George Washington High School were Chester and Duke. One day I walked into an empty classroom and there was a lone dark-haired boy playing the saxophone. Playing it well. Jazz. We looked at each other. My knees went weak. So did his. That was Duke. Duke's best friend, Chester, was a slim, funny, light-haired boy. They were attached at the hip. Duke did nothing without Chester. Romance fled. Together they were ten-year-old boys who played tricks on me, but I was fifteen and full of hormones. They pursued me on buses and subways. One afternoon they showed up laughing on a subway and I told the conductor they were pursuing me and had them thrown off the train. Their shocked eyes watched me from the platform as the train moved on. They sent me a book on charm. The cover had an inscription: *Although in beauty you do excel, in charm and discretion you sure do sm—! Signed, Chester and Duke.* Excel "in beauty" from two discriminating boys? My real report card was swelling my heart. Charm, I knew I had. Hadn't I been thrown out of Music & Art because of it? Discretion! Yes. I was guilty (of stranding them on a platform), but so what? Discretion is not interesting; it has nothing to do with being attractive. *In beauty you do excel.* Yes! My mother's daughter.

I went on to Juilliard after high school. I knew I was a minor, minor talent. I had no chest tone, just this tiny sweet lyric soprano voice coming out of me. My teacher, Madame Fouchard, gave me songs appropriate to my voice, and my age, which was sixteen: "My Love Is Like a Bubbling Brook" and the weirder "Daddy's Sweetheart." The end lyric goes, "Oh, if Mummy hadn't married Daddee [high note], Daddy might have married me! Tadum!" I sang these songs to great effect in my living room, my mother accompanying me, her eyes moist in appreciation of my talent. Even my father, the opera lover, approved of the direction my life was taking. Juilliard, after all!

I have a distinct memory of sitting in the Juilliard common room and receiving a phone call telling me Chester was dead. After graduation he had enlisted in the Air Force and was a pilot in training camp. He was eighteen when his plane crashed.

When I heard the news, I almost blacked out. I don't know how I got back to the apartment on Riverside Drive. I had to get someplace safe to wail, and I did as soon as I leaned against my front door. The apartment was empty. Sounds were coming out of me that I didn't recognize. Big, low, guttural heaves and openmouthed screams, hot and salty tears streaming down my face into my throat and down my neck. I howled in pain. I was sitting on the carpet in the living room, holding on to the leg of a chair, tasting my own tears. I rose to get something to blow my nose into and caught sight of myself in the mirrored wall above the sofa. I didn't recognize myself.

This is what grief is, I thought. *Remember this. This is what grief is.* I stepped closer to the mirror and looked at my contorted features and wet face. I became interested. I studied myself. I tried to cry for the mirror, but the moment was gone. Many years later, when my daughter, Dinah, was two and having a tantrum, I would grab her and carry her to the mirror, where her tears would fascinate her and she would study her pain as I had then. When my friend Chester died.

An Unsentimental Education

When I entered the Neighborhood Playhouse, I knew I'd come home.

In my half year at Juilliard I discovered the limits of what talent I had as a lyric soprano. If it were Jane Austen's time I might have shone as light after-dinner entertainment for guests. Facing reality, my undefeatable mother turned to the last art, acting. A lucky star led her to the Neighborhood Playhouse, then in the East Fifties off Fifth Avenue.

The atmosphere at the Playhouse was rigorous and strict. There were two extraordinary talents there: Sanford Meisner, a charter member and actor in the Group Theatre, which had revolutionized acting in America, and Martha Graham, the flaming talent who revolutionized modern dance. Both were cutting-edge artists with attitude.

Sandy was elegant and a snob. He looked down his nose at you from behind his square rimless glasses, hidden behind a cloud of smoke from his Pall Malls. I remember the brand because, as I became a favorite of his, he would send me to the corner drugstore on Fifth Avenue to buy him a pack. And of course Pall Malls were what I forced myself to try smoking on top of the double-decker bus on the long ride home at night. I hated the taste and it made me dizzy, but I was determined to copy Sandy in everything. Years later, Sandy would have his voice box removed because of those cigarettes. He would make weird, robot-like sounds holding a microphone to his throat, but his own need to teach, to communicate, was indomitable.

"You are spoiled!" Sandy said to me.

Our very first assignment was to look for an object. For a certain handkerchief, or book, or necklace, hidden in the furniture onstage. An upright piano, a chest of drawers, a bookcase, a bed, a waste-basket, and so on. I searched the chest of drawers. Desultorily, then the bookcase.

"I can't find it."

"You are spoiled," he said.

I understood. My first real education began.

I was my mother's and Fremo's beloved dolly. Marveled at within the confines of the brownstone and our apartment in 706 Riverside Drive.

When I sang "Embraceable You" to them on the couch, I dismantled them, trapped them with "You and you alone bring out the gypsy in me." Both of them gasping, overcome by my power, unable to escape my pointed finger, first at my mother—"No, no," she'd scream, hands up—then Fremo—"Lovey, stop, stop," overcome. Breathless. Leaning against each other for protection against my gifts.

Yet at fifteen, when my Aunt Anne set up an audition for an agent at the William Morris Agency, the magic didn't seem to work.

He, the agent, sat on a stool in this small audition room. I attacked him with "Embraceable You." Trying to engage his eyes. With each "you" and "you alone," his eyes averted, his stool turned. I couldn't understand why the power didn't work.

It confused me.

Outside my own living room, outside my own mother and aunt, I had no power, no impact.

In school I was a mediocre student. I had my friends on 148th Street, but was never the popular girl in school or in camp.

The dichotomy of my genius status at home and my slightly below par status in the outside world gave me a sense of instability and unreality throughout all of my life about exactly who I was and what I was capable of.

Could that be why I grabbed so ferociously at acting? Grounding myself in a structure that worked for me, the observant child?

To look for an object is the first exercise in the actor's bible, *An Actor Prepares*, by Constantin Stanislavski, the Russian director of the Moscow Art Theatre who brought reality into acting at a time when declaring and performing to the audience was in vogue. Stanislavski designed exercises that forced your concentration within the situation, within the character, that took your focus off the audience, off pleasing anyone. It gave me what I thought of as round white life preservers held together by a rope, which was the play, allowing me to navigate from one life preserver to the next and to keep my head above water.

When Sandy spoke about objectives and actions, my senses clicked into place. I saw a road to security as an actor. I understood that we all have an objective in life. We have an objective every day. Today I need to make dinner. My actions are to walk up the hill to Broadway. Go to Barzini's. Shop. Come home. Go to the kitchen. Cook. My objective is carried out. Dinner is on the table.

Transfer to working on a play: Find objectives within each scene for my character and the actions I need to take to carry it out. Objective: To borrow money from you. Why do I need it? How badly? When? Summer, winter, what time of day? What hour? Who are we to each other? Brother? Mother? Stranger? How much money are we talking about? What actions do I take to convince you to give it to me? Lie? Or tell the truth? Charm, threaten, seduce, make you an offer you can't refuse?

You get the idea. The essence of drama is conflict. What you choose to do with the conflict is unique to you as a talent, as an actor. And occasionally, particularly in the theater, your director's vision of what he wants from you. It's exciting and mysterious, talent is; that's why we keep going.

In speech class we had Mary Van Dyke, a talented and focused teacher whom I have to thank for my speaking voice. When we first arrived she taped us talking and played it back. I played my recording back to myself many times. Was that really me with that tiny, high bird voice? Like my mother's? Like Fremo's? No wonder they gave me those dumb songs at Juilliard. Mary gave us exercises that forced us to use the chest voice, every day, at home, at school, until the new placement became habit.

In second-year speech, the assignment was to listen to other people's conversations—strangers on the street, in stores, to capture the oddities in their voices, speech, or accents, and bring them to class, to train our ears. I listened to two girls behind me on the bus; I was so fascinated, I missed my stop. I brought one of the characters into class, and three years later I used her when I read for my first professional play, *Detective Story*. A fresh voice chattering away on the seat behind me blew open a fresh character who gave me an immense career.

In my second year at the Playhouse we put on a period, antebellum play of some kind, and I was assigned a dull brown dress. I hated its plainness. The other girls looked as if they'd stepped out of the Old South. Soft greens, pale lavenders, net and lace. I yearned to wear them. I approached Martha Graham.

"I don't like this dress; it's so plain. Can't I have one like theirs?"

"Why?"

"Because they're pretty."

She turned a terrifying face toward me. "Pretty? Pretty? That's what you want?"

Her face was mask-white, her hair black, her black brows frowned in a V, her mouth red.

"Ugly," she emphasized, "is better than pretty!"

I stepped back. She held my look. I ran to the stairs and burst into tears. Why was she so angry? What line had I crossed? What did she mean?

Pretty was one of my mother's favorite words.

I was not pretty in my Salem-witch-trials-brown jersey dress. Is angry better than nice? How could ugly be better than pretty?

Sandy gave me an improvisation. He paired me with a boy in class.

"You two have been going together," he said. "You, Lee, want to break up with him. You want him to leave. You"—he pointed to the boy—"want to stay!"

Conflict. I tried to get him to go. He wouldn't. The more he wouldn't, the more a storm built up inside of me, in places within myself that were new to me, foreign to me. Uncontrollable rage erupted from somewhere deep inside me and swept me away, until I pushed that boy, beat that boy out of my room. Ugly. I had a really interesting ugly side. Sandy's eyebrows were raised slightly.

"Well," he said. "Well, well, well. What have we here?"

Was that ugly better than pretty?

An actress I met much later in the Actors Studio, Vivian Nathan, was famous in our small circle for being able to cry on cue. If the script said, *She cries*, Vivian had tears falling down her face.

The rest of us have to work for the real pain that comes, the real grief that suddenly makes available our emotions, unlike the tears of

Merle Oberon and Norma Shearer, which rolled down the perfect faces on the black-and-white screens of my childhood.

All the restlessness, the intensity, the unnameable swirling storms, now had a place to go. And it was not only safe; it was worthy. There was a name for it. I would act. In a theater. From the time I was in the children's ballet troupe at the Metropolitan at the age of four through the Art Students League, Music & Art high school, and voice at Juilliard, my poor mother had doused me in every art form she could. She had finally hit on the right one, and this one was mine, mine alone.

When I played Electra almost two decades later, there was a place in me I knew I could go to as an actress. And a way to pour all my life experience into her.

Acting was to become my religion. A holy, safe place, a process that took place inside of me and that was to be protected at all costs. Nothing ever was allowed to get between me and the process I had given myself, to create in my own way, with the tools Sandy Meisner had given me. My truth. I had at last found my holy grail.

There is a time in a young girl's life, and a young boy's, too, when you are a perfect pervert magnet. Dreamily sitting in the front seat of a double-decker bus, I became aware that across the aisle a thirtyish man seemed to be stabbing himself between the legs. I looked. He smiled. His stabbing was fierce. I suddenly screamed and ran, calling for the driver. The man ran past me down the stairs and out the bus.

I stopped taking the bus home from the Playhouse. On the subway was a facsimile of the same man, big, angry, smiling, whacking off between cars.

In my second year at the Playhouse, sitting in my crowded seat on the subway, I became aware of a man standing over me. His newspaper was open. He seemed to read it. He concentrated on one spot. I real-

ized this man had been this near me before. The next day I found a
seat in a car in the front of the train. The following day, he was standing over me. I ran out at the next stop and took a local.

I was late to Sandy's class. It was past nine a.m. No one was allowed in after nine a.m. I sat outside by myself. I needed to catch my
breath. I went up to the closed door, turned the brass knob, and looked
inside. Sandy looked up, annoyed.

"I want to tell you why I'm late."

"It better be an interesting story," Sandy said.

"I think it is."

And so began an Arabian Nights saga. I was learning to use my
fears and real experiences to entertain. At least once or twice a week,
the well-dressed man with the newspaper loomed over me. He found
me in whatever car I was in, on whatever train. I tried to elude him.
Heart pounding, I thought, *I'm using you, scary man. And you're almost as afraid of me as I am of you.*

I could see that he couldn't confront me, any more than I, at seventeen, could confront him. But knowing I could use my fear as an
actor, to basically entertain Sandy and the class, was a great outlet. My
stalker abruptly disappeared for one week, two weeks. And then he
was gone, and I was free. I had a mini nervous breakdown in the girls'
bathroom.

The summer after my first year at the Playhouse, I got a job at
Tamiment, a famous summer resort in the Poconos with a huge
and famous summer theater and a great history of talented perform-
ers. Mervyn Nelson was the director, my first gay friend. At Tamiment,
at seventeen, I played the mother in *Ghosts* to Mervyn Nelson playing
my son, at thirty-seven; then played a thirteen-year-old in a Tennessee
Williams one-act; then singing, dancing, and musical comedy on the

weekends. Singing alone for a huge audience gave me my first stage fright. I started drinking martinis before I sang and ended up a very scared kid sobbing in Mervyn's lap at the end of the season.

Also hired that year was a cute Irish hoofer, Buster Burnell. Buster and I fell in summer love immediately. This is where my Uncle Raymond's joke comes in, about the midget lady and the giant in the circus.

I shared my two-cot bungalow with Mildred from the Tamiment office. She was a large young woman, with one wiry dark hair growing from her breast near the nipple. I always wanted to pluck it out.

The fact that Buster entered the tiny bungalow every night to share my cot didn't seem to bother her. She snored softly through our lovemaking. In my mind I was still a virgin. I knew there was a hymen, and I looked anxiously for bleeding many mornings-after. It never occurred to me that a childhood of ballet and the hard handlebars of my boy's bike might have deflowered me. Buster strenuously and rhythmically hit my insides while I lay there, kind of liking it but pitying him for not having a large enough, long enough member to devirginize me, to draw blood and reach my throat, like the lucky midget lady. I was seventeen and biologically really stupid. Unfortunately, the little bungalows were very close to one another. Next to mine was a bungalow with four mariachi players. The raw squeaking of the cot disturbed their sleep; they banged on the walls and cursed me in Spanish.

As July slid into August, Buster said, "I thought you said you were a virgin."

"I am."

"You're not."

"Oh yes I am."

I began telling him, with as much sensitivity as I could manage, how and in what way he was falling short. He regarded me in stunned silence, uncertain if I was sane or putting him on. And then he kindly put my mind to rest about the biology and the mythology with which I had deluded myself.

A ll the girls in the second year at the Playhouse were hot for Herbert Berghof, a Viennese actor then learning the Method from Sandy Meisner. Despite the fact that he was bald, Herbert was a fascinating, sexy man. All of us in Martha Graham's class fell like flies, writhing in our jersey uniforms under his tolerant and, yes, interested gaze. Somehow he promised each of us a great romance, without a touch or a word. He was an accomplished tease.

Herbert was always fascinating. A lit cigarette never left his mouth. His students watched, hypnotized, as the ash got longer and longer, before collapsing onto his chest and joining the rest of his ashes.

After graduating from the Playhouse, I was hired for the summer at Green Mansions, a wonderful little theater in the Adirondacks, a great job for a young actor. Idling in a rowboat on the lake after rehearsals, I fantasized about Herbert. Lying back in the rowboat under the summer blue sky, the clear cold water under my fingertips, I would romanticize our relationship.

"Herbert," I would breathe. "Heathcliff."

We had a few days off unexpectedly, and I was given a ride to the city. In the little mirrored phone alcove in our apartment on Riverside Drive, I called Herbert. He was glad to hear from me, his voice warm and provocative.

"What are you doing tonight?" Did I ask it or did he?

He said, "Do you want to come down to the Village?"

"Sure."

Then Herbert said, "Come to my apartment, but if you don't want to go to bed with me, don't come."

Silence.

"Lee, do you hear me? Don't come here if you're not going to go to bed with me."

"All right."

"All right, what?"

"All right I'll come down."

His apartment was small and grim. We sat across from each other in the living room. He was a jovial host, but who was this man?

"Have you had dinner?"

"I'm not hungry."

I wanted to leave, but I remembered that I'd promised not to come down unless I went to bed with him. A promise was a promise. There was absolutely no air in the balloon, no attraction, no romance, nothing. He opened the door to the bedroom. There was a large satin-covered bed in a small room. I guess we both undressed. I remember clearly, with my eyes closed, visualizing a Roman landscape, steps leading to pillars, the vertical lines on the pillars, a sunset backdrop behind them, and figures in Roman togas moving around on the steps.

I felt nothing. My concentration was focused on the images in my head. All I could think of was, *Is it over yet?*

When he was done, he was concerned. "Are you all right?"

"Fine, really."

It was stifling in his apartment. I had to get out to breathe.

All my one-night stands through the years would be a replica of that experience in one way or another: the anticipation—breathless and really hot, scorching to the touch. The actuality—the underwear coming off, the white body, the sheets, the strangeness. A total turnoff. Except for one, much later. No, two.

Within seven years I would call Herbert again. He had met, married, and opened an acting school with Uta Hagen, a remarkable actress and human being. My own life had undergone a radical change. Herbert and Uta opened their doors to me; their school gave me a home away from home.

On the Road

Right after I graduated from the Neighborhood Playhouse, Richard Rodgers of musical fame cast me in a play. I was eighteen. Since the play wasn't to be produced for another six months, he offered me the interim job of understudying Ado Annie in the road company of *Oklahoma!*

I took the train to St. Louis to join the company by myself. I wore a skunk coat and a red beret. The chorus people told me later that they all made fun of my snobby ways after they asked, "Are you a singer?"

"No."

"A dancer?"

"No." Pause, then, in the new lower voice I had acquired in speech class at the Playhouse: "I'm an actress!"

As it happened, Dorothea McFarland, whom I'd gone to understudy, broke her arm the day I arrived. I was desperate to go on in her place. I'd had no rehearsal with the cast, no rehearsal of the songs with the orchestra, but I had insane eagerness. Fortunately, wiser heads prevailed and the lovely girl who was the understudy I was sent to replace went on that night. I was never to perform Ado Annie. (Dorothea made sure of that.)

The company was spending two weeks in St. Louis. I'd been there just a few days when I came down with influenza. We were staying at some famous old hotel. For three days I was out of commission, sleeping most of the time, with a high fever. The doctor visited. Hotel maids moved in and out of my room. Waiters with tea and lemon. I slept.

Days later, there was a knock on the door. A man's head looked in.

"I brought you some soup."

He pulled up a chair and fed me chicken soup, blowing on each tablespoon to cool it off. He felt my forehead. Was he the doctor?

"You still have a fever."

"I know," I said, slipping back to sleep.

Later, I asked the maid if she knew who he was.

"Oh, they live in the suite next door."

Two men, nice men, tough guys, took turns feeding me. I felt very taken care of on my first foray to this strange new town, this strange new country outside New York City.

The real hotel doctor checked on me. I was more awake. He let me wash my hair. I was sitting up in my big bed now, but I had company. The men next door were friends now. They were my new family. Like uncles. And they were giving me a going-away party in their suite the night before the company went to San Francisco. These men fussed over me as if I were Beth, the poor dying sister in *Little Women*. They set me up in a big comfortable chair in their living room and introduced me, to my surprise, to a very handsome and self-assured boy, about my age, whose father, they said, owned the biggest factory in the state.

"Very rich," they said in front of him.

He nodded. I had a feeling *marriage* was the unsaid word here. Then, my two uncles put on a record with hot music that filled the room.

"I can't dance," I protested. "I'm still weak."

A girl younger than I, sixteen or so, pale, with a sloping chin and bent shoulders, stepped out from the foyer and started to strip to the music.

"What's this?" I asked.

The girl continued to take her clothes off, gracelessly.

"It's your going-away present," one of my uncles said.

I jumped up from the place of honor. "No! No, please! Don't!" I took the girl's arm and dragged her back into the foyer. "Don't do this." I was urgent and alarmed. "Please, you don't have to do this."

"They paid me."

"How much? I'll pay you."

"I want to," she said.

I looked at her. I went back to my chair in the living room and looked at the floor till the girl was naked. The uncles picked up her discarded clothes and told her to put them back on. They saw me back to my room two doors down.

"Sure, sure," they said when I told them I was still sick. "Sure, sure, you take care of yourself, take care now." Their big fingers patted my head, stroked my hair.

Later I learned there was a big mob presence in St. Louis.

When we arrived in San Francisco, I bought a pair of dangly rhinestone earings, one of which I still have. I went to the theater every night and sat with the chorus, makeup on, just in case Dorothea should slip and fall again. I learned how to bead my lashes with black wax and use thick #3 theater makeup. I begged to be permitted to stand on the porch with the rest of the cast for the finale of "The Farmer and the Cowman," and for a week had a wonderful time preparing, piling makeup on for my entrance on the porch. Apparently the makeup was so distracting that several audience members complained and I was sent back to the dressing room.

I had a one-night, or should I say a half-an-hour affair with my third lover, in San Francisco. First there'd been Buster, then my night with Herbert Berghof, and now the tenor from *Oklahoma!* We both lay half-dressed across the bottom of the hotel bed with its squeaky springs.

Within a few minutes his breaths were rapid and heavy, and suddenly "Mama" erupted from his mouth like a song. "Ma-maaaaa!" He was Italian.

When the company traveled to Los Angeles, my mother and father joined me at our hotel downtown. Two extraordinary things happened. I saw John Garfield in *Awake and Sing!* with other Group Theatre actors—he was stunning in it—and he drove me back to the hotel in his convertible. He talked about his wife, Robbie, and put his hand on my breast.

The other big event was about God. I was sunbathing on the roof of the hotel with my parents and maybe thirty residents in various stages of undress. The smell of suntan oil filled the air along with music from someone's radio. I was the only one sitting up.

I saw a girl a little older than myself with loose dark hair open the door to the roof. I had noticed her earlier in the day, arguing with a boy on one of the staircases near the elevator.

Standing by the roof door, she took off her skirt, her blouse, and her shoes, and hung her coral necklace on the doorknob. In just her white bra and panties she moved to the edge of the roof, climbed onto the edge, and jumped. Her beads were still swinging on the doorknob.

I went to the edge of the roof and looked down. There on the black tar of the parking lot, ten floors below, she was spread like a four-pointed star. I looked around the roof. People were talking quietly, tanning themselves, or dozing in the sun, Perry Como on the radio; a woman laughed. Had I dreamed this? No. Her clothes were by the door, the beads still swinging. The white star in the upside-down black night catapulted me out of all childhood certainty, introducing me to the unknown, Chance. The appointment in Samarra.

The casualness of the girl's death shook me out of a prolonged childhood. I ran down five flights of stairs to my hotel room. My father, sitting on my bed, tried to comfort me. I asked him about God. He said God was a force for good in the world.

For me, God had always been a kind of Christmas Santa. At night, I prayed, "Dear God, let me pass this test." "Dear God, make my legs thin. Make Stanley fall in love with me." He was a personal deity, there for me in all my important quests.

Now, God as I knew him left, and plain superstition crowded in to take his place. I couldn't go onstage without something to protect me. Knocking wood, a penny in my left shoe, someone saying "Good luck" three times, wearing a red string around my wrist. When my children fly, I light a candle. The fear of senseless chance disaster never leaves me.

After *Oklahoma!* I did a play in summer stock. The stock company was in Sayville, Long Island. I was still living at home. Also performing in Sayville that summer were John Randolph, his wife, the actress Sally Cunningham, and Warren Stevens, a young leading man who would play the juvenile lead on Broadway in *Detective Story*.

They asked me to go out with them one night. The journey in the car was a revelation. Warren Stevens drove, Sally and John sat in back, and I was in the front passenger seat. They were so passionate about something they read in the newspaper that day that I kept looking at them to see if they were putting me on. They were connected to some-thing totally foreign to me at that point, a political passion I didn't understand until I was blacklisted. I admired their connectedness, their young fire, and I loved John and Sally. John, the recruiter, never stopped trying to make a Communist out of me.

"Say you have two shirts, Lee. Wouldn't you want to give one to someone who doesn't have a shirt?" Completely earnest.

"John, leave me alone. I don't care about shirts. Take them both. It means nothing to me!"

John led me up two flights of stairs to a crowded room where young people were arguing. Stalin felt the music written by Shosta-kovich wasn't geared to the people. It was too elitist, or something. "Who is Stalin to tell a great musician how or what to write!" I turned around and walked back down the stairs.

John sent me a book to read. It was about conditions in the United States for working people, particularly women. I read it the week I had a bad cold, and it touched something in me. That was the day poor beat-up Mabel came to clean the apartment. I lectured her straight from the book, all the while blowing my nose into a clean hankie, not moving from my bed.

"Mabel." The sound of vacuuming in the hall outside my bedroom. "Mabel," I called, louder. The vacuum stopped. I was impatient. What I'd read was so amazingly appropriate. Young Mabel, not much older than I, opened the door. She was small, black, with one almost-closed puffy black eye. I read her a section from the book about the lack of living wages for working people and looked up to see her reaction. Blank.

Underneath, spoiled Lyova felt helpless. I couldn't say, "Don't go back to the guy who's been beating you up. Save yourself." I felt as helpless as I had been watching a man stalk a woman on Broadway, or when Mrs. Cherry hit Foster's open palms with her ruler.

. . .

Fremo had not one wrinkle on her face. She took my mother's dictum, "Don't frown, you'll get wrinkles," as an instruction to eliminate any movement of her face. Her limpid blue eyes were merry but wide, always. Her scarlet lips made a V for a smile, but never widened into a grin, so wrinkles never formed around her eyes or mouth. Her irrepressible laugh shot through the top of her head in a loud shriek— "Hoo! Hoo! Hoo!"

Try to laugh without moving your mouth; you'll see what I mean.

My mother and aunt were merry together, walking with their long legs, pushing me in front of them to instruct me to walk like they did, one foot in front of the other, or gossiping at the dinner table, my mother with expulsions of laughter, pink-faced and moist-eyed, Fremo hooting, genteelly, both squealing at times, so overcome by this and that.

They would be overcome with laughter at my taste in gifts for them, purchased at some specialty store on Broadway. "Darling, that's hideous!" holding up a blouse I'd given them, as if *hideous* meant *gorgeous*. "Lovey," they'd twinkle, holding the garment up to them, "this is hideous!" Peals of laughter, sisters as close as twins.

For all I was learning I was still my mother's daughter and Fremo's niece. Fremo had her ice skates slung over her shoulders. It was a warm June day, but she had taken up ice-skating. She was humming the Vienna Waltz as we waited for the elevator with my mother. From the seventh floor down she chirped out the Vienna Waltz to herself, unmindful of the five other occupants of the elevator. She didn't care.

On the subway we sat together, I between my aunt and my mother. Suddenly the train stopped between stations. There was that eerie quiet that follows when the brakes stop squeaking. A man standing over us hung on to a strap.

"Witia," Fremo said in her high, loud, rich-lady voice. "Doesn't that man look just like Hitler?"

The man reddened; people opposite craned their necks to look at him.

"Yes, yes he does," my mother called out calmly, like a loud, well-bred bird. "He certainly looks a lot like Hitler."

The man at the center of all the attention, now thoroughly traumatized, looked for a way to get away. When the train started up again, he moved as fast as he could away from my mother and Fremo.

In 1949, I was hired as understudy to the ingenue lead in an Irish play. My daytime rehearsals and nighttime check-in were all geared to the Theater District, between Broadway and Eighth Avenue, Shubert Alley. Gene Lyons and I understudied the leads. We delighted in each other. Love lite. He was elegant, charming, funny and, yes, Irish.

I wanted to move in with him, so my parents promptly left our wonderful spacious apartment on Riverside Drive, where I grew up, and moved the family to a small apartment on 52nd and Eighth Avenue near the Theater District, so I would have no excuse and not have to travel uptown to 148th Street. They would not let me get an apartment of my own. They would rather move to a grungy building. Above us, Betty Bruce, a singing star on Broadway, lived with her mother. Her two ratty little dogs would skitter down one flight, pee on our doormat, and skitter back up the stairs, their satin ribbons flapping in their eyes. On Riverside Drive my bedroom was on the seventh floor, high above the backyards of neighboring brownstones, including my grandmother's, and quiet. On 52nd and Eighth, the traffic beneath my little bedroom was incessant. Motors, buses, brakes, horns, the sound of wet splashing tires, were all magnified. It felt as if there were no wall separating me from the street. My mother tried to muffle the sound with thickly lined gray-green drapes. I lay in the crack between my bed and the wall, pulling the blankets over my head. I couldn't sleep. The doctor came and sat by the bed. I cried, I was so tired. He prescribed Nembutal and Seconal. I slept. I was nineteen. From that night until this I have never gone to sleep without a sleeping pill. Never.

Desperate for some independence, I spent a week at my friend Connie Sawyer's house. My mother checked in with Connie every day. I returned home. When I pushed the door open at two in the morning, the door would hit my mother, praying on her knees for me to come home safely. There were lots of lectures from my exhausted father, kept awake by his weeping, panicked wife.

My father lost the job he'd had for thirty years as director of the YM and YWHA. He'd never been out of work. Where does a boss apply for a job? He was shaken, his pride broken. He withdrew inside himself. This was a new alien home, new alien streets for both my parents. A sacrifice they had made for me, or that my mother forced on my father.

There was no other YM or YMHA to be director of. He'd been lured away by the siren song of the ladies of Hadassah. Said good-bye to all who'd known him as a young man fresh out of Columbia. He had waved good-bye with much fanfare, and then the Hadassah ladies fired him. He'd disagreed with them about policy. They didn't like it. Nobody had disagreed with my father at the Y or at camp. He didn't know how to handle the ladies.

He sold Pocono Camp Club. He sold his summers, his joy, his boss-ness, his way of life.

Detective Story

Fresh out of the Neighborhood Playhouse and with a recommendation from Hank Fonda, whom I didn't know but who had seen me in a performance showcase, I auditioned for my first Broadway play, Sidney Kingsley's *Detective Story*. There were two life-changing plays running that year, Tennessee Williams's *A Streetcar Named Desire* and Arthur Miller's *Death of a Salesman*, both directed by Elia Kazan. Offered the part of the ingenue lead in *Detective Story*, I turned down that part and asked if I could read for the part of the old lady shoplifter instead. (I was twenty; the shoplifter was described as fortyish.) The shoplifter was an unfortunate girl, a *meeskite* from the Bronx who wandered into Saks Fifth Avenue, took a bag, and was caught stealing and hustled off to the police station. The multi-action at this police station unfolding onstage excited the audience to cheers each night.

I was discovered that season and invited to join the Actors Studio. I became part of the pantheon of extraordinary, brilliant talents who poured out of their dressing rooms into great little late-night bars after the curtains came down on Broadway. My actor beau, Gene Lyons, and I were out at the bars every night after the show. The atmosphere was arty, raucous, and sexy. The handsome sons of Lee J. Cobb in *Death of a Salesman* were looking for action after the theater let out. The air in those theater bars crackled.

I was flirted with, recognized as a new big talent.

The play was a hit, and I was the surprise discovery of the 1950 theater season. Picture in *Vogue*, newspaper articles, the whole megillah. I had hit it out of the park with my first play.

About a year into the *Detective Story* run, I read *All You Need Is One Good Break* while going somewhere on a train. I loved the grittiness of the writing and the premise of the play.

Something in it called to me. My part only had one scene—it opened the second act—but I identified with her. Whoever had written it had lived that scene, and liked that girl, and valued her. I wanted to meet him. I wanted to play her. When I was asked if I wanted the part, I told my agents yes.

All You Need is about a struggling Jewish working-class family. The director and star was a charismatic street guy, John Berry. I was fascinated by him, as girls that age are by bad boys. John Berry was the baddest, worse even than Marlon Brando.

Marlon had asked me out the year before. Picked me up on his motorcycle—thrilling—and took me to a nightclub in the Fifties on Eighth Avenue. We sat on a long leather settee, had drinks at a small black table, and silently watched a naked woman on a small black stage do artistic and lewd things with a giant cobra.

Not a word exchanged. What can you say?

Back on the motorcycle, holding on to his back, to my front door. I had my key out, no kiss, thanked him, opened and closed the door. Out of love.

When I told Marlon, who had just had a triumph in *Streetcar*, what a fascinating actor John was, he challenged him to a boxing match at the gym. John showed his contempt by not showing up at the gym.

The leading character in *All You Need Is One Good Break* is a street guy, a gambler who has fallen for the American Dream, who lives dangerously and ends up its victim. My one scene with John opened the second act. For some reason we were on a blind date. I was babysitting at a friend's house, trying to amuse him by blowing up balloons and twisting them into animal shapes. John wanted to get laid.

It was a lovely scene, and I decided to leave *Detective Story* to do *All You Need Is One Good Break*. Sidney Kingsley, my director, and the other cast members were shocked. Horace McMahon warned me, "Hits like this happen once or twice in a lifetime—don't be foolish," and he was right. I thanked Sidney, my mentor, I thanked everyone in the large cast, which after a year had become family, and I bolted the nest. I had no idea what I was getting into, or that my acting career was about to go into a nosedive. I listened to no one, a course I have followed my entire life, and I paid for it. I also kicked open a door inside myself, a route to the questions I needed answers for in order to create a larger life.

John Berry's best friend was the guy who had written *All You Need Is One Good Break*, Arnie Manoff. Arnie's nickname was "the Silver Fox." His hair was white, his face tan, his eyes huge and brown-black. He had the long black lashes girls should have. His manner was deceptively soft and gentle. He said he was thirty-six. My girlfriends and I laughed at that in the ladies' room. He was fifty-six if he was a day. Why would a man need to lie about his age?

Arnie really was thirty-six. He'd been married three times; he had a nine-year-old daughter, Eva, with his second wife, Ruth. He was still married to Margie, the mother of their two boys, Tommy and Mikey, who were three and four at the time.

It was a heady time for everyone. We got great reviews out of town, in Philadelphia. I spent a lot of time hanging out with Arnie in the hope that proximity would do the trick with John, that his whirlwind personality would alight long enough to notice me. Nothing happened with John, but as Arnie and I talked and talked and talked, I became aware that he was falling for me. In thinking about it now, I know he must have relished the *Pygmalion* aspect of our relationship. He thought of me as a Broadway alley cat—which I guess I was—and thought he was going to make a revolutionary out of me, the raw material that had fallen into his path. In a way he did, but never in the mold that he wanted. I'll never know if that was the turn-on for him, or whether Margie, his wife, had been a radical when he met her, or a good-natured and good-hearted shiksa from Texas or someplace like that, equally ripe for conversion to Communism. By the time we left Philly, Arnie and I were an item.

Opening night in New York of *All You Need Is One Good Break* was a disaster, literally. The turntable that carried John Berry from scene to scene and from set to set broke at the beginning of the show. Stagehands scrambled to turn the set around in plain sight of the audience. John overcompensated for the disaster, railing at the audience instead of charming them. The reviews were scathing. One paper picked me out as "Best Actress in a Bad Play."

Every night for the rest of our short run, the entire cast—which included J. Edward Bromberg, a great character actor and a charter member of the Group Theatre—had to stand onstage after curtain calls while John begged the enthusiastic lefty audience to tell their friends to come so we could stay open. We all took pay cuts, but after four nights we closed.

It was about then that William Wyler asked me to play the shoplifter in the film version of *Detective Story*. Kirk Douglas was starring, with William Bendix and Eleanor Parker. I spent four or five weeks in an actor's hotel in Hollywood called the Montecito, a run-down five-story building. It was cheap and fun. My room had a Murphy bed. At Paramount I went through the huge costume floor and found a size-eighteen brown jumper once worn by Sara Allgood. Her name was still on it. An Irish character actress, Allgood had played the mother in *How Green Was My Valley*. I loved the idea of wearing something she had acted in and had the dress altered to fit the little shoplifter, as if I could absorb Sara's acting genes through the fabric.

I loved everyone in the cast and Mr. Wyler, whom I liked to make smile or laugh. Kirk Douglas was dazzling, both personally and in the part. The girl who played the ingenue, Cathy O'Donnell, was married to Wyler's brother and had the kind of sweetness the part called for and lines so gushy that when Sidney Kingsley had first offered the part to me I knew I couldn't say them without laughing.

Detective: (typing) What color are your eyes?
Leading man: Brown.
Ingenue: Brown and green flecked with gold.

Arnie came to L.A. toward the end of filming and invited a group of his friends to a party to introduce me. It was at the home of Ruth and Arthur Birnkrant, who were to become friends for life, particularly Ruth. The rest of Arnie's friends held me at a distance. I don't know how many of them knew Margie or were friends of hers. There were about twelve people, and they all seemed very glamorous and sophisticated, very grown-up, to me. One took her husband with her into the bathroom, laughing. I didn't know if they were laughing at me, or the situation, or making love.

When the film was finished, Arnie bought a two-tone Packard convertible and decided we would drive back to New York together. He had been teaching me how to drive on empty roads, and when we hit the desert he handed the big car over to me, then slid over to the passenger side to rest. I was too short to see over the steering wheel, so I kept looking down over the driver's-side window for the white line that separated the two-lane highway. I suddenly felt the wheel being grabbed away from me and looked up to see a shocked driver in an oncoming car, his mouth and eyes forming three O's, like Edvard Munch's *The Scream*, as Arnie yanked us out of the wrong side of the road and stopped the car. He was breathing hard, so frightened and angry he couldn't talk. I know these unthinking acts of mine provoked the distrust he always had for me.

What neither of us knew was how unprepared for adult life I was. I was still living with my parents. I had never cooked a meal or washed a dish. I wasn't allowed to. I'd never made a bed, except a cot at camp. I'd never done laundry, washed, or ironed. Or cleaned my room, much less a house. My mother had deliberately chosen not to teach me any of the practical skills that might have ended my dependence on her or her maids. My earnings were tended and protected by my parents for my own good. I'd never been inside a bank. I did not know how to write a check. I had no checks. Arnie had absolutely no concept of who I was or how I'd been raised. He had no idea how wrong for him I was at that tough, crucial time in his life. Miss Wrong meets Mr. Wronger.

Childish, reckless acts appealed to me, and the consequences rarely crossed my mind. As a protected child growing up on Riverside

Drive and 148th Street, I used to climb the steep hill up to Broadway wearing my roller skates, then fly straight down to the bottom of the block, speeding past the row of brownstones, with nothing to stop me but the moving cars at the bottom of the hill on Riverside Drive. Acting is filled with risk. You throw yourself into the part to see where it leads you. You jump without a net.

But driving the Packard, I had risked both our lives and I knew it. I was ashamed and badly frightened. I was twenty-one going on twenty-two.

I was on Broadway in *Detective Story* when Elia Kazan asked me to join his project. He was directing Tennessee Williams's new play *Camino Real*, rehearsing at the Actors Studio. He asked me to explore a very different character from the shoplifter in *Detective Story*, the gypsy girl, a seductive child/woman who was used to entrap soldiers and sailors and their paychecks. I was working on *Detective Story* nights and matinees and rehearsing with Kazan in between shows. At that time Kazan was the greatest theater director in the world. He'd yet to transform the film world with *Streetcar* and the many great films to follow. I don't use the word *great* loosely. He was that talented, that gifted a director.

Kazan would whisper directions in my ear. His way of directing me threw me off balance.

Sandy had taught me how to structure a character, personalize everything till I became one with the character. Kazan would whisper suggestions. I'd follow them, like the ballet dancer in *The Red Shoes*; her feet had a life of their own. Kazan loved my responses, and it was exciting and fun, but when I'd try to work on the character at home, I had no base. I hadn't a clue what I'd done. I began to feel very insecure. If this were film, the suggestions would be filmed immediately, but onstage, Kazan wouldn't be there every night and Saturday afternoon to whisper in my ear. I quit. He called and called. He was too great a director for me to admit to him I couldn't work his way. I felt unmoored.

This was a small beginning of future conflict between us. In a few years Kazan would give the names of his fellow actors and writers to the Un-American Activities Committee. We didn't speak after that for twenty years.

Arms and the Man

I was offered Shaw's *Arms and the Man*. I was the beautiful princess Raina opposite Sam Wanamaker and the charming movie star Francis Lederer. My friend and Neighborhood Playhouse alumna Anne Jackson was in it, as was Will Kuluva, another friend.

We were opening in the first theater-in-the-round in New York City, in the Edison Hotel. The seats were so close surrounding us that if I sat on one of the boxes onstage, my hand could touch an audience member or a critic.

Many full-length pictures of me appeared in the newspapers. "From shoplifter to princess" exclaimed an insert of the scruffy shoplifter appearing next to elegant Raina.

The opening scene of *Arms and the Man* finds Raina in bed in her blue nightgown covered by a thick black furry blanket. The Chocolate Cream Soldier, played by Lederer, climbs into her bedroom through a window and the scene ensues. She, shocked by the intruder; he, needing a place to hide.

Opening night as I lay under the furry blanket in the dark, before the lights came up, I could feel bubbles of liquid between my legs, so sudden and so wet, my thighs slid on each other. It flashed through my mind—I could be making theatrical history: "Actress gets period at opening of new intimate theater." I pulled the blanket around my body, played the scene, and exited, yelling for help to get cleaned up for the next scene. Sure enough, I was bleeding all down my nightgown to my lurid footprints. The reviews said I was "not Lynn Fontanne yet," but "on my way." They could have said, "Career over."

Grandmother Dora

My Grandmother Dora was now living with us on 52nd Street. She was ill with high blood pressure, so my mother moved her from the brownstone to care for her. An extra bed was put in my parents' room. My grandmother rarely spoke. When she did it was in Yiddish or occasionally Russian. She was not as tall as her daughters, but she was taller than I was, and slender. She had a classically beautiful face and light blue eyes. With four highly educated children, I'm sure she was ashamed of her lack of English. Her husband had schlepped off to create a Palestine for the Jews and left her. I never saw her with a friend she could just talk to. Neither Fremo nor my mother spoke Yiddish. It was clear, though, when Fremo came home from her late dates with various men and my grandmother flung *farshtunkena* and other strange words after her as she went up the stairs of the brownstone that she had an effect on her daughters. She was remote out of self-consciousness, but she deeply cared about them.

One bright day, I ran into the apartment after a meeting. A big, young, uniformed policeman was standing in the small hallway that led to the bedrooms. My mother huddled on the living room couch moaning, her hands clasped tightly in her lap. "Mother is in the bathroom. I can't. Would you go?" I walked past the policeman and down the small hall. The bathroom door was open. My grandmother was standing on her head in the tub. Dead. Her head at the drain, her legs extended up to the showerhead. Her nightgown had pooled around her head, revealing her naked body to me for the first time. The sight was so cruel and so bizarre that it didn't seem possible. I pulled her light nightgown down from her head to her legs and called to the policeman. "Could you please carry my grandmother to the bed?" I pointed to the bedroom. I couldn't watch. I went and sat by my mother in the living room. Her teeth were chattering.

"What happened?" I asked.

"She went to throw up. She felt sick, and she got a stroke that hurled her into the bathtub." Such indignity. So shocking, so mean.

"She's on the bed. Do you want to see her?"

"I can't, I can't." I think my mother was in shock. I went to my grandmother. She lay rigidly still. Her blue eyes were open and fixed, like a doll's. *Old doll's eyes*, I thought. Only her beautiful wavy hair was still lustrous and alive. I passed my fingers through her hair. I'd never seen it loose and spread out on a pillow before. I studied her features, frozen in midflight, surprised. I kissed her cool cheek and closed her light blue eyes.

Bromberg's Memorial

It was only after *All You Need Is One Good Break* closed, in February of 1950, that I learned that Arnie, John Berry, and J. Edward Bromberg had been named as Communists by former friends in the Party back in Hollywood. They were all being investigated by the House Un-American Activities Committee, known as HUAC, and had moved to New York in hopes of finding work on Broadway to support themselves.

They had a lot at stake and a lot of company. HUAC had been around for almost a decade before it turned its attention to Hollywood in 1947.

The Committee had since judged hundreds of Hollywood people un-American, triggering a mass exodus of the film community to safer ports—New York, Mexico, Paris, London. Well-known writers like Dalton Trumbo, Ring Lardner, and Michael Wilson went into exile. It was all news to me. I had never heard of HUAC or the Blacklist, knew nothing of this generation of deeply political artists, who were devoted to the labor movement, sympathetic to the Spanish Civil War and the Soviet Union. I had been raised in an apolitical household, where current events were rarely discussed. I knew nothing about politics. I was young, basically uneducated, and really ignorant.

By the summer of 1951, Joe Bromberg and I were working in stock theater together in *They Knew What They Wanted*. He had already been named as a Communist by the publication *Red Channels*, which issued a hit list of 151 members of the movie community in June 1950. A year later, he was called to testify before HUAC. Pleading the Fifth Amendment, he refused to answer the Committee's questions and was promptly blacklisted. The only work he could get was in the theater, but he was a wreck. He sweated in the wings before every performance, terrified that some right-wing organization would send militants to attack him onstage.

"What's the matter?" I asked.

"The American Legion. What if they show up? What if they stop the show?"

They didn't.

"The Committee wants me to testify again. I can't take it. My heart can't take it."

His fear and agitation frightened me. Onstage he plunged into character, jovial, expansive; offstage, he was consumed with fear.

Joe had a wife, three teenage children, and a heart condition. At the end of the summer, he decided to leave the country and took an acting job in London. He opened there in a play and got great reviews.

Arnie wanted to meet with me about something important. He said that he and his wife, Margie, were going to try to work things out. The tears streamed down my face, soaking the bandages from my recent nose job. He patted my sniffling head and took me in his arms. I understood this was the adult world and had nothing to do with me, but I was brokenhearted. I felt I was losing someone and something essential to me—the part of me that was missing.

. . .

I was offered the ingenue lead in a new play on Broadway, *Lo and Behold*, a good distraction, directed by Burgess Meredith, whom I had long admired. In the cast was Cloris Leachman, as madly in love with George Englund as I was at the time with Arnie. We spent hours lying around out of town pouring our hearts out to each other.

During the Theatre Guild run, someone called and told me Joe Bromberg had suffered a heart attack and died during the run of his play in London. Would I join the speakers at his memorial? They'd contacted all his associates, but they wanted a new young voice to speak about him as well.

When I heard the news about Joe, I remembered his terror. I was stunned that this kind, gifted man had been basically pushed to his death. The memorial service was held at the Edison Hotel on West 47th Street. Bromberg had been one of the few actors who had started the Group Theatre and he had tremendous cachet in the theater community. The place was packed, with two thousand outraged theater people, many of them standing. A fierce energy, an anger, was alive in the hall.

I was a very visible young actress at the time. I think the organizers wanted someone unknown for anything political to speak, in addition to the many who were well-known, including Clifford Odets, the playwright who reshaped the Group Theatre. The fiery Clifford Odets of *Waiting for Lefty*. Somewhere in the middle of the program I spoke, shakily. I had never spoken in public. I was very nervous, but also moved by Joe's death. I said, "The Un-American Activities Committee knew Joe had a bad heart and kept calling him to testify anyway. I feel the committee ultimately killed him."

Victor Navasky, who would later write *Naming Names* about the HUAC period, was there and recalls it as a memorable night. Speaker after speaker worked up the crowd until, finally, the man everyone was waiting for appeared: Odets. His passion brought the crowd to the boiling point, just like his union organizer in *Waiting for Lefty*. Almost two thousand people crowded into that room cheered him. They would have followed him anywhere.

A week after Clifford Odets spoke at Joe Bromberg's memorial, he met with the committee and gave names.

I went to a meeting at Actors' Equity. Leon Janney was sitting in front of me.

"Well, you made the list," he said.

"What list?"

He was holding the new *Red Channels*, a directory of left-wing actors and "subversives." My name was in it. I could feel the blood drain from my head. My remarks from the memorial were quoted. From that day forward, for twelve years, I was blacklisted from film and TV. And Arnie left Margie for the last time.

A few weeks after Arnie and I returned from California in the Packard, he moved into a nice residential hotel near the Theater District. I spent time with him there, but not sleepovers. I still lived with my parents and was careful not to reveal too much about him. It seemed Arnie was trying to figure out his family situation, his relationship with Margie. My friend Anne Jackson, with her woolen hat squishing her red hair, would stop by our apartment and ring the bell. "Can Lee come out to play?" she would call out, and the two kids we really were would escape the adult world and run down the street laughing, holding our stomachs.

Melanie and Darren McGavin had a little apartment above a Chinese restaurant on 52nd Street. They were married, which none of the other young actors were, and they tortured each other with their flirtations and flaunted their affairs. It made me swear to myself that in any future relationship, I would make a life agreement to tell nothing and ask to hear nothing.

One day, Melanie and I were heading somewhere and saw a big metallic sign in front of a kind of semi-mansion. It said PLASTIC SURGERY, RHINOPLASTY. We wrote down the number and called. I had a bump on my nose that I wanted removed. Melanie wanted her nose shorter. The nurse said the operation was done right there in the mansion, in a kind of barber chair. We should come prepared to spend the night, but if the swelling went down we might go right home. We looked at each other—cool! Let's do it and not tell anybody.

I was in my bedroom on 52nd Street, packing my little overnight bag, hoping to get out of the house before my mother came home, when she opened the door to my room. "Where are you going?"

"I'm going to get my nose done. It's all arranged. I'll be home later. Don't try to talk me out of it, blah, blah."

She sat on the bed very quiet, very calm. "Darling, you are going to a butcher. This is your face, and if you are determined to do this, let me call our doctor and find a surgeon and a hospital that does this operation."

"I told Melanie I'd meet her."

"Call her, stop her," said my mother.

The cold water hit me. I was frightened by the rashness of what I had been about to do.

Our doctor set me up with the medical group that had operated on the Hiroshima women. He scraped the bone. My face swelled. I spent at least two nights in the hospital.

Melanie McGavin heard my warning call but decided to go through with it anyway. The tip of her nose was cut off, operated on by a charlatan.

My Parents Demand
to Meet Arnie

My parents demanded to meet with Arnie. He agreed, since I wanted very much for them, especially my father, to see what an extraordinary man he was—how lucky I was to have him as a friend, how caring and concerned he was. Arnie came in the door. I don't think anybody shook hands.

My parents were on the couch. We sat opposite them. It was that time of day when they seemed in silhouette; the windows, hung with thin white curtains, threw a cool light. I don't remember Arnie's preamble, possibly something mild: "I really care about your daughter . . ." Trying to warm them, charm them. The arrows came fast.

"Aren't you a married man? Still married to your wife? Don't you have children? Are you leaving your wife? Who is supporting your wife and children?"

It went on like that until Arnie grew defensive and angry and walked out.

I confronted my father at the front door, wailing.

"How could you? How could you treat him like that?"

God knows what else I said, for my father slapped me hard across the face. It was the first time in my life he had ever touched me in anger, and it hurt me and made its impression.

A fterward, I moved with Arnie into a second-floor walk-up in the Seventies on Third Avenue, above a bakery. To see their child— and at twenty-four, I was still a child to them—leave their home for the first time, with a thirty-six-year-old, white-haired man on his third marriage, not divorced, with three children? A Communist writer who couldn't earn a living? They could not have dreamt a more tragic scenario, for themselves, for me. For all the advantages given me, the time, the love, yes, the money, the everything. Then this betrayal. This stealing of their child, their star. I was a big success on Broadway, written about, photographed in *Vogue*. My mother's dream come true turned into a total and unexpected nightmare by my choice to love Arnie. As for Arnie having a clue as to how I was raised? None, and he never asked. At the time, leaving my parents' apartment and moving in with him, I was still too much a part of my own past, still rebelling against my parents, to have any sense of how differently I was raised, or how absurdly—how spoiled, romanticized, focused on, petted, and worshipped I was. To me, that was normal.

Somewhere along the line, I did sense that I was to make my parents very proud. My father would have been content with a well-to-do, educated, conventional son-in-law and grandchildren who would perpetuate the Rosenthal bloodline. My mother wanted a star. Dance, song, acting, a child who would carry her longings to ultimate fulfillment.

I loved playing house. I loved being Mommy. Cooking. Laundry. I loved having an instant family.

My parents couldn't conceive of how wanted this made me feel, how needy an only daughter can be for freedom, to be the girl boss of her own family, with her own money, such as it was.

I felt liberated. All these new responsibilities, these little boys, liberated me. I loved my new life. It all clicked into place.

On weekends Tommy, four, and Mikey, two, would visit. I'd run to our neighbor on the floor below to learn how to cook spaghetti with tomato sauce. I'd run to her to learn where the Laundromat was and how to use it. I bought a sewing machine, yards of fluffy green material, and made a really ugly fitted bedspread. I sweated through the summer; our apartment was above a bakery. The best thing about living there was the divine smell of bread baking in the early morning.

One morning my father appeared at our apartment. His left hand never left his coat pocket. I know he had either a gun or a knife and was there to kill Arnie. His face was as white as paper, his eyes, very pale blue, fixed. He was saying nothing, his eyes never left Arnie, he kept moving in on him wherever Arnie went—we were in the kitchen of the floor-through, we were between the stairs and the stove. I never stopped talking: "Please, please, please, Dad, please, Dad, go, please don't do anything, please, I'm fine, please, please—"

Arnie just stared him down; his contempt for my father defeated my dad. Arnie shrank him, and he left. I cried for my dad. For his love. For his lifelong principles and manhood that had been dealt such a painful, shattering blow, that he felt he wasn't man enough to save his child.

Abraham Rosenthal's child, Witia's child, Lyova, was now a blacklisted actress, living with a married blacklisted writer with three children from two prior marriages, in a walk-up on Third Avenue in Yorkville. In 1951, when *Detective Story* the film was released, I was nominated for my first Academy Award. I won Best Actress at the Cannes International Film Festival that year, and I could work nowhere in film or television. I was twenty-four years old.

I would stay blacklisted for twelve years.

M y mother saved their lives financially when she found the ad for the nursery school in East Rockaway. They moved to East Rockaway. My mother ran the school, as she and Fremo had run the Haskell Nursery School at my grandmother's when I was a little girl. And she loved it. All those little girls to fuss over and entertain. Pop Abe would descend the steps of the house from their living space and serve the many adoring boys and girls fresh orange juice. They were both loved and respected—for my father, respect was everything.

A rnie was a mystery to me; I was a mystery to him. Neither of us knew anything about the other's childhood, youth, schooling, work, how the other was raised, what their parents did. No facts. During our relationship I met his younger sister and her husband one summer. She was warm, vivacious. I didn't know till years later she spent the rest of her life in and out of mental institutions.

He did tell me that as a boy on the way to school he carried a chain to arm himself against the kids in his neighborhood, in the playgrounds. Nothing, nothing about his mother. His father. I never met them.

When Arnie's father died, he sat in the backseat of the limo far away from me, against the window. Not sad. Grim, bitter. Never a word. His profile said, *Do not ask. Don't talk.*

His mother was never asked to our house; she never met his children to my knowledge. She was admitted to a hospital once, for a pelvic complaint, and I saw her on a gurney, but never met her. She was an unadorned, gray-haired older lady; the sheet covering her on the way to the operation slipped aside, and I was struck by the vibrant triangle of thick black hair covering her sex.

I didn't know if Arnie was attracted or repulsed by me, or both.

I think he was attracted by the prospect of me as fresh clay, open to being remodeled into his vision of who I should be. His Galatea. My talent was interesting to him, but that was the one area he was denied entry; that was mine alone.

His displeasure, anger, and confusion seemed to come from his inability to change me enough. And a total lack of curiosity as to what and who had formed me. My mother, of course, my Aunt Fremo. I was an uneducated high school graduate. Inspired by literature, art, and theater, reckless and passionate, unaware of boundaries or danger. Spoiled, my heart in the right place, indulged, utterly ignorant of money, housework, cooking, laundry, with an overwhelming passion for acting, and a passion for passion. Uneducated and inadequate in everything else practical, in life.

And as I was to find out in the coming years, I had my father's sense of justice, too. And my grandfather's, Lyov Haskelovich, Zionist, radical, martyr, whose blood ran through my veins. But I had to grow up first.

D arren McGavin had hit it big with a TV series. He and Melanie moved to Park Avenue. I walked from our floor-through on Third to their building on Park. Melanie was thrilled and excited, showing me everything. Park Avenue at that time was indeed a big deal. Only very rich people lived there, celebrated in story and song. But the apartment itself seemed an exact replica of the beloved one above the Chinese restaurant, with one addition: the maid's room. Except there wasn't an actual room for the maid, so inventive Melanie had turned the wide closet facing the front door into a kind of railroad berth. Levered doors opened onto a narrow built-in bed on a board. It had a small shelf with its own electric light. But it was still a clothes closet in size. Maybe five feet long, sixteen inches wide.

"How can you put a person in there to live, Melanie, in the middle of your apartment in a front hallway?"

Melanie protested, "The maid is happy there, she loves her room."

"It's a closet," I said, and walked back to Third Avenue. The class struggle had begun. I didn't have to be a Communist to feel for the girl in the closet. But my best friend Melanie and I had our first serious rift.

During our months on Third Avenue, Joe Papp wanted me for Sean O'Casey's one-act plays, to be done off-Broadway. I read them; they were delicious, sharp, and funny. I told Arnie I was excited about them. He said no. I was dumbfounded. Turning down work was something not in my gene pool, and to turn down the chance to act in something of this quality was inconceivable. I didn't know what to say or do. "Why?" He couldn't say, but he was angry. Looking back, I realize that he needed me to be there for his children. He and Margie were divorcing; he wanted custody. He never gave her money or paid child support. Margie was a mild person, a party person. She was principled. She wouldn't, couldn't ask a blacklisted writer to support her. So I suppose Joe's offer to me came at the wrong time.

Early on, Arnie would push books on me. Marx, Engels, and Hegel. I tried to read them—not very hard and not very willingly, but I found myself reading the same page over and over again till the print blurred. My tastes went to the arts and the great Russian novels I loved so much, the ballet, the theater. Arnie's concentration was on Soviet politics, on teaching me what was essential to him, but a piece of my brain was missing in that area. It frustrated him. How could I understand economics when I had never had my own bank account? How could I understand the masses? Who were they? The working-class people in factories? The exploiters? I'd never been exploited.

But with Arnie my sense of inadequacy grew and grew. Basically, outside of my talent as an actress, he had a kind of contempt for me, and my views on Soviet art and film enraged him. I had been attracted to—no, fallen in love with Russian literature early on. I couldn't get enough of Tolstoy and Turgenev. I gobbled them up along with apples on the window seat of our living room, overlooking the Hudson River and the George Washington Bridge.

That was the summer Arnie rented a big lovely house in the country. Ruth and Arthur Birnkrant were nearby. Was it all summer or for August only? I baked apple pies myself and somehow picked up cooking, because I marketed and had meals on the table every day. I loved that. I was the lady of the house. No one complained. Everyone ate, and I had two sweet little boys whom I was responsible for. I was learning how to be a real woman. There was even a small cornfield in back of the house. We had sweet corn whenever we wanted. I had suddenly embarked on a new, useful life, and I was good at it. And Ruth and Arthur were so brilliant and witty and warm. I had never spent time with people of that quality. I liked it. They liked me. They teased each other. They were fortyish but in love, in love.

Toward the end of the summer, Arnie climbed into my cot. (I don't know why we didn't share a bed—the children?) As he climbed in, he said, "I really used to love you."

I pushed him out of bed to the floor. "You used to love me? You used to love me and now you want to fuck me?"

Somehow summer was over. Arnie got into the big convertible car with the top down. The boys were in the backseat. They waved good-bye, facing me on their knees, as I stood in front of our summer house, sad, too stunned to say good-bye. I have no idea how I got back to New York.

Any thought of going home to my parents was out. I would never spend a night with them again. It was toxic, and to tell you the truth they were much more content without me. Where to go? I'd never lived by myself. I had no furniture or utensils. I had no friends. I couldn't work. I was cut off from the wild world of theater and actor friends that used to be. I was dangerous for them to associate with, and now I was cut off entirely from the community around Arnie that I yearned to be a part of.

So I moved in with Fremo. I slept on the couch in her small one-bedroom apartment somewhere in the East Fifties. Fremo was the dearest, most generous, different, uniquely crazy woman in the world. When I was growing up on 148th Street, Fremo would beat on the windows of the brownstones up and down the street and take the owners' cats home to our own, six houses down. I don't remember anyone coming after their cats; the neighbors were all afraid of her. She had a high, shrill, elegant, thirties-movie-star voice that screamed in indignation when she saw an animal abandoned.

She was an abandoned animal herself. She had turned from the waif I saw in her early photographs to a voluptuous five feet eight, with long beautiful legs with high heels attached to them. Her large breasts jiggled. Her hips swung. Her narrow, ascetic, pale face floated above, a gash of red lipstick, black eyebrow pencil around large sensitive blue eyes, and thin light brown hair in a short straight bob around her face. She worked all week as a social worker on the Bowery with the drunks. After work and on weekends she was at the Art Students League on 57th Street. Painting, painting was the love of her life, her true obsession. Fremo had no luck with men, certainly not the rich ones who would take her out someplace fancy, fuck her, and not call again. And she was crazy.

At the time I moved in with her she was married to Charlie. He was an odd Midwesterner who had something to do with oil, or building, or plumbing—depending on the day. The story goes, she was at art camp and he had put an ad on the bulletin board. *Lonely Midwestern businessman etc. wants to meet NY artistic type.* She snapped it up. I don't know where they married, but she adored him. He was a good old boy. She'd flutter around when he was there. "Charlie said I look like the *Venus de Milo*." Oh God, she loved being married, being a Mrs., finally breaking through to the 1950s Jewish American concept of womanhood.

Some years later she would learn that Charlie also had a wife in the Midwest with whom he split his time. Fremo and Charlie were at my parents' apartment when she found out. She grabbed my father's long black umbrella and hit Charlie over the head with it all the way down 52nd Street, screaming at him and crying at the same time. I think it was the only time I ever saw her break down.

Anyway, at that time she was happily married and I was happy to have a place to stay, with an aunt who was peculiar, and loved me, and left me alone. I was very hurt. I didn't want to see Arnie, and I missed the little boys terribly. I missed being a mommy, cooking and playing with them. I felt totally isolated. I sat in the apartment. I walked in the park. I didn't visit anyone. No one visited me.

At a certain point I decided to get my own apartment. I had money saved, thanks to my parents. My mother and I found a great one-bedroom on the first floor of an old brownstone in Chelsea, with a balcony, long doors and windows looking to the street, twenty-foot ceilings, and a fireplace. I had it painted eggplant with a white trim. My first apartment. My mother and I started to go to auctions to look for furniture. She was fun and the smartest shopper in the world; our apartments had always been furnished from her auctions. I was beginning to breathe.

Arnie started to call. I hung up. Over the next few weeks he called incessantly. I wouldn't, couldn't talk to him. Fremo told him I wasn't home. He sent an emissary. Who, I don't remember. Would I meet him at the apartment on Third Avenue? He just wanted to apologize— that's all.

I remember sitting on the ugly, furry, dark-green bedspread, sullen, confused, crying at last over my hurt and humiliation at Arnie's hands. He kept talking, apologizing, apologizing, thanking me for helping him to change, to alter his character flaws. Never before had he understood his weakness, harshness, wrongness, illadvisedness. I felt nothing. Heavy. Sodden. The room was smaller than I remembered it. I was ashamed I had made that awful green bedspread. I didn't trust him. I wanted to go back to Fremo's. I told him I was moving to my eggplant-painted apartment. I told him I didn't feel anything for him. I was not so much in love as I was in awe of Arnie.

A month later, more or less, we were married in Hoboken. Ruth and Arthur and my friend Mary Carver were witnesses. I wore a gray skirt and huge stripy jacket of Fremo's with big shoulder pads that I had to belt in. Arnie had a near fistfight with the judge who married us in his office. Arnie felt the judge overcharged him. Arthur calmed him down. Afterward, Arnie took me to Moskowitz and Lupowitz to celebrate. A theatrical middle-aged woman at the next table suddenly stood up and burst into song in Russian. The gentleman with her extended his arm toward her as if he were introducing her. He stayed like that all through her performance. My Russian roots were watered.

Arnie now rented a large dark apartment on the ground floor on

82nd between West End and Riverside Drive. The only room with light was the living room. Its windows looked out onto 82nd Street. The boys were with us, of course. Margie had them most weekends. She was married now to a man named Artie.

Kermit Bloomgarden was a huge producer on Broadway. Any play of real value, he'd produced. He had a new play, *Wedding Breakfast*, that he wanted me to do. Four characters, two men, two women, a comedy. Herman Shumlin was directing. Terry Hayden, whom I knew from the Actors Studio, was Herman's assistant. I wanted to play the funny girl part opposite Harvey Lembeck. No, they said. I was to play the leading lady part opposite Tony Franciosa, who had been waiting tables at Schrafft's when they hired him.

There was a gentleman's agreement between Actors' Equity and the League of New York Theatres and Producers. The theater would not permit a blacklist on Broadway. A tribute to a very brave board of principled actors and a great group of men and women, the producers who fought against the McCarthy tide.

I had convinced them to let me do the funny girl when they came up to see me in stock. I was playing the part Julie Harris had originated on Broadway in *I Am a Camera*. The part Liza Minnelli went on to film in *Cabaret*. From that performance they determined I was their leading lady. I fought, I left, I came back. Kermit said it was that part or none. You've seen those fifties movies: stuffy career girl, dressing gowns, love scenes (on proscenium in front of curtains, ugh)— boring. But Tony wasn't boring. Tony was as dynamic and talented as he was beautiful. He was grabbed and seduced by Hollywood when he belonged in the theater.

Our stage for *Wedding Breakfast* was divided into two apartments: My apartment was at stage level, the men's apartment four feet higher. Opening night, Tony and Harvey were doing their scene; the lights were on in their apartment. Tony had a long monologue. In the middle of it, he accidentally dropped his keys into my apartment (which was dark). Without missing a beat, he jumped down into my apartment, picked up the keys, and jumped four feet back up to his lit apartment. Without missing a beat or a word. Harvey watched him with his mouth open the whole time. Needless to say, the whole audience applauded him, and when the reviews came out Tony was a Broadway star.

But our director, Herman Shumlin, was a wreck. He was an old-fashioned director. He'd done great work with the drama *Watch on the Rhine*, working with seasoned Broadway actors. Our kind of Method exploration made him sick. His neck vertebrae dislodged, his head tilted to one side. He was in tremendous pain, especially from our proscenium love scene. Tony and I were supposedly in the park. We admitted our love and had many long kisses. This was an uncomfortable scene. We were two feet from the audience, unable to build that fourth wall, and the scene was gushy-romantic. On top of that, it was Herman's favorite scene, and he would conduct it like an orchestra for the level of passion he wanted. During the week while Herman was away recovering, Tony and I became comfortable with the scene and with each other in it. It was not high passion, but it was exploratory and really charming. When Herman saw it, he beat his fists on my dressing room door. "Betrayed," he boomed. "Betrayed. Betrayed." I locked my dressing room door.

Tony Franciosa was married at the time. Beatrice, I think, was her name. She adored him and was insecure about her looks.

Shelley Winters is bigger than life—was. It came through on-screen, an energy, a charge too big to contain. In life she could be a huge ballsy monster, running over anything in her tracks, or a funny, smart Brooklyn kid.

Shelley showed up on opening night, made a beeline for Tony's dressing room, and introduced herself. By the end of the run, Tony's marriage was over and he was set to star in another play. Mike Gazzo's *A Hatful of Rain*, in which he played a drug addict. Good play. Terrific performance by Shelley and Tony to great reviews. Love, lust, marriage, divorce.

I'd been blacklisted for about four years when Tony and I did *Wedding Breakfast*. It would be another seven before I saw Shelley again. About a year before I got off the Blacklist, around 1962 or 1963. We were like fire and dynamite together in an independent film.

I felt I was caught in a Red Queen world, the Cheshire cat zooming at me from the trees. I was falling, falling, into a strange, bizarre world where Joe McCarthy was the Red Queen, screaming, "Off with their heads, off with their heads!"

The sane people were the elegant couples I was coming to know: Ring Lardner, his wife, Frances (who had first been married to Ring's brother, who had died young in the Spanish Civil War); Zero Mostel and Kate of course; Fra and Sol Kaplan; Waldo and Mary Salt, Zelma and Michael Wilson, who wrote *Bridge on the River Kwai*; Jules Dassin; John Berry, who'd moved to Paris; Dalton Trumbo, who would write for Kirk Douglas, and who finally broke the blacklist; Walter Bernstein and Abe Polonsky, who with Arnie asked a non-blacklisted friend to front for them in television. Abe, Arnie, and Walter wrote for *You Are There* and for many brave producers in TV who worked with great blacklisted writers through a front man. The "front man" was a hero in the business. It was a sly game for Arnie, Walter, and Abe to maneuver, and a delicious way to outsmart the enemy. Walter later wrote the movie *The Front*, based on himself, Arnie, and Abe, with Woody Allen playing the go-between. It was a great comedy and absolutely true. The three writers were good friends, stimulated one another, and had some very loyal, remarkable friends in the industry, producers who made it possible for them to earn a living and support their families undercover. *The Front* also told the story of Phil Loeb, a veteran actor who played Molly's husband on a popular television series called *The Goldbergs* for many years. Loeb was fired from *The Goldbergs*, and a few years later, suffering from severe depression, he took his own life in a New York hotel room.

While I was on the Blacklist, I continued to drop in at the Actors Studio. I was staggered by the worship given to Lee Strasberg. The tape recorders were taking down his every word, and Lee could talk and talk and talk. If there was no exercise or scene that day, he would stand in the acting area and expound on who really represented the Method, the right Method. Guess who? Not Sandy Meisner or Bobby Lewis; not Vakhtangov, not the Russians who started it, not the Group members who discovered and shared it, and particularly not Stella Adler, who studied with Stanislavski in Paris. Stanislavski wrote *An Actor Prepares*, the Method actors' bible.

All the actors were poised in a breathless, lean-forward position. The worship bothered me and turned me off. I couldn't breathe. One morning I left the studio in the middle of Strasberg's drone and came on the sight of General Charles de Gaulle, being pulled on a platform of some kind to a parade on the East Side. Voilà! General de Gaulle himself, on 44th Street between Eighth and Ninth. History was passing by. I thought about running back inside the studio and telling everyone, "Come, come, history is passing by!" But the platform was moving too fast. I ran up to two adolescent girls deep in chatter. "Look, look," I said, "that's General de Gaulle—history is passing by!"

"Who?" they asked, looking around.

"History, history!"

They continued on, talking their way up the street.

444 Central Park West

Alot of Arnie's friends were living at 444 Central Park West at 104th Street: Waldo Salt and his wife, Mary, with their daughters, Jennifer and Debbie, and Ethel and Buddy Tyne. (Ethel's daughter Judy later married Hal Prince.) On the first floor were Tanya and David Chasman with two children, and Gladys Schwartz, my future best friend.

Sol Kaplan, a brilliant composer, lived two floors above us with his wife, Frances Heflin (Van Heflin's sister), and their kids, Jonathan and Nora. Fra was a working actress. She had a role in the great William Inge play *The Dark at the Top of the Stairs* on Broadway. Fra was my other significant girlfriend at 444 Central Park West.

Sol had a musician's hot temper. Jonathan, their son, either inherited it or, as the only other man in the house, competed with his father from the time he could talk. Fra tried to keep the peace, throwing herself between her son and her husband.

Sometimes I'd hear my front door open. Fra would quietly come into the bedroom, put her head on my shoulder, and sob. When she had cried it all out, she'd go back upstairs to her tempestuous husband and son.

Our apartment was on the eleventh floor, overlooking the park, with a small terrace. The dining room had glass doors; we curtained them to make a big bedroom for the boys. In addition there were two bedrooms and a maid's room. The larger bedroom became "our" bedroom, the smaller one Arnie's room, where he wrote at his desk and slept on a brown flat couch. I had the bigger bedroom to myself, unhappily.

Some nights Arnie would stumble from his room next door to mine, lean with his arms high on my open door, wearing saggy white underwear, and say with disdain for himself, "I need to be satisfied." Arnie's approach to sex was not intimate. The need for sex put him in a humiliating position. The need for it gnawed at him, until the only way to deal with it was to get it out of the way, and he came to my door with the inner weakness of a priest. Each time I welcomed him with open arms, as if he were a poor sick child with a fever.

"Yes," I'd say, "come here."

I was proud he wanted me. Sometimes pleasure would come, sometimes not. There was no conversation. There was no touching, no kissing. I longed for him to touch me, to kiss me, to let me kiss his mouth. I longed to talk, to whisper, to touch him, to have him put his hands on me, hold me, hug me, kiss my head. Love me. He fucked for release. Quietly, the sounds of the bed linen shushing, bedsprings, car sounds from the street. Afterward he would lie spent beside me before returning to his room.

I wanted to say, "I love you." I'd look at his wonderful tanned face, at his closed eyes with thick black eyelashes. *I love you,* I'd say silently, practicing to myself. But I felt he'd think I was corny. So I never said it. I never heard it. Afterward, I'd watch his resting face. Distant. The disappointed mouth. The closed lids hiding his world from me. I was too much of a coward to cross the heavy silence. I lay quietly, watching him breathe, till his eyes opened, black-brown.

"Thank you," he would say, and stumble out of bed into his own room.

I was grateful, like a Mormon wife, to be visited by the household god. Grateful the way Geraldine Fitzgerald was grateful to be with Heathcliff, even if she would never be his Cathy.

So began a nine-year residence at 444 Central Park West. The boys grew to fourteen and fifteen; Eva, Arnie's daughter, became a young bride. Dinah, my daughter, our daughter, would be born there. And from that foyer I would leave forever.

When I was out of work, I called Herbert and Uta and asked if I could teach a class there. I'd never taught before, but there were no questions or hesitation. "Yes, of course." My name joined their list of teachers, and students began to sign up for the class. I had an income, I had an outlet, a passionate outlet, talented people to work with, a door to unemployment insurance, a legitimate reason to leave the house for hours once or twice a week—and most important of all, money to pay Vi, our housekeeper.

I still get excited when I talk about this period. In my first class at HB Studio were Sandy Dennis, straight out of college, little Mike Pollard, whom you saw later in *Bonnie and Clyde*, a passionate and talented young woman named Rosemary Torre and her husband, Mike, a great Irish guy, and about eight others.

Every play is a situation—a situation you have encountered before or a situation you are entering for the first time. The job of an actor is to make the imaginary circumstance given to them as real as anything in their lives. That and, if you're onstage, to stimulate yourself in fresh ways to reproduce this reality night after night after matinee.

But in my HB class, by the end of our first year together, I was giving my students improvisation situations that took each actor into dangerous inner places. I gave Sandy Dennis a date with Mike, Rosemary's husband. His need: to get into her bed. Her need: to steer the relationship into friendship, not sex, or end it. Well, Sandy was such a sensual being, with such powerful yearnings rushing through her, that after his first kiss she was gone, gone—on the bed, pulling him to her, Mike looking back at me helplessly till I stopped the scene. I gave Mike and Rosemary a situation: She was cheating on him. He was to confront her; she was to deny it. That night after class in their own home, Mike had a heart attack. This terrible lesson for me as a young teacher changed me, changed us all, forever.

I was horrified. I was responsible. Rosemary kept calling me and came to see me. She told me that Mike had an existing heart condition. He'd had an attack before, but he didn't want it known because he loved the work so much. It could have killed him, the work he loved and the places it took him. The places every actor has to go to experience each new situation, each new life, was for him, for his fragile heart, like swallowing dynamite. A year later Mike died. Beautiful Mike. I became a very careful teacher. In those days my students were my age or older. We both learned. I have been teaching to this day. My students are friends and family; we give back. Not long ago, preparing to act in a film, I went to an ex-student of mine and asked her to coach me. She was brilliant. I can only hope to give others what she gave me.

I did *A Hole in the Head* the year before Dinah was born. Garson Kanin directed it. Paul Douglas starred. My friend for life Joyce Van Patton was in it, and Kay Medford. The script was a drama, but the way Garson cast it, we came into New York a comedy. I think the playwright was in shock. It was his own family he had written about, but one didn't argue with success. *A Hole in the Head* was a hit. Garson never gave a direction, except to suggest where to move. On the train when we left for Boston to try it out, I asked him for some sort of discussion about my character. He said he never discussed; everything was in the casting. If he cast correctly, his actors would know how to play their parts. My part was that of a lonely lady in blue who comes to meet Paul Douglas at his hotel, hoping for romance. It was a twenty-minute scene, the only one I had in the play. But it was a lovely character. I loved doing it.

One night after the show I was in my dressing room on the fifth floor, taking off my makeup, when a British gent burst through the door, threw himself at my feet, literally, introduced himself as Ken Tynan, an English critic, and proclaimed that my performance was the best he'd seen in years. Please, please come downstairs and meet the lady who had accompanied him to the theater. She, too, was dying to meet me.

We clanged down the backstage steps. There on stage level was a pale blonde with a wispy voice. It was Carol Saroyan, later Carol Matthau, who was to be the best whispering advice giver a girl could ask for. The next day, she and Ken Tynan ran off from their respective spouses to Spain for a romantic interlude. When he returned to London, he wrote a lovely piece about me, which he sent.

The Committee

The main thing about *A Hole in the Head* was that the Un-American Committee finally caught up with me. I'd been avoiding strange official-looking men, or pairs of men showing up in rehearsal halls, outside stage doors, even when I was pushing a baby carriage; now I was finally caught, served with a subpoena, and a date was set for me to go to Washington to appear before the Committee. Bob Whitehead was the producer, a gentleman from handsome head to polished boot. I told him I had to speak to him. We met in his office. I told him Leonard Boudin was representing me, I was taking the Fifth, and that I understood that he might need to replace me—to protect his show, his investment. Anyone who refused to answer questions in front of the committee was absolutely considered to be a Communist, a threat, and in the wider community, persona non grata. I certainly didn't want to endanger the show or have American Legion groups harassing our actors because of me.

Bob said, and my throat closes as I write this, "You do whatever you have to do. When you come back, your part will be here waiting for you."

My visit to Washington was like a visit to the dentist's office. *Is it gonna hurt? Are they gonna drill?* I saw myself squirming in the dentist's chair, mouth wide open, black like a cartoon.

"Ow! Ow! OOOOW! Stop!"

Pulling teeth, blood, spit, drilling, loud—all the crazy dentists shoving for a chance at my mouth.

I actually wasn't sure whether I was a member of the Communist Party or not. As far as my husband was concerned I was a hapless bourgeois, unschooled in Marx, Lenin, or Hegel. He was a writer, an intellectual; I had my own ideas, and to him they were simplistic, unideological.

One afternoon, Arnie passed me in the foyer of our apartment.

"I think it would be a good idea for you to join the Party. It would make some of our friends more secure around you."

I understood the truth of his logic.

"Okay," I said on my way to the kitchen. By the time I turned on the faucet, I was a member of the Party, since Arnie to me was God, his suggestion a reality.

We went on our respective ways. I doubt my name was added to an official list. I was never given a card saying I was a member of the Communist Party. But I crossed an invisible line somewhere between the foyer and the kitchen. I was one of them. I liked it.

So I was surprised when I met with Leonard Boudin to find out that more steps had to be taken to become an actual Communist Party member, and I wasn't one, he said.

I was being readied and prepared for the House Un-American Activities Committee, and the Fifth Amendment was my defense, Leonard told me.

My intellect was challenged. My emotions were my ally, part of my equipment as an actor, but Leonard told me feelings must be put away in a secret drawer and forgotten. They would only get me in trouble.

Leonard impressed on me strongly that if I answered any questions that involved the past, I could open myself up to answering questions about the beliefs of other people, my friends, my husband.

Leonard said, "Don't engage in conversation; you're not smart enough to sense a trap. They are professionals. That's why I'm there. If you're not sure, ask me. I'll be sitting right next to you."

I understood that if I made a mistake, had a slip of the tongue, got angry or silly, I could jeopardize myself, my family, even go to jail, as the Hollywood Ten had.

I still don't understand the Fifth Amendment. "I refuse to answer on the grounds that it may tend to incriminate me." It worked, when someone invoked it, but it made no sense. This was Wonderland and the penalty was: YOU CANNOT WORK FOREVER IN FILM OR TV.

But I was already not working forever.

All of us blacklisted actors understood that this was for the rest of our lives. This was what forever looked like in the fifties.

Change was inconceivable; that the fifties would eventually become the wild sixties nobody in their right mind would have ever believed.

I wasn't scared, I was curious; I would see the monster in its lair. With Leonard Boudin to protect me and a hit Broadway play, *A Hole in the Head*, to return to.

Going to the committee was like being taken to the zoo by my dad when I was a little girl. I'd hide behind his legs when the lion roared, when the gorilla shook its cage.

Leonard was my dad. Instead of the real lion's roar, these men reminded me of Mr. Forster, my fourth-grade history teacher, who sweated too much and kept touching the back of my neck.

They asked nothing about American Federation of Television and Radio Artists, where we were organized and at war.

The committee was incredibly, laughably ignorant about everything show business—television, theater, agents, and especially Communism.

Interestingly, looking back now, there was a similarity between the mind-set most Communist functionaries have and that of the Soviets and the HUAC. People who are accustomed to taking orders, whose minds are so closed, thinking restricted, limited. The writers deported to prison camps by Stalin, the fear of free thought, the preening and arrogance of the former KGB. Shocking, really, that these men investigating enemy activity in the entertainment industry, the infiltration of foreign spies, should not know anything about the shows on TV, that actors have agents who sell them in these shows. That they didn't even know I was in a play on Broadway or the name of it. Who appointed these men who set the rules for the whole country?

"Talk! Talk!" they yelled. "Do you know a person by the name of Morris Carnovsky?" "You know a person by the name of Alan Manson? Lou Pollan? John Randolph?" "Name someone! Anyone!"

Well, my dear, I recommend the Fifth Amendment, and my attractive and mysterious lawyer, Leonard Boudin, who is no longer with us. I entered the chamber—why do I remember a kind of three-tiered stand?—and a fiftyish-year-old man sitting on the top tier said to me, "What's a nice little girl like you doing in a place like this?"

Pleasantly I replied, "What are you doing in a place like this?"

I was seated behind a table with Leonard Boudin at my side. About eighteen men asked questions, but mostly one man. To most questions, Leonard said, "Take the Fifth. Say 'I refuse to answer on the grounds of my Fifth Amendment rights.' "

This was curiouser and curiouser. My body could rise like a balloon over the proceedings. And what did they know? Nothing. It made my head shake from side to side in amazement.

TRANSCRIPT FROM THE COMMITTEE HEARING

Mr. Arens: Have you been engaged in the last few years in a play called *Danger*?

Miss Grant: It is a television show.

Mr. Arens: Was your employment in the production *Danger* procured for you by any person who, at any time, was known to you to have been a Communist?

(The idea was so funny, I laughed. Leonard nudged me.)

Mr. Boudin: The answer with respect to that, and generally, would have been the same, namely, that Miss Grant got the job through the routine way and is not prepared to say who were and were not members of the Communist Party.

Mr. Arens: Do you know a person by the name of Sidney Lumet?

Miss Grant: Yes.

Mr. Arens: Did he have anything to do with your appearances on *Danger*?

Miss Grant: I refuse to answer that question on the grounds of the Fifth Amendment.

Mr. Arens: Do you know whether or not Sidney Lumet has ever been a member of the Communist Party?

Miss Grant: I refuse to answer that question on the
   grounds of the Fifth Amendment.

Mr. Arens: Are you presently under Communist Party
   discipline?

Miss Grant: I am not a member of the Communist Party.

Mr. Arens: Are you presently under Communist Party
   discipline?

Miss Grant: I am not.

The Committee was so out of touch and awash in ignorance that I was thinking, *Get a good director. This wouldn't pass for a dangerous committee on TV. They're really bad actors, not the least in touch with reality.*

I left the chamber. The senator who thought I was a nice girl didn't look at me. I now had the stamp of disapproval. Officially OUT. I went back to the play. Not a ripple; every day was the same as it had been.

Dinah. My Dinah.

Dinah. My Dinah. Arnie wanted a girl so badly. He hung pink and blue cords from the ceiling light in the maid's room, which was to be the baby's room. He'd turn the tassels to see which would end up toward him, the pink or the blue. When pink, he was excited; when blue, sad. Yes, children, in those days doctors couldn't tell the baby's sex in advance.

I didn't get a small round belly. I had a yard-long belly stretched out way in front of me. I wore my old camel-hair coat all winter; the button on the coat was pulled so far that the frayed thread stretched across my stomach. From the back one could see nothing; from the side I was formidable. I went to the unemployment insurance office one morning with my belly and coat. There was a Hispanic man who sent the people in line who arrived at his post even two minutes before the time printed on their cards back to the end of the line. It was a cold, gray winter day. Maybe five hundred people were lined up, maybe fifteen lines with fifty or so people shuffling forward. Everybody switched with the person behind them as they approached the counter so they wouldn't be sent to the back of the line again and wait another hour. I reached the man a couple of minutes early, but I needed to get home. I had been carrying my belly in line for forty-five minutes, and yes, he told me to go to the back of the line. Suddenly I became La Pasionaria. My voice boomed: "I'm sick of being treated like shit! Who the fuck do you think you are? I'm not going to the end of any line. I'm pregnant, damn it. You take care of me right now. What's your name? I'm reporting you for cruelty." Rah rah rah.

Suddenly I had a revolution on my hands, and I was leading it. The place was in an uproar. People were crowding out of lines. Screaming at the guy: "Yeah! Yeah!"

"Petty power," I yelled at him. "Petty power, that's what you are!"

I had an army behind me. All the civil servants were scared. I was trying to think where to go with this when a warm arm came around my shoulder and a kind voice said, in a very "there, there" tone of voice, "I'm the supervisor. What's the problem, dear?" He sounded like my childhood doctor, Dr. Berkowitz.

I pointed at my enemy. "He's sending people . . ." My voice cracked, hot tears poured down my face. La Pasionaria shrank back into a pregnant, sobbing lady.

"Yes, yes," the supervisor said as he led me to a cot in one of the offices. "Lie down. You can rest. I'll take care of everything."

I didn't want to rest, but I had to. I was so ashamed of my blubbering, I couldn't face my followers. Finally I crept out.

A month later, January 25, Arnie took me to Mount Sinai, sat around for a while, then left. I didn't blame him. It was such a kind of boring anticlimax to wait, wait in white rooms. The day before, the newspapers had printed the Pope's opinion on childbirth. "It's a cinch," he said in Italian. "Women drop babies in the field; it's the most natural act in the world." An hour later I was lying one leg hither, one leg thither, begging for anesthesia, screaming, "Fuck the Pope, put me out, fuck the Pope." When I came out of it, they brought my baby to me. Red-faced, dark-haired, her head came to a point, her mouth stretched from ear to ear. She looked like Edward G. Robinson. I'd been going to call her Darya after my Grandmother Dora, but it was too fancy a name for that little face. "Dinah, I'll call you," and Dinah it was.

Tommy and Mikey sent cards across Central Park to Mount Sinai. Sweet little-boy cards. Eva slept over. Everybody wanted a baby in the house. The baby was big, I was small, so for months I carried around an inflatable ring cushion to sit on. My mother and father were exploding with joy. Arnie let them visit once a week. Early on Arnie had agreed to one feeding of Dinah when she woke up screaming at one or two in the morning. I wasn't breast-feeding, so it was all formula, heating bottles from the fridge and putting the nipple into her greedy mouth. When Dinah wailed, it was a cartoon wail. A big black hole, with a surprisingly loud noise coming out of her little red face. On one of those two a.m. feedings, the wails didn't stop. I made my way from the bedroom to the baby's room. Dinah was red with rage. So was Arnie. They were both screaming. I took her from him quietly. We didn't exchange a word. He went to bed. From then on, I took all the feedings.

Nothing, nothing could get between Dinah and me. She was a strong, funny baby. Even when I could feel myself sinking in my marriage to Arnie, she delighted me. She made me laugh. Fra Heflin had her little girl Mady at the same time I had Dinah, so Fra and I had each other, and the two babies visited in the building and in Central Park.

Dinah screamed her way out of her room into a crib in my room. She screamed out of her crib into her carriage, with me rocking her all night, then out of her carriage onto my bed, and finally from lying next to me to lying on top of my chest. When I couldn't breathe anymore, I put her back in her crib, next to my bed, and shut the door to my bedroom. In the hall, encouraging me to stay outside and let her cry it out, were my three stepchildren. It was a hot night; the sweat was pouring down. As the hours passed and Dinah's screams grew hoarse, the boys and Eva kept me from turning the knob on my bedroom door and picking up my furious baby. So hoarseness turned into laryngitis. I entered the bedroom. Dinah was still standing, red-faced, tear-strewn, indomitable, wide-open mouth still going *Wha!* But soundlessly. I lay her down in her crib, patted her back, sang to her, and she crashed. She slept in her crib in my room from then on.

As the tension between Arnie and me continued, Dinah was a great fun outlet for Tommy and Mikey; they had a funny baby sister to play with. Eva was conflicted. Dinah was yet another reason why her father wasn't paying any attention to her. Eva would cry at night. I would sit on her bed. She wanted her daddy, not me. Arnie didn't like tears, needy tears; he'd had enough of them. Eva was fifteen, a difficult age, and she was slightly overweight. Three strikes.

Two for the Seesaw

Arthur Penn and William Gibson sent a script. Come in and read for *Two for the Seesaw*, the part of Gittel. Gittel was like a second cousin to the shoplifter of *Detective Story*, so I knew why Arthur wanted me.

Arnie asked me what I thought of the script.

"Terrible," I said. "He has her going to the potty onstage. Tasteless. It's only two characters onstage all the time. It's awful."

How could I get out of it without hurting Arthur's feelings? I knew. I wouldn't go into character. I'd read Gittel like the upper-middle-class girl I really was. I just wouldn't get her. I wouldn't have to tell them I didn't like the play.

It worked. I walked into the room. Arthur and William Gibson, who wrote it, were there. Over and over I read for them. Over and over Arthur tried to reach me. Finally he gave up.

I was thrilled with myself.

I ran into Paddy Chayefsky on Sixth Avenue and told him the whole story. He thought I was very clever. Needless to say, two or three months later *Two for the Seesaw* opened to rave reviews, changed the face of theater, and catapulted Anne Bancroft to stardom. I was in shock. The last vestiges of respect Arnie had for my opinions were gone, and I was so jealous of Anne, I cried.

I was married to a sexy, charismatic, intellectual Jewish guy who loved me off and on, mostly off. After the five-year mark, mostly off. He basically needed me as an au pair for the boys and an added source of income. He was coping with keeping afloat financially with a dangerous heart problem. Also trying to fight a political assault as a deeply committed Communist.

I found I was making a fool of myself often, like a child vying for his attention. As I moved toward the end of my twenties, I became unattractive. At the unemployment insurance office, the young man checking my files asked my age. Coyly, I said, "How old do you think I am?" I was twenty-nine.

He said immediately, "Twenty-nine."

I blinked, went home, and got in bed. Almost thirty. I was old.

"Nothing," I said when Arnie asked what was wrong with me.

I was too insecure. He told me once I looked young with my glasses on.

"Really?" I said.

The glasses stayed on for weeks while I waited for another compliment. How boring was I? How bored was he!

He was my mirror. I had no career. At home I became dumber and homelier.

I was offered the London company of *Seesaw*, which of course was out of the question. Arnie suggested I ask about understudying Anne in the part. So the understudy went off to star in London and I filled her job.

I was resentful. I was impossible with Arthur Penn. Every direction he gave I fought because I thought it was to make me more like

Anne. I'd never seen the play. I didn't want to until I'd found my own Gittel. I asked for the stage manager, Porter Van Zandt, to show me the stage moves, for Arthur to give me more time alone, away from him. He didn't know what to do with me. He had a hornet on his hands, an insecure, resentful actress who was venting the rage she couldn't feel or show at home.

At my wits' end, unable to find the character, I finally sneaked into a matinee. The dawn broke, the sun came out. It was a love story! They loved each other! Remember love, attraction? Liking people? Enjoying them? Remember having fun? Poor Arthur! I never told him this. I never apologized for being impossible, but that wasn't the end of it.

I had just about mastered the first act of the play, maybe walked through the second act once or twice, when a phone call came.

"You're on tonight! Annie has her period."

I could feel the blood draining from my brain. I looked at where I had been sitting a second ago. The children and Arnie were sitting around the table eating dinner. Spaghetti marinara; the children's mouths were red with it. Arnie looked at me questioningly,

"They want me to go on tonight. Annie has her period."

Tonight. I will leave the pasta and this family and in two hours go onstage at the Belasco Theatre in a play I don't know, for an audience that has paid good money to see a wonderful play with a different actress—who's gotten rave reviews.

I'd been accepting a salary. I'd utterly blocked out this possibility, and it was here.

I don't know how I got in a cab, but I remember the ride, how cold I was. Marie Antoinette on the tumbrel could not have faced the guillotine with greater disbelief or dread than I faced this night. *Unprepared.* There is no more shameful and reprehensible word for an actor. I didn't know how I was going to get through the night.

Aside from the fact that I had never learned or blocked the second act, there were turntables for each apartment, Gittel's and Jerry's. One had to know how and when to get on and off in order to land in each apartment. Then there were clothes changes I'd never gotten to. Tights, skirts, pj's.

I entered Anne Bancroft's dressing room, where a very efficient, but officious, large woman took charge. I was trying to learn the lines for the second act. She was telling me I had to wash my feet between scenes. I called Porter Van Zandt.

"Let me concentrate."

She left the room.

Henry Fonda looked in. His face was trusty, his eyes were corn-flower blue. I spilled my heart out. I had to let him know. We had never as much as read a line together, and suddenly he would have a partner, inadequate, who should not be on that stage with him.

Porter announced, "The understudy for Ms. Bancroft will go on tonight."

A few people in the audience left, and then childbirth began— blurry, jumping off turntables, clothes torn off me, clothes thrust on me, shoes, clothes, white peroxide on my upper lip in Gittel's apartment that wasn't wiped off for Jerry's apartment.

I sensed a fascination in the audience, a kind of horror at being present at the scene of an accident. Nobody knew when the crash would take place. Hank said, "I'll take you through it. Hold on."

I never took my eyes off his strong, steady, blue, blue eyes. He never took his off me. He was holding me and leading me like a dancer, a doctor-dancer, and I made it to the end. He got an ovation at curtain; the audience had watched him make this happen. It was his night. Hank had once told me that he was more comfortable onstage than any other place in life. To experience that real strength and intimacy with him was a life lesson and a privilege. No other actor after him could have done it. I know.

Anne left the show and I stayed on, stepping into my own Gittel finally. A series of different Hollywood leading men followed—Dana Andrews, Jeffrey Lynn, Hal March. But it was Gittel's play. The audience was on her side. Except for that one night when Hank Fonda saved Gittel's life.

Burt Lancaster

I was offered two independent movies while I was blacklisted. As I buzzed around our new apartment at 444 Central Park West in my uniform skirt and sweater, the phone rang and it was John Frankenheimer, a charismatic, successful young director who offered me the lead opposite Burt Lancaster in *The Young Savages*. I became dizzy. I had to sit down. I was scared. I didn't realize how comfortable I'd become in anonymity. To step out of it into a big, blazing, mainstream film was to risk the abyss. I knew that Burt Lancaster had worked with Waldo Salt, that he was one of those progressive good guys, like his good friend Kirk Douglas. Did I meet with John Frankenheimer? I must have. The part, I think, was a social worker raised in a tough neighborhood who had once had a thing with Burt's character. I could be wrong, but that's what I remember.

Day of the shoot. A car took me to a street set. One Hundred and Sixteenth Street somewhere, teeming neighborhood, mostly Latino, black. My first scene was to be shot on that street. The neighbors had their chairs out; the kids were running around, screaming. I was packed into the backseat of a limo with John and Burt Lancaster, whom I'd never met, to go over the lines for a scene where we bump into each other on the street for the first time in years. Someone said, "We need to get this shot"; the windows of the car were open to the street. Burt Lancaster, bigger than life, godlike in beauty and power, movie star, was saying his lines, and suddenly I felt all the Method reality I'd worked on leak out of me, never to return. It was all too much, too fast, and too public, and Burt's presence so big and unreal and startling that I was outside myself watching from the bottom of a well.

They took me to makeup and hair, which was set up in the classroom of a public school, then released me to the street, to the crowds, the lights, and eventually Burt, whom my character hadn't seen in a long time. He and I exchanged some flirtatious words and exited. It was my shot, long shot, walking up to Burt, his back to the camera that is facing me. Action! I worked on moving my legs. I felt my hips pushing them to move. My heel caught on the concrete. I wanted to die. At the end of the walk stood Zeus, the sun—or was it the lights?—blazing behind his golden head, making me squint as I forced my mouth to say lines I had absolutely no connection with. Later, as they put me in the car to take me home, I knew that it was my first and last day, and I was relieved. Shelley Winters quickly replaced me, and the film went on.

When I was fired from the Burt Lancaster film, Arnie took pity on me. I was so humiliated, I couldn't stop crying. I was talentless in front of everybody, the whole block, such a pitiful klutz in front of Lancaster. Arnie took me with him to the racetrack. He always went with his friend Norman Shelley. I sat on a wooden bench out of the loop, but happy to be asked, happy to be part of his outside life.

Much later, in another life, I was on *The Dick Cavett Show* with Richard Rodgers and Burt Lancaster. I said something to Dick Cavett like, "This is the first man who ever hired me"—nodding to Rodgers—"and this is the first man who ever fired me"—nodding to Lancaster. It

felt sweet. I was in the catbird seat. Years later, Frankenheimer attacked me in a restaurant, screamed at me, "Why?" It was all a jumble
at the time.

I didn't get it. Now I do. I don't know what strings they, especially
Burt, had to pull to get a studio to hire me, but they did. He had to fire
me. I couldn't step up to the job. I have a lot of people to apologize to
in my life. I wish I had done it when I had the chance.

Arnie's Heart Attack

Arnie had a heart attack. Walter Bernstein's brother was his doctor. The minute Dr. Bernstein told me, I hated him—"the doctor." I resented him. He could have prevented this. "Save him," I told him. Arnie was in a hospital on Long Island. I took our car and drove there. I have no sense of direction; I don't know how I got there. When I did, I sat in a chair opposite the bed and stared at Arnie. I had no words. None. After a couple of hours, he said, "Go home." How intolerable those visits must have been for him. To have to deal, in his precarious health, with someone like me—inadequate and shell-shocked. I knew I couldn't drive out by myself anymore without rearranging life at home, with anxious children who needed me. I was fine with that. I had a language with them, feelings, motherliness, normality. I was real. I had none of that with Arnie. I did not know how to talk or what to say.

Until Boris Pasternak and Aleksandr Solzhenitsyn, there was no real art coming out of the USSR. The Soviets made movies with happy peasants singing on tractors. Great composers were being reprimanded for not writing music for the masses. Only the ballet was left alone. The people loved the classics. *Swan Lake* was safe.

I learned not to express these opinions to Arnie, since they made him furious. "You don't understand," he'd say. He would reprimand me in front of company in our living room for joking about something he considered sacred. I felt shamed, minimized. When I tried to talk to him about the way he made me feel, he would go to his room and slam the door. I would write boring three-page letters trying to pour out my heart, as close to Marxism as I could get. They would be slid back under the door, where I waited. Sometimes with small grammatical corrections, but always, "Unless you can write me in acceptable terms, don't write!" That, of course, meant with a knowledge of Marxist philosophy. I tried rereading Marx, but I didn't know what I was reading or how to apply it.

Eventually, I stopped talking and started painting. I had a lot to get out of my system. Because Fremo was a painter, there had always been art in my life. I'm a good second-rate painter, and painting became a necessary passion for me. I did an ink and watercolor of a woman, her back to the viewer, sitting at a small square table in the middle of a room. There was a Persian rug on the floor. The windows and door were too high on the walls to be reached.

I knew I needed help. I started going to Dr. Austin, a psychiatrist. I was beginning to disassociate. I'd find myself staring out the kitchen window, startled when Arnie entered, when anybody entered. The children and Dinah were a life force; so was teaching. When I wasn't connected to them, I felt myself floating in a balloon that would rise, unmoored over the city, out, out into the unknown. What I was most afraid of was causing Arnie to have another heart attack, of causing his death by some unthinking, thoughtless act of mine.

When Arnie came home from the hospital, he was worried about working, about his health, about money. *Seesaw* had closed. My teaching money was just enough to pay Vi. We both felt the pressure.

Marty Gang

Just at this time, one of the bad lawyers, Marty Gang, who had gotten Lee Cobb and others to give names, got in touch with my aunt Anne Rosenthal. Anne was the top entertainment lawyer at William Morris. She worked with Abe Lastfogel, the head of the firm. She told me Marty Gang had called her, they had discussed me, and he felt he could get me off the Blacklist because of his contacts with the committee.

Arnie and I talked about it. I thought it was a trick. I knew it was a trick. Arnie felt we could use it. If together we went over everything I said to Gang, maybe we could use him the same way he was trying to use me. We knew it was a trap, but he had the wrong actor. I was not so desperate for work that I would turn anybody in, as he pressed his other clients to do.

As I'm writing, I suddenly want a cigarette. I haven't wanted a cigarette in thirty years.

I met with him twice at someone else's law office, in a small dark room. I felt safer meeting with him as Gittel—an open New York girl, not too smart, a girl who instinctively followed her heart. A creature of impulse, warm, sunny. Arnie and I went over his questions. They were about my AFTRA meetings. Gittel could handle them.

Marty Gang and I took a plane to Washington, D.C., to meet with the lawyers who worked with the Un-American Activities Committee. It was like an audition. It was a cool, sunny day, and there were about four men huddled around the edge of a long table in a large committee room. They activated a recording machine. The questions came fast. Gittel answered them with her usual bumbling innocence. Marty took over the questions, showing off for them or trying to justify bringing down such an innocent but dumb, uncooperative witness. My impression was that the Committee had run out of theater and film people and was casting around for a way to justify its existence. Marty focused on a meeting I had had around the selection of the president for AFTRA. Who did I meet with?

Gittel: They changed, you know what I mean? Different people all the time. Nice people, very educated. Yeah, I gave money, a couple of bucks, dollars, I mean. It went for food, lunch, you know what I mean?

Them: Where'd you go after the meeting?

Gittel: Go someplace—have coffee, you know?

Them: Who with?

Gittel: Different people each time, nice people.

Them: Just coffee?

Gittel: Oh you know, go shopping, shop around.

Them: Who did you go shopping with?

Gittel: *(squirming)* Who did I go shopping with?

Them: You must know who you went shopping with.

I cast about furiously for an answer; who would I go shopping with? Who had nothing to do with the Party and the union? My mind went to two women who were totally out of the loop, but who were helpful, sympathetic, and had no careers or jobs to lose. The men at the table were observing me.

Me: I think Elaine and Mary and I shopped in a dress shop after the coffee—

Them: Who?

Me: Yeah, we didn't buy anything, just shopped.

Them: Who?

Me: Elaine Eldmore, Mary Murphy, and me. We went to the dress shop.

Whew. I got away with it. Gittel did. Ditsy Gittel. But I realized it was an exercise in futility. A fishing expedition for Martin Gang's next informant. The lawyers clearly thought I was a waste of time, either a charlatan or an idiot. They were barely civil. Martin Gang was grim. We flew back to New York in separate seats, across the aisle from each other.

It wasn't until I was on the plane back to New York that it hit me. I gave them names. The names of two real women. I could feel my heart sink inside me. I burst through the door of the apartment and broke down crying. Sobbing. Arnie was lying on my bed. "I gave names." I told him what had happened. "You didn't give names." I had been so easily tricked. What would happen to those poor women? Out of the blue. I don't even know what made me think of them. I'd felt cornered, as Gittel had been cornered, and thought, *What a smart way out*.

But in my mind on that plane and forever afterward, I felt I had put two innocent and real women's lives and careers in jeopardy. That I couldn't trust myself.

The next time I introduced one old friend to another, my mind went blank—I literally could not remember their names. I know one part of me is forever punishing another part of me, for life. My throat closes when I think of the guilt and panic I feel, and felt from then till now. It's no accident that I went from years of not being able to remember or say names to the sudden inability to remember lines or, worse still, the fear that I would forget them. Fear. Without meaning to, I realized that I could say something unforeseen that would damage and cause untold destruction to another person.

I just reread what I wrote about that afternoon. What I feel is missing from that description was the depth of my desperation and guilt. The slip of the tongue that haunted my conscience affected my memory for names forever.

That afternoon in Washington, in the lions' den with the Committee lawyers and Martin Gang questioning me—no, pushing me to incriminate myself as a Communist, to incriminate other actors, Gang pushed the idea that our union meetings were really Communist cells, with money contributed for Communist causes.

Why did I go to Washington? Why did I put myself in such a dangerous position? Arnie felt it was worth a shot. If I was cleared I could earn a living, hugely important after his heart attack, which had changed everything and frightened both of us.

My choice was to use the character of Gittel to see me through the experience. Gittel was an innocent. A brave, funny girl who took chances. Gittel was disarming, charming. Audiences loved Gittel. I ought to know; I played her on Broadway every night for a year. She was a great cover for my fear. I feel a near faint still when I think of that fear. We had gone over any possible question they could ask me about him, our friends, the meetings—in Gittel's character and out. We knew from the outset that Martin Gang just wanted to bring them another trophy. For his own reasons, Arnie felt there was a slim chance that these lawyers would recommend lifting the Blacklist on me. It was basically an audition session. Writing this, I realize the extent of the idiocy on all sides.

In another life, many, many years later, I would discover that Elaine Eldmore worked in children's theater and did extra work on television.

And Mary, I was told, married a general.

But for me, in saying their names in front of the lawyers, the damage was done.

AFTRA

My new education began with the Blacklist. Learning to think outside myself, learning a new talent that was to serve me all the rest of my life. To fight the bad guys.

I may have been confused at home with Arnie, but I was very clear and motivated about this enemy from the time my name was listed in *Red Channels*.

I'd spent the past ten years taking action against the Blacklist in New York. My focus, talent, and passion went into that fight. It was my job to work through Actors' Equity to keep the theater free to hire any actor who was right for the part—and to vote the current board of AFTRA out of office.

Kim Hunter and I were both members of the Actors Studio, very celebrated, very young. Both in our early twenties when I acted in *Detective Story* and Kim acted in *A Streetcar Named Desire*. We both originated the roles on Broadway, appeared in the films, and were nominated for the Best Supporting Actress Oscar in 1952. Kim won for her moving Stella in *Streetcar*. I won the Cannes International Film Festival award for Best Actress of 1952 for *Detective Story*. We were golden girls with great lives and careers ahead of us. There's a line in Shakespeare's *Cymbeline*:

> Golden lads and girls all must,
>
> as chimney-sweepers, come to dust.

Kim and I came to dust early as working actors.

Working actors lost the best years of their lives, some never knew why, and in New York, two men, insignificant, and in one case downright stupid, actually ran the television and radio blacklist business. Giant corporations allowed two unstable, insignificant guys to exercise power over the choice of talent and content on television and radio for twelve years.

One of the men, Vincent Hartnett, created *Red Channels*, the pamphlet I was listed in. Hartnett also created AWARE, Inc. Private, anti-Communist entrepreneurs created the blacklist business in New York not just to catch Communists, but liberals. They set the standard for how far left an actor was, what Hartnett considered to be Communistic. The tide and absurd rules set by HUAC and McCarthy allowed it to happen nationwide. In New York it was a witch hunt. Only Hartnett and his cohorts decided who was the witch. It was also a lucrative business. Vincent Hartnett was a smart businessman; he was hired by ad agencies and networks to clear names for them. Anywhere from five bucks to twenty bucks a name, and there were hundreds of names daily to be cast.

Our union heads at the American Federation of Television and Radio Artists, the president of our union, Vinton Hayworth, and the rest of the board were also all members of AWARE, Inc. They partnered with Mr. Hartnett to dominate the television actors' union, to blacklist fellow actors in our union and the entire New York television and radio industry.

This meant that any actor who rose at a union meeting and spoke his mind took a calculated risk. If they rose to speak against the Blacklist in any way, some member of our AFTRA union board would give that actor's name to Hartnett at AWARE, Inc., and that actor would be added to the blacklist, his name sent to the networks as unhireable.

So the responsibility of those of us already blacklisted became to speak for the vast majority of television and radio actors who couldn't. Tentative at first, as we lived it, year in and year out, we funneled our passion into our war, our cause.

Slowly a small but steady group evolved of actors of all political stripes. Two lefties, Madeline Lee and me; Florida Friebus, a centrist member of the Actors' Equity board; some rarely working actors who helped with mimeograph machines; some working actors with family responsibilities. We few planned our war. To get AWARE, Inc., out of AFTRA and elect a new democratic slate.

We discussed actors without known affiliation who were smart, brave, and respected enough by their fellow AFTRA members to vote into office. Strong enough to oust this board of blacklisters.

Fighters get wounded. This is about an actor I involved in running for the board of AFTRA who lost everything because of it.

John Henry Faulk was a successful radio humorist on CBS, with a lot of sponsors and a high listening audience for two hours a day. He had come to New York from Austin, Texas, a sweet, funny, good ol' boy on air covering a highly educated, moral man. As Willy Loman would put it, "He was well liked," very. And he had kept that kind of Will Rogers unassailability, that un-Jew folksiness that we saw as a tough act to attack. He was America.

Madeline Lee and I called John Henry and went to his apartment to talk. He sat back and listened, his fingers making an arch below his eyes.

Before we left, he'd committed to run against the AFTRA board.

I turned at the door and repeated all the warnings. I owed him every warning that was not given to me when I spoke at Bromberg's memorial. "This is your one life. It could be changed forever; they have all the guns. They could wreck you!"

John talked about his father, who'd been a constitutional lawyer in Austin. "I was raised by a dad who looked out for the underdog, went to court and protected them. That's who he was, and he knew his Constitution."

I felt really privileged to know him, as I did with so many of my new friends.

Our next strategy was to shake the AFTRA board to its roots by calling for a vote against AWARE, Inc., and blacklisters in our union meetings. One blacklister listened to private conversations of members and reported them to AWARE, Inc., and the board.

The lefty actors could not get recognized to speak at AFTRA meetings; they were all too well-known to the board. Madeline Lee in particular, who had a smart mouth, could raise her hand forever and never be permitted to speak at a meeting.

I, on the other hand, was a new face, not quite placeable yet, and although I couldn't work in television I had been the leading lady on Broadway in *Wedding Breakfast* and either appeared or starred in one play after another on Broadway.

There was a huge AFTRA meeting at which I spoke, my first AFTRA speech.

"I think the fact that our board members [board members of AFTRA] are sitting with a man, Vincent Hartnett, who is the author of *Red Channels* and helped to put out lists is a shameful, shameful thing and should not be tolerated in our union." Applause.

The board stared out at us from the stage, a still life, their eyes and mouths like O's, startled and shaken.

Later, on May 24, 1955, we called for and seconded a reprimand of AWARE, Inc., and those who collaborated with them. A member of the board interrupted with a telegram from Kim Hunter, which they said she requested to have read at the meeting.

As a good American, Kim Hunter said she endorsed AWARE, Inc., and deplored Communist efforts to invade television.

It made me sick to imagine the duress she'd had to have been under to send that telegram and the shame she must have felt.

The vote to chastise AWARE, Inc., was 514 for AWARE, Inc., and 982 against. We won. A big, startling win. The hall erupted like a Dodgers game. The danger for the slate that John Henry was putting together was rising exponentially. The board and AWARE, Inc., would be fighting for their very existence.

We were euphoric, of course; our little secret group of ragtag actors had our first triumph. It was amazing.

John Henry named his slate the "Middle of the Road," opposed to both Communism and blacklisting. He was running for vice president, his friend Charles Collingwood for president. Collingwood was a very respected news correspondent for CBS. Impeccable. Other friends of his agreed to run with them. Almost twenty in all.

Our job, our group's job, was to gather the necessary signatures for each candidate to qualify to run for office. Spreading through the Theater District, we urged scared, reluctant actors to put down their signatures backing the candidates of "Middle of the Road," who were putting their professional lives on the line.

I remember getting a call from CBS asking if I was available to work on *Danger*, one of their shows, at the time.

"No, no," I protested, "you don't mean me, check your records."

The nice network girl called back, flustered. "I'm sorry, you're right, cancel that offer."

Then, through some wonderful oversight, I fell into a job on a soap opera. Ira Cirker was the producer-director. Soaps were big business, many of them with huge casts. I think it was *Search for Tomorrow*. I do know Mary Stuart, the leading lady who played Joanne Gardner, had been on every day since the show began. At the time my character was her friend Rose, who had a big grudge against Joanne for some reason. The last shot viewers had of me, I was holding a salt shaker containing poison over a soup pot in the kitchen. Would I or wouldn't I poison the soup and kill Joanne and her loved ones?

I felt really lucky. I was working live every morning, the show went straight into the television-watchers' homes, the cast was like family, and I hoped that maybe the show was below the radar. I was going to work every day and nobody said anything.

And my job was so fun. It was such a guilty pleasure to be below the visibility line on daytime television.

Then Ira called me in. The network, CBS, had been threatened by Laurence Johnson, a grocer from Syracuse, New York. He'd read *Red Channels* and found me. Johnson owned a few supermarkets in Syracuse. A few markets, that's all—not in New York City, not in Los Angeles. He threatened the advertising agency who represented Crest toothpaste, one of the sponsors of *Search for Tomorrow*. He would track down actors working on TV and threaten the sponsors—in this case, Crest—with a display in his markets in front of their merchandise: DO YOU WANT TO BRUSH YOUR TEETH WITH A PRODUCT FROM A COMPANY THAT EMPLOYS COMMUNISTS?

It was very effective. Johnson also had a strong connection to a group of veterans in Syracuse, who he threatened would start a mail campaign.

It put me out of the soap opera business and effectively stopped any paycheck I could count on, or Arnie could count on. Arnie had

angina, and he needed help paying the bills. Losing the soap opera
was a real loss for him and for me.

Mike Wallace, who hosted game shows back then, passed me in
the hall on my last day of work. "How ya' doing?"

I told him I was fired that day and how and why.

Mike said, "You tell me you're not a Communist; I'll go to bat
for you."

"Mike, the whole point is to be whatever you are, Communist or
not, as long as you don't hurt anybody. One is supposed to have the
freedom to believe anything in this country and still be able to earn a
living."

Laurence Johnson, the short, fat grocer from Syracuse, would
come to New York City, go to the Madison Avenue advertising agencies and, floor by floor, introduce himself and threaten them with en-
dangering their accounts. The accounts ranged from Lipton tea to
Campbell's soup to Crest toothpaste. Advertising agencies certainly
didn't want the publicity, so little Mr. Johnson became a very important man. Madison Avenue was not political, just anticontroversy.

Mr. Johnson and Mr. Hartnett became friends and partners of
sorts. They would be in contact, they would discuss strategy, and
Hartnett even brought Mr. Johnson to a hotel in New York to meet
with our union leaders, union president Vinton Hayworth, and members of AFTRA's board.

I was chosen by our group to rise at our AFTRA meeting and
confront our board with this information. It was given to us by a *Herald Tribune* reporter when the newspaper was afraid to print it.

It was a thrilling journey down the aisle, down the carpet, con-
fronting President Vinton Hayworth and the AFTRA board. As exciting as any theater experience I'd ever had. Facing the enemy.

The "Middle of the Road" slate won the election, with about eight of the old slate still serving. Collingwood was now president, Faulk now vice president of AFTRA. An overwhelming win for our side.

After the victory, several things happened. The new slate discovered they didn't have a clue as to how to run this huge union; AFTRA's old lawyer, a Mr. Joffe, continued in the same bad old way; and Vincent Hartnett revealed to John Henry's bosses at CBS suspicious Communistic connections in the leftist activities of John Henry Faulk.

John Henry lost his radio show, all employment stopped. He went broke. He tried selling bonds back in Austin. Friends gave money for him and his wife to live on. He went to a big lawyer, Louis Nizer, and convinced him to sue AWARE, Inc., Hartnett, and Johnson. Edward R. Murrow gave him $7,500 to pay his legal bills. Murrow considered the money an investment in America.

Six years later, July 29, 1962, John Henry was awarded three and a half million dollars, one million more than he and his attorney had asked for. The jury had asked the judge if they could give him an extra million.

Louis Nizer, John Henry's attorney, brilliantly exposed Vincent Hartnett's assumptions of John Henry's connections to Communist causes. All of which turned out to be lies. One of the dinners he was accused of attending was also attended by Eleanor Roosevelt.

Hartnett's lawyer, who was attached to Roy Cohn's law firm, was hopelessly outflanked by Nizer and by John Henry's appearance on the witness stand, his wounds so deep and unfair, his own decency and clarity so obvious.

Hartnett's insane rise, his bizarre inaccurate charges, his money-making on the backs of his victims, were exposed to the jury and the newspapers. Everything was printed for the world to see. After all, it was the sixties. The *Herald Tribune* was no longer afraid to comment on what they called the "unholy alliance" between the leaders of AFTRA and the Blacklist.

Laurence Johnson was the principal person in the suit. He was the one with the supermarket millions. He refused to show up in court or to testify. The day Louis Nizer made his brilliant summation to the jury, Johnson was found dead, of natural causes, in a Bronx motel.

There were to be no millions for John Henry Faulk or Louis Nizer. All that was left was about $160,000 from Johnson's estate.

Some interesting grace notes—John Henry talked Kim Hunter into telling her own story, her encounter with Hartnett, to the jury. She testified that after *A Streetcar Named Desire* and her Oscar for acting in the film, she was finding it puzzlingly difficult to find work as an actor. Someone suggested she contact Hartnett.

She testified that he asked for and received two hundred dollars from her to clear her name, and he demanded that she appear at that AFTRA meeting and speak in support of AWARE, Inc. When she refused, he demanded she send in a telegram in support of AWARE, Inc. She agreed. She was blackmailed for work, pure and simple.

Louis Nizer put into the record my speech at that meeting when I accused the AFTRA board of collusion with AWARE, Inc., and Hartnett.

John Henry never climbed back to where he was when he was taken down. Austin loved him, and he was surrounded by supporters and family. Friends like Molly Ivins, Studs Terkel, and Governor Ann Richards. He was their good old boy, but it was never the same. His confidence in himself was badly shaken. Was it his talent that was gone, or had the Blacklist affected him? The most evil aspect of attacking an actor's confidence in himself is that we're so fragile. John Henry lost confidence in himself. That was the tragedy. Nearly twenty years later, in 1975, CBS would broadcast *Fear on Trial*, a movie based on the book John Henry wrote about this defining chapter of his life.

Paris and Comeuppance

Arnie had been offered a job in Paris through John Berry, who had become a great colorful fixture there. Arnie had been gone about ten days when he called and said to come. I was thrilled. My time in Paris when I was a small girl had been full of sun and gardens and adventure, and now I could give Dinah the same. She was about four then. When our plane hit bad weather, we landed in Ireland and stayed until it cleared, drinking Irish tea with milk in the airport before we set off for Paris later in the evening.

I saw Arnie's truly concerned face as we got off the plane and received a genuinely relieved hug. He carried Dinah to the car on his shoulders. Friends of his drove us to a café. Dinah ate so much French spaghetti that she threw up her whole dinner a block away. It happened to be at a tree right in front of General de Gaulle's official residence. Armed guards ordered us to move on—"*Vite, vite!*"—while one of Arnie's friends argued with them in French, pointing to my poor baby, who had had a rocky long flight and night. "*Elle est malade, malade!*"

We finally reached our apartment. It was very large, everything very white, and a little tacky. Dinah's bed was a large oval wicker basket with a straw mattress—sweet-smelling straw covered with white muslin. I have no memory of our bedroom or our bed, or of sleeping with or without Arnie.

I have a memory of the bathroom because that is where I spent all of my time. There was a step-up toilet with a seat made of brown wood and a flush chain with a brown wooden handle. I spent most of my daytime hours sitting there reading *The Story of O.*

We enrolled Dinah in nursery school, so I saw her off in the mornings and welcomed her back late in the afternoons. Arnie was away all day writing. Paris at that time of year was the opposite of my childhood memories of the sunny Luxembourg Gardens, puppet shows, children running rolling hoops, and exploring with Fremo. Close to thirty years later, it was gray winter, a cold that entered your bones, and a gray sky that never let the blue break through. I was not so much starved for sun as for a break in the gray, gray pall that covered the city. I couldn't take a deep enough breath.

I don't remember cooking. I remember going to the little neighborhood grocery, carrying the red mesh bag to put milk and fruit in, but I was so self-conscious about my French that I didn't get that neighborhood rapport.

My first night in Paris, I'd called the hotel operator. An old friend of mine, Ellie Pine, had moved to Paris and married a Frenchman. I said the number two, *deux*, in my best high school French accent. *"Pas Dieu! Deux!"* the operator screamed at me. *"Deux, deux!"* I hung up quietly, completely intimidated, and put my high school French away in a secret drawer.

About a week later, Ellie came to our apartment to pick me up for lunch. Ellie had been the open, eager young actress who played John Berry's sister in *All You Need Is One Good Break.* Now she was Madame. She picked me up in a tiny red car. She was pressed for time, but was charming and very elegant. We squeezed her little car into a parking space and somehow offended a huge Parisian, who screamed at us and grabbed the top of the car, shaking it easily from side to side. Ellie and I gripped our car seats like two Helen Hokinson cartoon ladies in *The New Yorker*.

Afterward, she took me to her big, sprawling flat. Her husband was just leaving. He was handsome, aristocratic, and impatient. He was a wealthy manufacturer who voted straight Communist—apparently not that strange or uncommon in France.

They had a woman servant, imported from Spain or Portugal for a pittance. She would return to her country after a year, and they would hire another young woman. Ellie dropped me off and I said good-bye to a true *femme du monde*, off on her errands.

The next evening, Arnie arranged for a sitter for Dinah, and we went out to dinner. John and two other friends picked us up and drove to a street off the boulevard. We walked a block or two in high spirits, passed a little Russian restaurant, and decided to go in.

The room was small, maybe three or four tables for small groups of people. The waiters wore the high-necked red silk blouses, belted at the waist, that were the uniform for Russian male dancers. My grandmother had once made one for me. There's an oil portrait of a young Fremo wearing the same Russian blouse.

The three waiters all seemed to converge on us at once. They suggested the beef on skewers. They brought red wine and drinks. Arnie and John and their friends became happy and comfortable. Their stories piled one on top of the other. Arnie and John had outsmarted some bastard; they broke each other up. Their friends were drinking and laughing. So was I; they were such fascinating guys.

Suddenly we heard crowd sounds. We looked around. We were

still the only ones in the little restaurant. The waiters were coming in with the skewers of meat, making low *blah, blah, blah* sounds in their throats, like someone had hired them to be the crowd in a movie. You know the sound Arab women make when they are celebrating or protesting? Like that, but low. Then one would say, *"Le baron,"* which was picked up. *"Le baron." "Le baron."*

The baron was coming, and the waiters were creating a buzz of excitement and a crowd to welcome him. The refrain was sustained, and we became very excited about the baron coming ourselves. We all watched the door in anticipation. The waiters were proud, all three of them facing the door. Suddenly, the door opened and a small gentleman stood framed in it. The waiters now broke into proud announcements, calling out, *"Le baron, le baron est ici!"*

The noise continued as the little baron nodded, accepting their adoration, and permitted them to show him and his companion, a young blonde wearing much makeup, to their seats at the table next to ours. The hubbub died down, but not the admiration.

So here we were at two tables in a white Russian restaurant. At one table the American Communists; next to us a relic of the czar's reign. After ordering and exchanging a few words with his companion, the baron turned to us. He looked exactly like the actor who played Topper in the black-and-white comedy. Roland Young, was it? The raised eyebrows, the thinning brown hair, the clipped mustache. Mildly he introduced himself and asked about us.

"What do you do?" he asked.

"Writer." "Writer." "Writer." Then me, "Actor." He nodded sweetly.

"What do you do?" we asked.

"Moi, je souffre." Me, I suffer, he said, smiling.

The next night I saw the woman who triumphed over suffering, Édith Piaf. It was her comeback performance at the Olympia Theatre.

Before Piaf emerged from the wings, there was a kind of throaty acoustic furor. People yelled things. Shouted sounds. The orchestra played "Allez-Vous-En," the introduction to "M'sieu" over and over, the big red velvet curtain was lit, and then suddenly she appeared from the wings, facing front, looking out at us, half smiling. She wore black, with laced-up old-lady shoes, her ankles so swollen she could hardly stand. Still facing us, she took small side steps, her hands stretched out on each side, clutching the curtain for support. The audience roared, giving her strength until she finally stepped from the curtain to the microphone, and then—my God, that little woman filled all of us, all of Paris.

Arnie had no problem with my leaving early for New York. I stepped out of the plane holding Dinah. "Look up, look up," I said, and she did. The New York sky was never so blue, never so warm and familiar as it was at that moment. We bathed in the blue.

Arnie followed us home soon after. He had only been back from Paris a month or two when the newspapers carried Khrushchev's revelations about the regime under Stalin. Not only had Stalin held power over every Soviet citizen, every man, woman, and child, but his treatment of artists, poets, writers, was devastating. Millions condemned to gulags, to prison forever, or to be shot, all on Stalin's orders.

Arnie shut the door to his room. He stayed there for hours; the principles he'd lived by, his faith, his religion if you will, had been destroyed by one of his heroes. Stalin destroyed Arnie's world. When he came out of his room, he didn't discuss it. I don't know who he talked to. Walter Bernstein, one of his closest friends, told me they never talked about it. But the shock and the pain had to have been awful. Other friends said that up till then they never believed anything printed in the newspapers because the news was so biased, so controlled by the anti-Communist climate in Washington, and that was true. But this was Khrushchev, the new head of the Soviet Union, who was giving names, and the name he gave was Stalin. The hero of World War II; the hero of 444 Central Park West.

I'd become one of "the wives of" the Communist men of 444 Central Park West. The men were the ones with real identities; the wives were in the shadows politically, standing behind their husbands.

As Karen Morley once whispered to me, "We're pillow Reds"— women who happened to fall in love with a guy who happened to be a Communist. The girls were hooked by attraction, not politics.

I wasn't aware I'd become one of the wives, pathetically searching my husband's face for approval, alienating him in the process.

I don't think the word *love* applies.

I wanted him. I yearned for his approval. Very much. Too much. Boringly, I'm sure. He gave me a failing mark in everything but being a satisfactory mother. In almost everything else he gritted his teeth and went behind his eyes.

And I was dwindling. I had lost my luster, gotten shabby in a kind of land of the formerly wanted, now forgotten, sinking into married quicksand. I had no tools to reach him and slowly fell inside myself. Not when I taught, not when I fought. Normalcy returned, need returned, and passion.

In the apartment, I moved in slow motion.

I had married my mysterious Heathcliff, but I was isolated on the moors of the apartment; it was grim. I was the miserable Geraldine Fitzgerald whom Heathcliff now despised.

Outside was life and breath. In acting, in teaching, in learning to

fight the enemy. There, I found my passion and family. In every theater I found family. Actors are always there for each other, and my
students, and my ragtag fighting friends in Equity and AFTRA.

But at home someone was winding the key in my back and I went
through my days and nights on automatic. Watching myself, floating
over myself.

I didn't feel.

We live with our mirrors. The more I lost my originality, my funny,
comedic, outrageous side, the more I tried to fit into my idea of what
Arnie wanted, the more I lost him—and the more I lost myself. This
isn't something I knew; it's what I'm discovering as I write.

Arnie became my mirror. I became totally dependent on his vision of me. Once, he'd been attracted to me—the me that was foreign
to him, that was sexy, mysterious.

The me that became one of the wives of 444 Central Park West
didn't interest him. I annoyed him. The Pleaser is always boring and
annoying.

Voices weren't raised in our house. No one yelled. No one got anything out of his or her system. Doors were slammed. Cheek muscles
clenched. Eyes averted. Breath was uneven. It was all sucked inside,
like poison.

Once, just once, Arnie was so angry, he threw an open container
of cottage cheese at me, which landed facedown on the awful, thick,
rose-colored carpeting in the living room. Cottage cheese curds found
their way down the long, two-inch-thick rose threads and settled there.
I stood there nonplussed, my mind screaming, *You pick it up! You
threw it!* My mouth said nothing.

Finally, with a pail of soapy water, pillowed resentfully on the
carpet, I began the task of removing hundreds of curds nestled at the
root of the wool strands. I shrank into the curds in the carpet. But I

was not charming Alice shrinking into Wonderland. I was bulky, clumsy Lee, who sweated over the squishy, elusive cheese curds. I was disappearing.

Little Lyova Haskell Rosenthal, the pride and joy of 706 Riverside Drive, her mother's dream of glory and riches and fame, got her comeuppance.

The Summer House

That summer Arnie drove us—the boys, Dinah, and myself—to Lake Mohegan. He stayed a few restless days and left to return to the city. The bungalow we rented each summer had few amenities. The week before I'd packed carton after carton with bed stuff, linens, toys, pots, and pans in a stifling apartment. We filled the trunk of the Packard.

It was Dinah's third summer there. I'd been pregnant with her on the beach in Lake Mohegan; she'd stretched my belly in my ugly green bathing suit. The boys were returning to Camp Mohegan with their old friends (they loved it). I was painting on the porch when the telephone rang. Dinah was dipping graham crackers in milk at the kitchen table. Joe Anthony was on the line. Charming, talented director. Kind.

"I have a play for you," he said.

My heart dropped. I sat at the kitchen table, Dinah's spilled milk dripping on my thighs.

Me: When do you start?

Joe: We rehearse in San Francisco end of August, work our way across the country, open in New York early November.

Me: Sounds great.

Joe: You're available?

Me: Send the script.

I didn't care what it was. I lived in the land of the forgotten. Lost my luster. Shabby.

I put Dinah down for a nap and sang her to sleep, my mind and heart racing close to her warm little body.

A rnie's voice sounded trembly.

"If you go through with this, I'm driving up to get the kids. You understand me? If you take this job, we're through."

He was sitting on his anger, his rage. I don't know what script he was working on in the city, but the idea that I would leave home and do this play was an outrage. It was unacceptable.

I could hear his breath angry on the phone. Click. I sat like a slug, the blood pounding in my ears. I spun my chair around. I was wearing dark blue shorts and a light blue shirt. It was so hot, they were sticking to me. I looked outside the screened-in porch. Everything looked the same—the bungalow across the way, the swing set, the high, parched summer grass. Nothing moved. There was no breeze. The sweat trickled down the side of my nose to my upper lip.

Arnie was in the city, writing, going to the races and, I heard, having an affair with Lulla Adler. (I loved Lulla. I once saw Lulla and Pearlie Adler sunbathing by a lake. Against the dark ground, her skin shimmered like the belly of a fish.) I was here in our summer house, alone, with the children. That said something.

I was painting on a big piece of dark gray cardboard and had almost finished a full-length portrait of myself on a swivel chair. I looked into an old full-length mirror, flecked with gray undercoat, which I used for shadows on my face and body, thick dabs of light blue shirt, dark blue shorts, flesh with dabs of white and pink, orange-brown my face and arms and legs.

The heat and sweat made its way onto the cardboard. The high dry grass was still, the swing set creaked a little, the bungalow opposite had an open door like a yawn.

Inside on an old brown corduroy couch, my stepsons, Tommy and Mikey, were singing along with Pete Seeger and the Weavers, "Goodnight, Irene." Dinah was taking her afternoon nap in our bedroom, Arnie's and mine.

I was painting, waiting for him, for Arnie, to call me back.

I called our friend Walter Bernstein. Walter was a fellow writer and close to Arnie. I explained I'd been offered a play, rehearsing in San Francisco and coming to Broadway. I asked him to intervene.

"Please, Walter, please, please . . ."

He called back and said, "Arnie will absolutely not back down. If you take the play, he'll take the children and he's finished."

"Walter, listen. This is the first offer I've had in two years. I'm gone, forgotten. This is the only way I know to earn a living."

I had no money of my own. I had that certain knowledge that I had become expendable. This was the first summer Arnie hadn't come to Lake Mohegan. I was alone with our children, sweating on the porch of our summer home. Drowning on the porch of our summer home.

Lake Mohegan was a mecca for lefties like us. Fifteen minutes from Peekskill—where Paul Robeson had been run out of town—two hours from our apartment in the city, 444 Central Park West, referred to by us and the FBI as "the Kremlin." That's where Arnie would be in sole charge of Tommy and Mikey, his twelve- and thirteen-year-old boys from his previous marriage, and Dinah, his four-year-old daughter with me, the love of my life. Dinah.

My heart was thumping in my ears. I stared at the self-portrait of a hopeless, sweaty, blank-faced girl wearing the same blue shirt and shorts, sticking to the same chair I was sitting on. I took the job.

The Captains and the Kings was about Eddie Rickenbacker and nuclear submarines, and it starred Dana Andrews. It had an all-male cast, except for me, playing a spunky secretary.

I'd accepted a play in which I was to be the ingenue—a cute secretary in her twenties. To bring sex and romance to the austere all-male cast.

I had one talent. Only one.

I'd played "the pretty girl actress," the female lead in everything I'd acted in on Broadway, in stock, on television. A wanted talent, even through the blacklist. A respected talent. Even an honored one.

I was in two independent movies through the blacklist. One gave us enough money to have our daughter; the other, *Middle of the Night*, gave me a sense of doom. I played Kim Novak's best friend and confidante in her romance with an older man, played by Fredric March. Maybe because Kim was Cover Girl–beautiful, maybe because I just looked like hell, but I suddenly saw myself for the first time cast as the "friend," "comic friend," "understanding friend" of the leading lady, the Nancy Walker part, the Thelma Ritter part.

When the director, Joe Anthony, called with a description of the ingenue lead, I was no longer an ingenue. He hadn't seen me. I was thirty-one. I had been blacklisted by my industry and rejected by my husband. I looked sad and bad.

I threw myself into remaking myself into a commercial entity. My outside was what producers would buy. The talent was inside; I just had to look the part—young. I'm not vain. I'm not.

As soon as I returned to the city I went to see Dr. Blumenthal, the plastic surgeon my mother had found when I'd wanted to straighten the bump on my nose ten years earlier, when I was still living at home; the year I met Arnie. I threw myself into the doctor's office.

"Change me. Save me. I need the part!"

I asked Dr. Blumenthal to stop my face from sagging down, because when I looked in the mirror, all I could see was sad. Nothing was up anymore. I wanted up. Because I was only thirty-one, he insisted I bring him a letter of approval from my psychiatrist.

Dr. Austin was worried about me. He told Arnie he was concerned; I was floating, disassociating from life. I saw myself crouched inside a big pink balloon floating listlessly above my life, unmoored, uninvolved. In his office his desk lamp moved toward me and then back again. It scared me. Dr. Austin, who was more or less head of psychiatry at Mount Sinai, napped in his chair through most of my sessions, but he knew I had been sinking into myself more and more, and his office visits had been totally unhelpful. I couldn't find a way to climb out of myself.

He called Dr. Blumenthal, the plastic surgeon. Together, they approved the operation.

Arnie went up to Lake Mohegan to stay with the kids. I borrowed money from my parents on my condition it would be paid back out of my earnings. The earnings were crucial. Any money I brought in went straight into Arnie's bank account, since he paid for everything: the apartment, the food, the children. Now I was desperate for my own money. I needed to get an apartment for myself and Dinah. I told my agents at William Morris to have my checks sent to their office, to be held for me until I came back to New York.

Dr. Blumenthal gave me a face-lift. I spent August in our empty apartment with a swollen face, bandaged at first. Then, as the swelling subsided, another face emerged. The face of ten years earlier; a girl again. This new girl did not have the downward pull of rejection and atrophy. I had repainted the self-portrait of the sweaty girl on our porch.

Arnie called. He said he was going to call the newspapers. That everyone would know that I'd had plastic surgery.

No one in the 1950s had their faces altered, in particular no young women with reputations as serious actresses. No women were getting face-lifts unless they were scarred, beaten, burned. If newspapers printed, "Blacklisted actress gets face-lift at thirty," I'd never work again. Particularly because of the Cannes award and the Oscar nomination I'd won for *Detective Story*. It was not the act of a serious actress. Nor of a particularly sane woman.

I ran to Walter Bernstein's apartment, crying so hard, I couldn't talk.

"No," Walter said. "No, Arnie wouldn't tell the newspapers."

I was sitting on the edge of his bathtub with the bathroom door closed so no one could hear me.

I know I was driven to have my face done—driven. There was no thinking, no analyzing. I felt I was starting over again. Beginning again. Twenty-one again. What instinct made me so determined, at that time, in that year? I wanted to save my own life, to remove what the blacklist and ten years with a man who didn't like me put there. And I was panic-stricken, worrying that it wouldn't work.

Rehearsal for *The Captains and the Kings* started in San Francisco a few weeks later. On the first day of rehearsal it was a new girl who walked into the room.

I don't know how I got to San Francisco. I must have flown. I do remember lying on the bed of my hotel room having taken two Seconals, holding on to the sides of the tilting bed, then running in a full panic attack to Joe Sullivan's room. Joe was an actor I liked and trusted, and I asked if I could sit on a chair in his room for the night. I was afraid to be alone. I still hear his kind voice making me quiet, his kind eyes. I'm starting to cry as I write this, more than fifty years later. His kindness was so crucial for me that night.

For two months we played theaters on the way back to New York. From Philadelphia, our last stop before New York, I had arranged for Arnie to meet me at Grand Central Terminal with Dinah so I could spend the night with her. I had left my little girl with her father. I had good reason to fear he would keep her. Arnie could take Dinah; he had the power. Through all the panic and fear, the fierceness of my protectiveness and yearning for Dinah was the most powerful force of my life. I could do anything, would do anything to be with her and make a home for us. It was animal and it made me strong and fierce.

I waited at the station, and I waited. I telephoned. Arnie picked up. Dinah was sleeping. I don't know how I got to our apartment. I was on fire with rage and need for my child. I rang the bell. He opened the door. I pushed him.

"Where is she?" I screamed.

I steamed through the house. Arnie had never seen this side of me. He opened our bedroom door.

"She's sleeping."

I looked. She was asleep in my big bed. I picked her up.

"I'm taking her."

"She's sleeping," he repeated.

Dinah was now rubbing her eyes in my arms. I couldn't run with her to a hotel room. It was stupid.

"Don't you dare try to keep her from me," I said.

Arnie smiled, hands palms-up in a *Who's trying?* gesture. I left.

Arnie didn't have a problem in the world taking the boys from Margie. It was his right, his boys. Their mother was inadequate. Even I, their new young mother, could see that. I was competitive with Margie. It never entered my mind in those days, those years, that she might have yearned for them. I knew Tommy and Mikey were very protective of her. Did they yearn for her? They must have. When I look back now, my marriage was based on raising and caring for the children. It was the one area where I was given plenty of approval from Arnie. It was the one area we could have fun, joy, together.

The biggest part of saving my own life was Dinah. Without her I was in a vacuum, without motivation, no raison d'être. I was hers. She was mine. Love is not a word that describes it.

The next day I called William Morris. I told my agent I was coming down to get my paychecks.

"Oh," he said. "Don't you have them? They were sent to your apartment."

"What? I told you to keep all my checks. I was living on per diem."

"Your husband told us to send them to the house."

I hung up, the blood drained out of me. I couldn't breathe. I knew Arnie kept the money. And I was broke. I confronted him. I lost. I was his wife. He had expenses. I hated him for the first time. I had wanted him, wanted him to want me, love me, approve of me, think I was smart. He never could. I'd escaped with my life. But to take every penny I'd worked for these last months was despicable. Arnie had absolutely no problem justifying it—the rent, the children, the bills.

He was even attracted to me again. He pushed me up against the wall, his lips on my neck. When we sat on the couch, his fingers played on my shoulders. He was in love again, like nothing had happened.

The show opened and the show closed quickly. I had no money. I moved in with my friend Gladys four floors below. I slept on her couch. During the day I would bring Dinah and the boys down to her apartment. Gladys begged me not to reenter the relationship with Arnie, who was now barraging me with notes and phone calls, wooing me.

There was a dark space that Arnie inhabited. An inky-black, smoky space that he looked out from. He would leave it and join us for dinner, for games, for guests, then retreat, as easily as closing the door to his room.

I feel so damned sorry for him. Under the charm, the camaraderie with fellow writers, Walter Bernstein, Abe Polonsky, with his deep friend John Berry, he carried so much heavy, dark, irreversible stuff. His stuff. He never chose women who could fill that space or cope with it. He chose innocents like me, like Margie, or Eva's mother, Ruth. I don't know anything about his first brief marriage.

He would be the teacher. I was the bad pupil, ultimately disappointing and failing him, as we all did.

The dark space, I'm thinking these days, may not have been in my power to reach. Was there a connection between it and his sister's mental illness? She spent years in hospitals. Both Tommy and Mikey have coped with depression, both needing much more than we could have dreamed of in those days.

Long before, when we had just moved into 444, I remember asking Arnie some innocuous question as I crossed the foyer, and he said, "How do I know? I'm not God." I stopped in my tracks in the foyer. *You're not?* I thought. *Then who is?*

Now God was beaming on me again. God wanted me again. I was valuable. He was shy, tentative, and tender. God really wanted me. Gladys pulled one side of me, Arnie the other. I went up to my apartment to move my makeup case to Gladys's. I sat down on the couch with Arnie. The more he wooed me, the more I thought, *This man wants to kill me. I won't get away so easily next time.* I took my makeup case and went to the door. I think I said, "I can't come back."

He turned on me with the rage I feared, with the ferocity of Rumpelstiltskin.

"Go! Go! Get out!" he spewed. "Get out of my house." His arms were around his sons' shoulders—one over Tommy, the other over Mikey. He was armored with his boys. They were never to be mine again. They held him up as he screamed, red-faced, weak-kneed, an endless stream of hatred for me. I was so stunned that I felt nothing. I was the observer, watching me watching him. Feeling relief it was over. I went down to Gladys's apartment with the last thing I had left in my own house. I was safe.

The first time I saw Gladys Schwartz was at a fund-raising event at someone's apartment. There were many money-raising events, since no one was working. I was auctioning my Cannes International Film Festival award for Best Actress for the third time. The kind benefactors who bid for it had always given it back. It was a guaranteed little money-raiser. I hadn't a clue to the high honor of the Cannes award; neither did the nomination for the Oscar really impact me. It was in Hollywood, California, a site as foreign as Paris to a born-and-bred New Yorker. I looked around the room and there was an interestingly beautiful woman. She was wearing a black off-the-shoulder dress. Her shoulders, neck, and heart-shaped face were white surrounded by black curls, eyes cornflower blue, with thick black lashes and a curling, smiling, endearing red mouth. She was married to Herschel Bernardi at the time, a good actor who was to make a name for himself replacing Zero Mostel in *Fiddler on the Roof*. She was small, built like a boy, and generous. Lorraine Hansberry, the young, elegant playwright of *A Raisin in the Sun*, was a close friend, and a number of well-known artists whose names I didn't know at the time hung around. Gladys painted big canvases. One is on my wall now—extras sitting around the set for *The Day of the Locust,* the screenplay that Waldo Salt would write years later.

Gladys painted compulsively, inexhaustibly. Her apartment smelled of turpentine and wood frames and oil paint. She had planted an avocado pit that grew into a huge avocado tree that stood in her living room. She was a little red Commie to her toes. Both her parents were Garment District workers, and she was raised at union meetings, sitting on her father's shoulders. Gladys and Hersh split the year after I met them, and we became joined at the hip. I don't know how she made money. Her paintings weren't in demand. It was a tough time.

I must have borrowed from my parents again after *Captains and Kings* closed. I managed to salvage my last couple of paychecks. I had to find a place to stay. I knew Gladys needed the space for her students.

Someone told me there was a summer ad for an apartment in the front of the building. Two young gay guys were going to Costa Rica for two months. Yes!

Vi, my housekeeper, and Dinah and I visited the apartment. I gave them two months' rent. Vi and I prepared to clean on Monday.

The apartment was a spacious two-bedroom, overlooking Central Park. I had it for June and July, plenty of time to look for a permanent home.

Vi and I made the beds, brought Dinah's clothes and toys over, and started on the kitchen. I opened the utensil drawer. It seemed to be moving. Brown feelers between the forks and knives. We opened more drawers. They were all crawling with roaches. I sat in the living room while Vi ran to Arnie's apartment on the other side of the building to get roach spray. I told Vi to go back up to Gladys's with Dinah. I positioned myself at the door of the kitchen with two cans of spray and covered my face like an outlaw. As I sprayed I could hear the splats of roach bodies hitting the linoleum floor from the tops of the cupboards near the ceiling. The living room and the bedrooms were behind me. I wasn't going to let one roach past me through the kitchen door. My repulsion mixed with my sweat. Into the night I emptied the cans—the smell suffocating, the dead and dying roaches revolting. I cursed those fucking guys who'd dared to hand over this filth. The next day Dinah and I moved in.

Two months later I heard a key in the lock. One of my landlords entered the apartment. From the foyer a stream of insults left my lips; words I didn't even know I knew were hurled straight at him. Pale, his arms stretched against the door, he was caught. "Dyke!" he screamed. "You dyke!" A moment of incomprehension—then I fell to the floor laughing. Our whole exchange was so hilarious to me. Our exchange helped me to extend our stay for the couple of weeks I needed before we moved to the most wonderful apartment in the world, on the seventh floor on West End Avenue and 83rd Street.

A New Life

When I first moved with Dinah and Vi to 83rd Street, Tommy and Mikey would come over and visit. They hurt. I had been a mom to them. I'd loved them and they had loved me. Not like they loved their mother, but we'd been together since they were four and five and they were now adolescents. All our hearts were heavy.

One day Tommy said to me, "We have to choose sides. He's my father. I have to choose my father."

"Does that mean you're not coming to see me anymore?" My heart was sinking. *Does this mean you don't love me anymore? What about listening to your music? What about talking at bedtime, telling you about sex with Mike falling off the bed in laughter, what about bringing down your fevers with alcohol and water washcloths under your arms and knees, what about dinner every night of your life, what about me?*

"I don't think so," Tommy said.

Mikey kept coming. Mikey was the baby; he needed me more. He was the neediest. From the first time he sat on my lap on Riverside Drive, when he was only three or four, and we looked out at the river together, I knew we were a couple. Sweet little arms around me, sweet little V-shaped smile.

I was making the bed in my bedroom on 83rd Street when a heavy object fell onto the floor under my bed. I reached into the darkness underneath. The mattress seemed to be slashed. Something had fallen from it. When Mikey next came to my apartment, I showed it to him. "Did you put a tape recorder in my mattress?" He looked down. I waited. He nodded. I gave it to him.

"Here," I said. He left.

Eva came into her own when I left Arnie. She mobilized her forces to protect her father. She was his general; she was jubilant. At last he wanted her; at last he needed her.

I don't know if the tape recorder was Arnie's idea or Eva's. If Arnie caught me in bed making love, was he thinking he could win custody of Dinah? Within a few weeks, Arnie would have a new live-in girl-friend. Dinah said she was nice. I was no longer a mother to anyone but her.

My last few weeks at 444 Central Park West, while I was waiting for the occupants of the apartment on 83rd Street to leave, the phone rang. "Lee, this is Alan Foshko. I'm having a party for Marilyn Maxwell." "Who?" Who indeed. Foshko was calling from a different world. Handsome Alan, as he preferred to be called, was a high-flying young publicity maven. He gave parties to end all parties. He took over a New York City subway; he rented Coney Island. He had an office and apartment on 52nd Street and Eighth Avenue. The same building my parents had moved us to when we left Riverside Drive. We shared a knowledge of Nameless Fear together. I was living on the edge and so was Foshko in his own way. Fear pervaded us as we jumped into the unknown. He in business, me in life. Nameless Fear he called it, so real that "nameless" became a real character in our lives. Handsome Alan would telephone. "Is Nameless there today?"

"Sitting on the end of my bed. Do you want to say hi?"

"Nah," he'd say, "get rid of him."

"I'm trying, I'm trying," and I was trying each day.

Handsome Alan had a friend who was also called Alan. A tough, cute cookie who sounded like Gene Kelly. He seduced me in no time flat. On the bed, the couch, the floor, simple straight sex. It was a revelation. I was hooked. Then I noticed that he was attracted to any interesting girl who walked by. At the diner his eyes were constantly moving from my body parts to someone else's. Finally at a party he crowded under a coffee table we were all sitting around with a pretty girl, and the coffee table was glass so there was no escaping that they were making out right in front of me.

I was hurt. I was insecure. I called Carol Matthau. She said, in her whisper, "Lee, you can have any man you want. So, be very sure you want him, because you can have him." I thought, *How do those women manage it? To accept living with someone who always has eyes for someone else? I've just gotten away from a man who didn't want me, who didn't like me, much less love me.* Carol said, "Be very sure you want him, because you can have him." We made love one more time. It was great. He was a talented man. It was over.

Carol lived across the street from me on West End Avenue. She was the great white pussycat, wise, practical, mythical, and unpredictable. She had beautiful skin, white as cream. She and Gloria Vanderbilt, best friends at the time, put white, white makeup on their faces. Carol's was sweet and rosy under the makeup. When I sat in her bedroom listening to advice, she held a mirror up to her face. Her brown-black eyes never left the mirror. She was almost satisfied with what she saw in the mirror then; much later her need for perfection almost destroyed her face.

I loved her dining room, her eye for charm. She had green vines on white paper on her walls, Woodson wallpaper, and a lemon-colored floor. I imitated her. I made my home charming, too.

Ever practical, Carol set me up with the legendary theater producer Billy Rose. "He's got lots and lots of money, Lee," she whispered. First Billy had me sing for him, alone, on the stage of—what else?—the Billy Rose Theatre. He sat up in the sound booth. I sang my heart out to a totally empty house. I had been taking lessons that year from David Craig, a brilliant teacher, great friend, and husband to the born-onstage Nancy Walker. I would try to knock 'em dead, anywhere, anytime.

When I finished Billy stomped down the aisle toward me. "Kid," he said, "you're built like a brick shithouse!" and invited me to a week-end at his island. I asked who else he had invited. He said, "Senator Jacob Javits and his wife, Marion, are coming, good friends of mine." Over his strong objections I insisted on taking Dinah, then five or so, and a nanny. "I don't feel comfortable coming alone," I said. "I won't come alone. I can't."

He called later and said he wanted to come and see where I lived. "Come on up," I said. I was living across the street from his friends the Matthaus. He wandered around the house, stopping to look at my paintings. I had some lined up on bookcases on either side of the fire-place. "None of these are any good," he said, waving his hand at most of my work. Then he picked up the old watercolor of me at a table in the middle of the room, with the door and the windows too high to reach. "This is good," he said. "This has something."

We met at the wharf Saturday morning, the Javitses, Dinah and me, and Norma, friend and nanny, and took Billy's big yacht to Billy's big island. A red flag with his name and a rose flew over both. The five grown-ups had lunch at a small table. Marion and I were forced to ex-change small talk, because all of Billy's attack conversation was directed to Senator Javits, and it was all about money and numbers. The two men disappeared; Marion and I played three games of Scrabble. She was a tough, clever player and beat me easily.

I wandered around looking for Dinah. She and Norma were playing pool happily. I joined them. Suddenly Billy was at the door of the game house. "Take that pool stick away from her!" he barked. "She could rip the felt." We three looked at him. "The stick. The stick—take it away." Norma took the cue from Dinah. Billy disappeared. We wandered down to the water until dinner. I was so grateful Dinah and Norma were with me; this was boring. We ate late, and the Javitses retired early. Then there was just Billy and me.

He brought over a gold box and opened it. Inside were chocolates wrapped in foil. Billy sat down close to me. "Life," he said, "is like a box of bonbons. Some dark with chocolate filling; some with cherries. But you never know till you open the silver wrapper what life holds for you." He held my hand and squeezed it. I squeezed back. I knew this was some kind of mantra for him, the opening of his moves on the lady of the evening, which was me, I realized. He said, "Come," and started up the steps, still philosophizing about life and chocolate and bonbons. I was racking my brain how to get out of this without hurt feelings or rancor. I was in his house on his island. I had to spend the night in his guest bedroom. Billy suddenly pushed me against the wall hard and pressed his mouth to mine. His mouthwash was so strong and recent that my own mouth sizzled unpleasantly from high-dosage Listerine.

I heard myself babbling all kinds of nonsense, I was so uncomfortable. I didn't know how to get this little Chihuahua, this intense little animal off me. Billy may have been in his sixties then, shorter than I was, and I'm five feet four. Somehow we were sitting on my bed in his guest room, and he was trying to get me down. I bounced up. "I would, Billy, I really would, but I have my period—I had no idea, awfully sorry." Suddenly his hand was at the back of my neck. Trying to bob it toward his zipped fly. "Dinah's in the next room, Billy, I couldn't do that with Dinah in the next room." Bob head, bob head. I didn't even get it at first.

"Wouldn't you like to live in my princess room?" said Billy. "Be a good girl, you can move into the princess room." Billy had taken me on a tour of his Manhattan mansion after I sang for him. He showed me his own room. An ascetic chamber for a monk, with a single narrow bed, like a cot, which he said had belonged to Napoléon, and then showed me my future room—if I was a good girl. A large, tasteful beige girl's room, with a big four-poster curtained bed. This was the bonbon I was refusing as he tried to push my mouth to his fly. Finally he figured it just wasn't worth the time and effort and he left. I stepped into Dinah's room and climbed into bed with her and slept and felt safe. The next morning the Javitses and Billy were back on the boat, the Rose flag flying, Billy a lonely little figure sitting in the middle of the boat holding his tiny dog with a red coat.

Several months later Carol called. Billy was marrying a well-known society matron. Billy told Carol, "She comes with her own money."

"You could have had him, Lee," she whispered.

One of the great understandings that came out of those two years alone was that I never wanted to live in anybody else's house again. I never wanted to take my place in somebody else's life. No matter how wonderful or beautiful. I wanted only people who fit into my life, whatever it was. I felt suffocated at the very thought of fitting in. To someone else's home. To someone else's career. To someone else's hours. To someone else's children. I wanted my life. My child. Me.

Two for the Seesaw—*Boston*

I was asked to do a short run of *Two for the Seesaw* in Boston. This was a welcome job. I loved the part, I missed Gittel, and I was always desperate for money. John Lehne was directing, a very easy and knowledgeable guy. Gittel and I melded again. It was an easy, unstressful, happy run, and Dinah was with Arnie and the boys.

Boston was a great town for time off. It has its own buzz, a mix of colleges, upper-class art, theater. The last time I had been there, Gene Lyons and I found each other, both understudying in our first play. Now, Maureen Stapleton was here on an upper floor of the hotel, and Laurence Olivier, also staying at our hotel, was playing the mad and unpredictable king in *Becket*. He'd played the title role of sober Becket on Broadway. Anthony Quinn had played the king and gotten all the reviews. Realizing he'd chosen the wrong character, Olivier was giving himself a chance to explore the king here, in Boston.

I had to wait till the *Seesaw* run was over to see him onstage. I'd been blown away by his performance as Archie in *The Entertainer* the year before. When it was over, I just sat in my seat while the audience filed out of the theater. Archie was an over-the-hill song and dance man. His pathetic need to please an audience—a dwindling audience since both vaudeville and Archie were on their last legs—was an incredible stretch for a powerful classical actor. Olivier gave it everything he had and found that dim place in his head that Archie saw out of. It was brave. I wonder if that's where *Bravo!* comes from— the root. I can certainly see jumping to my feet and crying, "Brave! Brave!" and meaning it. Theater people are brave.

Joan Plowright was also in *The Entertainer.* She played his daughter. Vivien Leigh and Olivier had split. Plowright was to be his next wife. The very antithesis of Leigh, who in this period was at her most fragile, and to me most exquisite. Plowright, down to earth. Sensible. A nice, sensible woman.

Jim Frawley, a friend from the Actors Studio, played a small part in *Becket.* He told me about an afternoon rehearsal in Boston. Olivier stopped rehearsal and said to the director, "Tony"—it seems most English directors are named Tony—"give me a chance to walk around a bit and work this out." The cast backed off or sat down while Olivier went into himself onstage. He walked, he talked, he suddenly kicked the can full of water that held the cigarette butts, kicked it downstage into the orchestra pit, and began to wail—undistinguishable words, angry, loving, longing, while walking the entire stage. Within himself. Exploring himself. Suddenly he called out, "Vivien!" and began to cry. He stood within himself, as the hushed actors watched, afraid to breathe. Then suddenly he turned to the director. "All right, Tony, I think I've got it." "You want more time?" "No, no," he said, and slowly the actors went to the positions they'd left onstage earlier.

I didn't learn about this from Jim until years later. What I saw onstage in Boston, in one matinee, was so powerful, I nearly fainted. I could feel the blood leave my head and come back, my hands on both sides of my seat to steady me. Like when a plane suddenly drops and you grab for stability, or like when you're four and some passionate tenor lets loose with *La Bohème* and it makes you dizzy in a new way. It never happened to me before or since in the theater.

I gave my name to the doorkeeper backstage. I imagined Olivier knew my name from *Seesaw*, which had been at a theater near his. All actors know who's in town. I was determined to throw myself at his feet, as Ken Tynan had thrown himself to his knees in my dressing room when I played in *A Hole in the Head* on Broadway. I understood the gesture. It was beyond words, and that's what I felt.

The door to Olivier's dressing room was opened. He was alone in the brightly lit room, wearing a silk dressing gown. "Lee," he said cheerily, "would you like a drink?" He was pouring white wine into a wineglass. I shook my head no. I realized I didn't know how to get to my knees from a standing position. Ken Tynan had thrown himself across the room. I bent my knees a couple of times, still standing by the door. Olivier kept talking, chatting really, nervously, like a host with a shy, dangerous guest.

There was a footstool by his chair. If I could make it to his footstool, I reasoned, I could slide from there to my knees. I walked to the footstool and sat on it, facing him. I still couldn't speak. He had almost exhausted his small talk and was dying for me to leave. From the stool I said, "I understand you don't like the Actors Studio." I don't know why. I had given my heart to this man, Heathcliff, when I was a child, and suddenly I was a child again. Some part of my brain was chattering about the Actors Studio, arguing with Laurence Olivier about its good points. I could not throw myself at his feet and tell him he was the greatest actor in the world and had, that afternoon, given the greatest performance I would ever see. He chatted about Joan Plowright, anything to fill the void. Suddenly I got up from the footstool, thanked him, and walked the long distance to his door, opened it, walked out, and closed it behind me.

I'm sure he gave a gasp of relief. I'd also heard that Maureen, who drank a bit, had called him from her room in the hotel at two in the morning, telling him how much she wanted to fuck him. After she woke up and realized what she had done, she walked up and down the stairs for the rest of her stay so she wouldn't run into him in the elevator.

For many years I wanted to write to him, to tell him. I never did. I have a picture of the two of us taken at some Hollywood event years later. I don't resemble the actress in his dressing room—Gittel. In the photograph, I'm wearing brown chiffon and long earrings; my hair is auburn. We're looking at each other, posing for the camera.

The Balcony

A millionaire trucking company owner, Joe Strick, decided to direct Jean Genet's *The Balcony* as an independent film. It had played for two seasons off-Broadway. An original take on our society by comparing it to a well-run house of prostitution.

Shelley Winters and Peter Falk were the leads of the film, Peter the chief of police, Shelley the madam. I was head prostitute and her special favorite. In essence the house of prostitution mirrors the world outside its doors; eventually the illusions that take place, the presidents and popes and police chiefs, pour into the streets and take over society.

I flew from New York to Los Angeles. Joe Strick introduced himself to me at the airport and insisted we go to his new studio office to view what he'd filmed so far. He was a tall, fiftyish, regular guy, eager, making the crossover from millionaire truck impresario to director of an esoteric film.

"Joe, can I see it tomorrow? It's been a long flight."

"No, no, I need you to see this at the studio."

I was told to look into a small screen when he turned a switch. The film he'd shot came on; I couldn't make heads or tails of it. The room was dark, and suddenly my foot felt wet. I looked down, and Joe Strick was on his hands and knees licking my toes. I was wearing tan flat sandals. I was shocked. I pulled my feet under my chair. "Stop it! Stop it!" I ordered Joe, still on his knees.

"I just want you to experience, blah, blah."

As a brand-new director, sincere and earnest, Joe had carried his version of the Method too far. He was an innocent. Experimenting. Excited.

The next day I joined his family for lunch at his beach house in Malibu. His nice wife and two small boys were there, and some of the actors. The table on the patio faced the sand and the ocean.

I don't remember what word I used—*bitch, bastard.* Joe sharply stopped me. "There are children present," he said. "Please watch your language!" The other lunchers stopped eating and looked at me. I apologized. And meant it.

Ten minutes later, one of the eight-year-old boys pointed to the beach excitedly. In front of Joe's house in the sand, one big dog had mounted another medium-sized dog.

"Are the dogs fucking, Dad? Is that what they're doing?"

The younger boy chimed in, "Dad, Dad," his tan little hand pulling Joe's shirt. "The dogs are fucking, Dad, aren't they? Dad? Dad?"

We all, maybe seven of us at the lunch, looked straight ahead, begging silently for the dogs to run, to move, to finish. "Dad, Dad— aren't they?"

Like a fifties dad with a pipe: "Yes, son," Joe said calmly, "the dogs are fucking."

I felt a little cross. My word had been so tame. We watched the dogs for the next long minutes, and I thought, *This is the movie!* The ham sandwiches lay on our plates as nature danced before us. A huge red doggie thingy seeking its target, missing, seeking, till Joe

Strick finally jumped up and chased the dogs down toward the ocean and away.

The next day we would begin a movie about simulated sex, very French, very political. No dogs.

Shelley was a serious actress. And I was to find out in *The Balcony* that Shelley was a serious bully.

The scene between Peter and Shelley was coming up. The chief of police and the madam. It was Peter's scene. He was enacting all of his master needs to Shelley's willing madam.

We were working on a huge soundstage in Hollywood. All our trailers were within it, tucked to the sides.

Shelley Winters, in a long glittering dress hugging her voluptuous body, pushing out round full breasts, was lying on a chaise longue on the set, her bedroom, where she was about to entertain her best customer, the chief of police, played by her costar, Peter Falk.

The bedroom set was in the middle of the soundstage, about twelve tennis courts long, wide, empty, with its silent black floors and high, high beamed ceiling. A camera crew stood by the bedroom set along with Peter in his police chief uniform and cap, ready to do the scene. Simple, seductive scene, madam and patron.

"Quiet!" Shelley yelled to the crew who were setting up the shot, the crew quietly working on lighting. "I'm preparing. Nobody move!"

The set froze. Shelley had a small record player on a table next to the chaise. She moved the needle arm to the record. A scratchy "Lili Marlene" sung by Marlene Dietrich could be heard, thinly. The small crew stood like statues next to the set.

A group of extras walked by outside. "Close that door!" Shelley had suddenly turned into the Red Queen from *Alice's Adventures in Wonderland*. Door closed. "I saw you with the white sneakers, stand still." The crew guy with the white sneakers stopped in the middle of the set, frozen.

Suddenly: "Stop combing your hair!" I jumped, deep in my trailer in front of the mirror. She saw through walls.

"Lili Marlene" ended and began, ended and began; the crew was still, as was the boy in the white sneakers in the middle of nowhere. The doors closed. I could hear myself breathe.

Peter, sitting in his canvas chair with the camera crew, quietly stood to look into the camera, focused on Shelley. On tiptoe.

I heard screaming, shouting, then a man's voice. I went to the door of my trailer. Shelley, sitting up in the chaise longue now, was screaming at Peter something like, "I've got money in this movie, I can hire you and I can fire you, blah, blah . . . !" Peter's neck turned red and he leapt at her from behind the camera. Joe Strick jumped between them and threw his script up in the air to distract them. The pages, swept up by the air-conditioning, were floating all over the studio, everyone scrambling like kids at a party to pick up or catch the festive pages falling and flying through the air.

I now hated Shelley, and we had a love scene between us coming up.
     "Action!"

Shelley smiled. Both provocative and motherly as she grabbed the back of my head and pulled me to her for our kiss. "Don't touch my hair," I hissed.

I had so much nervous hair spray on my short dark hair that it would dent if you touched it. Hard as nails.

"Did ya hear that?" Shelley turned to the assembled crew. " 'Don't touch my hair,' supposed to be a Method actress, what kind of actress is that? 'Don't touch my hair,' blah, blah . . ."

I was unfazed; I had her in my rifle sights. I looked in her eyes, waiting for the camera to roll. "You can put your hands anywhere you want, just not in my hair!"

Did I glimpse a little fear?

We filmed the scene. We kissed. She wasn't a bad kisser.

My loathing of Shelley became my character's secret loathing of the madam. Good. Something to work with. I found my objective that morning: to throw over the madam and run the house myself one day.

In a photo shoot at the end of filming, Joe placed me slightly in front of Shelley. She blew up. "Who's the star here, anyway?"

Shelley had been the dictator of the set, telling everyone what to do, how to do it, we were cowed by her, all of us, the director and the actors.

Fade out. Fade in. The leads in the cast assembled at the Playboy Club in New York. We'd been asked by Hugh Hefner to celebrate the breakout hit movie of the summer. Audiences thronged to drive-ins to see this indie film, *The Balcony*, which was kind of a dirty movie, but not.

We were sitting in this little pen at the bottom of many flights of wide steps with aluminum railings and black marble floors, waiting to be introduced at the Playboy Club. Shelley entered with her assistant and began to sit. She caught my eye—startled, she began to run from me up the steps. Suddenly my body was chasing her. I was a loose cannon. Shelley took the brunt of all my resentment and hatred, all the unsaid stuff. Something in me broke open and I was screaming at this unexpected moving target. "Cunt," a word I'd never used, burst from my throat as I raced up the steps of the Playboy Club, closing in on a terrified Shelley.

The Playboy bouncers stopped me at the landing, not unlike a boxing ring. Shelley, scared, holding on to the aluminum railing. I'd burst through something in myself, at the wrong target but it felt great.

I left and went home. Content. To 83rd Street and West End Avenue.

I t was 1962. Everybody knew the Committee was dead. They had no public image anymore. Joe McCarthy himself had been beautifully and publicly shamed and disposed of on television by Joseph Welch and Ed Murrow years before. My agents at William Morris contacted the Blacklist office at CBS. Yes, the office in charge of keeping dangerous actors from working on TV.

"Come in, come in," a nice man said, "let's clear Lee and get her back to work!"

They agreed with my agents that I seemed to be no threat. We met at CBS one morning so that they, with my agents and me present, might talk to the head of the Un-American Committee by phone, to clear me and get me back to work.

It all looked extremely positive. If the office in charge of blacklisting was on my side, I was in. The voice on the other end of the phone said, "Not until she names her husband, Arnold Manoff." The CBS person said, "But a wife isn't allowed to testify against her husband." They were defending me! Amazing. Once more the committee person said, "Not until she names her husband, Arnold Manoff." The head of blacklisting at CBS hung up. He could barely look at me. I almost felt sorry for him. My agent took me home.

It's interesting that the committee never called Arnie to testify, though he had been named by one of the Hollywood Ten who had been jailed and later reversed his stand. They only wanted me to name him.

How American is that? So their job was to get vulnerable people to rat on one another. Some did with the other's consent—"I'll name you and you can name me"—in order that they both could work.

If we all named one another, this would have been a comedy, but my friends were sick at the very idea. And to me it was like killing a friend. Putting a gun to his head and pulling the trigger. But why didn't they ever ask Arnie to testify? Why me?

I called the lawyer Leonard Weinglass. He was a strong and clear voice for all the things and people I cared about.

He said, "Lee, you need a powerful voice in Washington, a moderate voice. Not anyone who's associated with the left. Someone connected in Washington. Someone inside the system."

"Who?"

"Let me think about it."

That's how I came to know Max Kampelman.

Max Kampelman

We arranged to meet on a bench in Central Park. I was wearing a chiffon flowered dress. It was romantic but appropriate, the kind of dress that was so distracting to the husband in the Irwin Shaw story "The Girls in Their Summer Dresses." Shadows cut through the sunlight, smoky and shifting on the graveled pavement. I sat alone and waited for Max Kampelman.

Max was cautious. Caution served him well. He declared himself a conscientious objector in World War II, worked as lawyer and advisor to Senator Hubert Humphrey, and would later be appointed ambassador and head of the United States delegation to the negotiations with the Soviet Union on nuclear and space arms. But on this spring day in 1962, he was risking his good name to meet with me on a park bench. He was drawn to my case. And to me.

I've found that there are two times in a woman's life when she is irresistible to men. First in adolescence, between girlhood and womanhood, ages twelve to nineteen. Young men catch the scent of possibility and will follow a young woman anywhere. But men are also attracted to a woman when she's sincerely crazy, vulnerable, and in trouble. But still young. And pretty.

I was desperate, and Max Kampelman, a big connected lawyer in Washington, seemed like my last hope.

Max showed up. I saw him walking toward me from the east side of Central Park, blending in at first with the children on tricycles and couples holding hands in the fresh spring air, everyone dappled with leaf shade. Max, a forty-something, solid man in a gray suit, the businessman cutting through the children and romantic strollers.

I stood up. He stopped. We looked at each other for a short couple seconds. There was an electricity, not quite attraction, but something momentous. We sat, knee to knee. I asked him, did he fly in that day? Where was he staying?

I was auditioning for my life.

Central Park was sunny and breezy. People walked by us clutching kids or lovers or balloons, but Max and I were in a bubble. He asked all the questions that a smart, well-connected lawyer would. I answered as truthfully as possible. I understood that a good part of my future depended on this stranger.

I told him that I spoke at Joe Bromberg's memorial service in 1951 and accused the House Un-American Activities Committee— HUAC—of driving him to his death; that I was listed in *Red Channels* as a suspected Communist one week later; that I hadn't been allowed to work in film or TV for the last ten years; and that I myself had been called to Washington to testify and had taken the Fifth in front of HUAC. I told him that I wasn't a Communist. That the blacklist seemed to be over for everyone but me. That I needed to work, that I couldn't pay rent, and that I had a six-year-old daughter at home to support.

He understood, I could see that.

Kennedy was president, for God's sake. Bob Dylan debuted his first album, Andy Warhol premiered his *Campbell's Soup Cans*, the world was moving, art and expression were alive, and everybody knew that the HUAC was next to dead. At this point, McCarthy himself had been dead for five years, but the committee trudged on. So the Blacklist still controlled my fate, and I was still a hostage. I had spent the last ten years fighting the Blacklist, the blacklisters, and the Committee. Through Max, I was hoping to get action.

The day was breezy, and the skirt of my chiffon dress moved against my legs. I told Max that my agents had fought for me, about the meeting with CBS and the phone call to try to clear me. And some five hours after I met him in Central Park, by the time the air turned chilly, I knew he was a principled, serious man. I realized I had an important, influential ally.

I think he left first. I'm certain I walked home alone in the chill of late afternoon, hopeful. Breathing deeply the scent of earth and cut grass.

How could I know then that years would pass before I would reclaim my life, before I could reinvent myself to compete for my role on *Peyton Place*, for my Emmy, for *Valley of the Dolls*, for *In the Heat of the Night*, for my Golden Globe nomination, for *The Landlord*, for my Oscar nomination, for Hal Ashby's *Shampoo*, for my first Oscar?

How could I know then how much had yet to change?

Lenny Bruce

While I was still blacklisted in 1964, I was hanging out with a journalist who took me to see Lenny Bruce. Of course everyone in the audience laughed, but they were laughing at the kind of stuff I'd never heard before. I was stunned by his truths—original, dangerous truths. After Lenny's show the cops came out of the wings and arrested him. We just happened to be there the night the Irish-Catholic cop mafia ended Lenny's career. Not only his career; the man he was. We became friends, hung out at his place in the Village. My reporter friend, Gary Gates, and I loved listening to Lenny. The stuff coming out of him so unexpected, exposed.

He showed up at my door once. Out of it. Slept on the couch. Crashed when his head hit the pillow, mouth open. I covered him like a child. A brilliant, out of control, sick boy. In the morning, gone.

I attended one of his days in court. Even Dorothy Kilgallen, the tight-assed columnist for Hearst's *Journal-American*, testified for him. Marty Garbus was his lefty lawyer.

> *Garbus:* Miss Kilgallen, in the transcripts the words
>   *motherfucker, cocksucker, fuck, shit, ass* are found,
>   isn't that correct?

Kilgallen: Yes.

Garbus: Is there an artistic purpose in the use of language as set forth in these transcripts in evidence?

Kilgallen: In my opinion there is.

Garbus: In what way?

Kilgallen: Well, I think that Lenny Bruce, as a nightclub performer, employs these words the way James Baldwin or Tennessee Williams or playwrights employ them on the Broadway stage—for emphasis or because that is the way that people in a given situation would talk. They would use those words.

Lenny stood up before this Irish-Catholic judge and abased himself. He lost his soul right there and then. "Please, Judge," he said, "just let me do a piece of my act for you. It's not what you think!" He was practically crying.

Slam, slam, went the gavel. "Will you please sit down, Mr. Bruce, and behave yourself? No, we are not listening to your act."

"Please, Judge, please, Judge." I left.

There's a postscript to our short friendship, Lenny's and mine. After the trial, Lenny went into the hospital. He was very sick with a lung infection. After a few weeks, a friend of his called and said he wanted visitors. The next day I took a subway down to some big New York City hospital, found Lenny's room, and walked in. He was in a white room sitting up in bed, as white as his white sheets.

There was a young couple sitting by his bed, heads bent, taking turns reading an entire page of *The New York Times*, the contents of which Lenny was absorbed in. He nodded to me, his concentration on the young woman stumbling though the words.

I sat against the wall for about twenty minutes until she finished. They said their good-byes, worshipfully, and left.

Me: How are you?

Lenny: Getting there.

Me: Good.

Lenny: Read this page for me. *(Pointing to the page in the* Times *the young couple had just read to him.)*

Me: Read that page to you?

Lenny: Yes.

Our eyes locked. I felt suddenly in a battle of wills. The test was, would I read a page of *The New York Times*?

Me: No.

Lenny: If you don't, I don't want to see you again.

I was still sitting against the wall, my coat in my lap. We looked at each other silently. Then I nodded, rose, and walked out the door. I'd known other brilliant men who tested me.

Been there. Done that.

Lenny wasn't attracted to me. In his act he riffed on how turned on he was as a boy by the burlesque girls he hung around with backstage— the legs, the Max Factor #32 sponged onto their bodies, the strippers. He'd been married to one, whom he'd loved madly. Had a daughter with.

And I wasn't attracted to Lenny. I recognized a genius when I saw one, heard one, but the pasty face, the sweat, the whiff of strange inner sickness, was not something I wanted to be close to, intimate with.

But I loved him. His blacklisting was fatal. His voice was stopped along with the *fuck*s and *shit*s and whatever key words he used to open his brain. He worked little clubs where people paid to see him, hear him. His livelihood was taken away, along with his originality and brilliance.

His manager said, "Lenny sinned against his own talent" with all the drugs he had used and died from, too soon. But Lenny was sinned against first, and most sinned against.

Never, never will I need the enemy's approval. And by "the enemy" I'm talking about people like the judge. He, as a moral compass of what is right and what is wrong!

"Fuck the Pope!" I screamed in childbirth. And fuck the Taliban who behead their women for baring their heads, and fuck the crazy Orthodox Jews taking land away from a people so like themselves and for teaching nothing but myths. Fuck them for making proud Lenny crawl. Fuck them all!

In August 1966, Lenny died of a morphine overdose in California. After his death, one of his New York prosecutors, Assistant District Attorney Vincent Cuccia, was quoted as saying, "I feel terrible about Bruce. We drove him into poverty and bankruptcy and then murdered him. I watched him gradually fall apart. It's the only thing I did in [District Attorney Frank] Hogan's office that I'm really ashamed of. We all knew what we were doing. We used the law to kill him."

In 2003, thirty-seven years later, Governor Pataki pardoned Lenny Bruce. It was the first posthumous pardon granted in the state's history. Governor Pataki described the pardon as "a declaration of New York's commitment to upholding the First Amendment."

So?

Joe McCarthy had been the poster child of the period. I picture Roy Cohn, legal advisor to the McCarthy committee, blowing up this flat balloon every morning till it swelled to about ten feet around. The head bobs, the mouth roars: "Communists, Communists, all around us—the teachers, TV, the newspapers, the government, the Army."

For ten years this ranting alcoholic terrified thinking men and women into complete submission, all the while manipulated by the slimy, revolting Roy Cohn. Then one day, right there on our own television sets, we saw a slight, balding gentleman, who was defending a lieutenant in the Army, rise from his seat and walk across our black-and-white TV screens. He shook his index finger at McCarthy. "Have you no shame?" he asked. "At long last, have you no shame?" His name was Joe Welch. He told the millions of people watching, their mouths hanging open, that the king was naked; he had no clothes on. Like David, Joe Welch brought down our Goliath with a slingshot and a little stone. The king was not only naked, he was stupid.

On March 9, 1954, Edward R. Murrow addressed an audience of millions on a special edition of his show, *See It Now*, and tore down the rest of Joseph McCarthy. A political attitude that had come to be known as McCarthyism began to lose steam.

Intro to Joey

This was the second summer that I was on the Guber, Ford, Gross circuit. I was playing the lead in *Silk Stockings*, the musical stage version of the great Garbo comedy *Ninotchka*. It was a tent circuit—many more could fill a tent than a theater—and the audiences were huge. Dinah was five and traveling with me. Norma, her babysitter, rounded out our family. It was perfect. I had started teaching private classes in the winter in addition to classes at Uta and Herbert's studio. I was touring all summer and I was able to pay for everything.

"I shoulda stayed a plumber."

"What?"

"I shoulda stayed a plumber."

Something in me perked up. A plumber. Interesting, really interesting. Much more so than a dancer. Nothing is as sexless to me as a male dancer. I know, I know, Baryshnikov, but I was raised in dance, so plumbing was infinitely more interesting and provocative.

Joey Fioretti was standing onstage, trying to catch his breath after a hard rehearsal, in black tights and a white underwear shirt, and he was real. As real as a tomato.

When I was in the supermarket shopping for my sizable family while I was with Arnie, I would take so much comfort in just looking at the fruits and vegetables. They were so down-to-earth, so real, so cheerful, so simple. I would pick up a tomato. Its skin was tight and smooth, but it had weight in my hand. The color was simply red, with a green belly button. There was no subtlety, no shading, no hidden prickliness. The tomato was what it was. It wasn't proud of what it was, it just was. I wanted very much for my life to be like that. As simple as a tomato. I now saw that tomato standing before me.

I was painting in my living room on 83rd and West End Avenue. It was a self-portrait. I was painting over one of the desperate, unhappy self-portraits I'd painted earlier. I was painting over the image of who I once was, not realizing at the time that underneath it was a much truer reflection than the superficial makeup application that transformed the painting into a perfect flawless image that was pure wish-fulfillment.

"Dillinger's balls are in the Smithsonian Institution," Joey said.

"What?"

Joey was constantly interrupting my painting—my life, actually. He hung around, bugged me, bothered me, and watched my apartment from the phone booth across the street all night. Asked my dates for a light for his cigarette as they left my apartment building at two a.m.

Joey and I had become friends the summer before, when I was doing *Silk Stockings* on the summer circuit. He had his dad's car and offered to drive Dinah, her nanny, and me to the many theaters we performed in over the course of the summer season. It was not only convenient. It was fun. It was easy. Joey worshipped me. And Joey was, at that time, the tomato. Uncomplicated, uneducated, unsophisticated. The plumber-dancer of my dreams. Ten years younger than me, a boy. We had no future together. He was a great friend and a great pain in the ass. Did I mention that I easily submitted to him, at the Baywood Motel in Maryland? He wore me down.

And he protected me. I had to take a train into the city at some point. He went with me. We were the only passengers on a train of railroad cars that must have been retrieved from the train graveyard. The old green cloth seats exhaled clouds of tan dust when you sat down. The windows were clouded with filmy brown stuff. It felt weird and claustrophobic. Suddenly an energetic young conductor walked through. I signaled him.

"Am I on the right train? This one is so dusty, it looks like it hasn't been in use for years."

"If you don't like it, get off," he said.

I sat back. He walked through the train toward the next car. Suddenly there was a flash of movement, so fast it was a blur. Joey was pushing the conductor toward the opposite wall. The conductor's eyes looked frightened, his mouth a black O. Joey's arm was under his chin.

"Don't you ever talk to her like that!"

It took a minute for me to grasp what had happened, Joey had moved so fast. The conductor apologized. Joey let him go, came back up the aisle, and sat down. But something happened in that instant. I was impressed. By his passion, by his reflexes, by his basic instinct to guard me. All of that washed over me in an instant. I felt safe.

So Joey said, "Dillinger's cock and balls are preserved in the Smithsonian Institution."

"Are you crazy?" I yelled. "Why would a reputable institution like the Smithsonian show Dillinger's cock and balls?"

I was constantly screaming at him. He was constantly shocking me with how his mind worked and what he believed.

"Call them," I ordered.

"What?"

"Call the Smithsonian in Washington and find out if Dillinger's balls are there!"

"What do you mean?"

"Never mind." Enraged, I reached for the phone, dialed information, and got the Smithsonian's number in Washington, D.C.

"You're going to ask them," I hissed, "not me. I'm not going to ask them that question."

"Good afternoon, Smithsonian Institute."

"Hello, sir," I said, ignoring my last command. "I know this is a strange question, but my friend and I have a bet. It was rumored that John Dillinger, the gangster . . . that his private parts—this is not a joke—were preserved in some way and are stored at the Smithsonian."

There was a pause and an extended silence at the other end of the line. Finally, a kindly, avuncular voice answered.

"No. There is nothing of that kind here." Pause. "I did hear rumors of that kind of thing traveling with one of those tent shows, though."

"Sir, sir, I know this is an intrusion, but would you please repeat that to my friend?"

I handed the telephone to Joey and watched his face.

"See! See!" I hissed.

He hung up smiling. "Well, they have them in a tent show. I was right about that!"

"No you were not!" I screamed.

Joey smiled more and relaxed.

He felt more at home when I screamed. In his Italian working-class home in Little Italy, Wilmington, Delaware, everyone yelled. Nobody talked. They yelled over recipes, over incidents, over what time it was! Joey said things that were so outrageous to me, I was constantly reacting with unbridled fury.

"I think Mussolini did a good job."

"Huh?"

"The trains ran on time."

"Get out!"

"What did I say?"

"Just get out!"

"When can I come back?"

"Never, learn your history!"

"All right. Tell me what I said wrong?"

And I would tell him and we would yell some more.

I had never yelled before in my life. I never remember my parents raising their voices. I had discovered my endless rage in an exercise at the Neighborhood Playhouse at sixteen or seventeen. In acting I had plenty of anger. In life it was dangerous, up to that point, to express anger and not hurt someone's feelings deeply, like my parents'. I certainly couldn't show anger to Arnie. Actually, I never felt anger toward Arnie. I was completely cowed and confused, but never allowed myself to feel angry. I was angry at my country, and had found a way to express it, in a way. With Joey it was like kindergarten anger. It was real, but not bitter. It was fun. It was kind of normal. We were good enough friends for me to yell at him. And it was for his own good. For us to be friends, he'd better bone up on Mussolini, and on everything I'd lived through. I couldn't abide the ignorance.

But this was a very comfortable relationship for me. It could never go anywhere permanent, but it was a new kind of being together that felt interesting at the time. I was the older one. I had a child who came before anyone else. I had a career that came before anyone else. I had to make money, to be independent of any man.

Max Calls

In the fifteen years since HUAC had invaded the movie business, the victims of its accusations had become older, sicker, poorer, stressed out of their careers, marriages, and lives. The world had changed. I still couldn't get off the Blacklist. It seemed like the only people who couldn't get official sanction were Morris Carnovsky and me.

One day, Max Kampelman called. He had been at lunch with the head of the Committee. The man asked Max to do him a political favor. Max said to him, "I'll do it if you let Lee Grant go."

The committee man said "Okay," and that was it.

The world ends with a whimper, not with a bang. It was 1964. I'd been twenty-four when I was blacklisted. I was now thirty-six.

A couple of days later I received an official letter on government stationery. In the vaguest of terms, it said I was a "good citizen." And that was that. I sent it to my agent and had offers almost immediately for TV shows in New York.

In those days most TV was still shot in New York. There was a big studio in Queens. And there were many, many decent producers waiting in line to employ me—David Susskind, Herb Brodkin. I did an episode of *The Doctors and the Nurses* directed by David Brooks, which no one today could get permission to do with his concept. It was about a woman who checks into a hotel and wants to commit suicide. He shot all day long, no breaks, and all night long, so that the character would enter that state of exhaustion and vulnerability. Then I went right into E. G. Marshall's *The Defenders*. Stu Rosenberg directed that one. It was about a prostitute who sues her client for rape. After that there was a drama starring George C. Scott. I put my salary checks in my bureau drawer, then couldn't find them. I called my agent, Phyllis Raab.

"Did you send my checks?"

"Yes, two weeks ago."

"Oh."

They had piled up amid my underthings and slipped down into the bureau. What a wonderful problem to have.

The Fugitive

In September of 1964, while we were living on 83rd Street, I was called to do David Janssen's series *The Fugitive*, which everyone in America tuned in to. It was a big deal for me. It would be my first step into the Hollywood mainstream. All the other TV shows I did came out of New York. I watched an episode that guest-starred an actress friend of mine. She looked awful. Her makeup was thick and overdone. I had been taught makeup by a genius. When I first moved into 83rd Street, my ex-boyfriend Alan filmed me there for about three weeks for an independent movie. I'd wake up in my bedroom, my friend Dick Smith the makeup artist would arrive, I'd move from the bed to the makeup table, then straight out to the crew and the director in the dining room, the living room, or wherever they'd set up, and go to work acting and filming. Not a bad job! And I learned exactly what was right for my face from the master.

Back to *The Fugitive*. I arrived in Hollywood, where I stayed again at the wonderful, sleazy actors' hotel, the Montecito. I looked out the windows. Across the street a big sign said BACH APARTMENTS. *Wow,* I thought. *This must be an artistic area, like the Village in New York, to name your building after Bach.*

I went to the set ready to work, and of course went first to the makeup room. A nice man in his fifties showed me to a big chair, like a barbershop chair. It was still dark out. I said to him, "Thanks, but I do my own makeup."

He stared at me, then left the room. In a minute the director of photography entered and introduced himself. "George does the makeup for everyone here. He does David Janssen's makeup."

"I'm sure he's wonderful," I said. "I know he's wonderful. I've seen the show, everyone looks great. It's just that I prefer to do my own makeup."

"We don't do that," the director of photography said. "George does the makeup."

I was beginning to squirm. I felt guilty and very uncomfortable. I also felt resentful. I wanted to do my own makeup. I had entered into a phobic phase that would never really leave me. How I was lit and how I looked came before the actual work many times and took away from the work I should have been doing. The gift that Stuart Rosenberg gave me on *The Defenders* in concentrating on my face turned out to be a blessing and a curse. I wanted to look like that forever and ever. I remember passing the editing room on *The Defenders* set and seeing this face fill the screen. I stopped in my tracks.

"Who is that?" I asked.

"You!" Stuart answered.

I've searched for that miracle ever since. But it was that face (and performance) that was bringing me everything I wanted.

George the makeup man was watching with big eyes, watching the camera guy do his fighting for him. This was the worst possible way to start a job, with the DP against me. "I'm sorry," I said. "It's no reflection on George. I don't know George. I'm used to doing it myself." The DP gave me a long contemptuous look and left the room with George. I was shaking. I made myself up. There was no one else in the small makeup room. I went out to the set. George was there. The crew around him. None of them looked at me. The director, Billy Graham, was oblivious. His head was deep into a book about boats, which I was to learn was his passion.

David came on set. He was, well, David Janssen, in the flesh, right in front of me, with a deep brown tan—or #23 Max Factor makeup— groggy from all-night partying, but a pro. He would fall asleep standing up when the camera was on me. My jaw dropped. This was a new world. We shot for about five days, and in all those days no one from the crew would meet my eyes or say hi. The set was frozen to me. At the craft service table, George's back would be slapped, coffee handed to him. He was loved. I, the actress from New York who did her own makeup, was hated. George's reproachful eyes followed me. He powdered me when I got shiny. When the DP called, "George, her nose is shiny," he dutifully crossed the set, watched by the crew, took a long time carefully pressing powder to my face, then slowly walked back to the crew.

At night I would lie on my couch at the Montecito, dreading the morning, trying to think of a way out. I slept on the couch because the Murphy bed scared me. I thought it might slam me back into the wall while I slept, swallow me up like a giant mouth. Finally I came up with a plan. *Why don't I simply lie?*

We had a night shoot before our last day. We were in cold, dark woods. I was walking back and forth to keep myself warm. The DP walked past.

"May I speak to you for a minute?" I asked.

"Sure," he said.

I pulled him off to the side. I had difficulty talking. Tears sprang to my eyes.

"I want you to know something; it's hard for me to talk about this."

"Go ahead," he said.

I took a dramatic breath.

"I was once almost raped by a makeup man."

Silence.

"My God!" he said.

I envisioned myself fighting off a crazed makeup man, him pushing me down on the big makeup chair, trying to separate my legs, his hand over my mouth, suffocating me, the two of us alone in the makeup trailer.

"I'm sorry," I said. "I don't want to—"

"Oh, you poor kid . . . No wonder—"

"Please, I don't want people to know."

"Oh, sure. Poor kid—why didn't you say something? Jesus!"

"I couldn't."

"Sure. C'mon, get some hot coffee in you, you're shaking!"

"I'm just cold. I'm okay."

"No, no. Hank, get some coffee for Lee," he said, patting my back. Oh, it felt so good being loved again. Why hadn't I thought of this before? All that night and the next day, men were jumping to help me. Chairs pulled out, food pushed in. Hellos, good-byes, concern all the way around.

Billy, the director, whom I was to work with fondly on many projects, remained oblivious, still immersed with his ship book. David was friendly and funny. There were lots of hugs at the end of the show, especially from the DP and even one from sad George.

When I got back to New York, my agents telephoned. The producers of *The Fugitive* had called.

"They said they know you lied about being raped by a makeup man, and they never want you to work on *The Fugitive* again."

"Almost raped. There's a big difference, you know . . ."

. . .

A telegram came the day after. It was drizzling outside. Dinah was composing a song on the piano with a single finger. "Oh my! Sigh, sigh! Nowhere I can play, play, play on this rainy day, day, day. Oh my. Sigh, sigh." I opened the telegram. It had black letters on white paper, not the usual yellow telegram. It said, *I know you named me—that's why you're working.* Signed, *Arnie.*

My mouth started working, but nothing came out. The blow took the air out of me, as that little blond boy had on the *Île de France* when he punched me hard in the stomach when I was five.

I sat down on the chair near the desk, waiting for the buzzing in my head to clear. For this heavy sensation to lift. This fog of something like pain or shock or surprise. Stunned, slack, I fell in on myself.

Arnie didn't know that at the very least I was a decent person.

How could he not have known me? All those years.

I felt struck to the heart. In limbo. Dinah left the piano and came over to where I was sitting, on a straight chair near a desk. She looked in my face, put her hands on my face. "What's the matter, Mommy?" I shook my head. I couldn't speak to comfort her. My throat was closed. She climbed on my lap, so warm and round, and petted my face. "It's all right, Mommy, it's all right."

Arnie's Death

Arnie was fifty-one when he died, and our friends focused on me as the widow. Arnie and I had been divorced for a year, but they needed to honor the struggle of all of our lives together. Solly and Fra pushed in the door and told me.

"Arnie had a heart attack. He is dead."

I thought of him lying cold and alone on a gurney in a hospital hallway. Suddenly my living room filled with his friends. My friends from another life. A nice psychiatrist, whom I didn't know, must have seen how dazed I was. Old friends coming in the front door like a dream, outside of Fra and Solly, people I hadn't seen in years. The psychiatrist asked me where my bedroom was, steered me in, and closed the door, talking all the while.

"You're in shock," he said as I sat down on the edge of the bed and stared out.

I should run down to the hospital and put a blanket over him, he must be cold, I thought. *So cold on a gurney in an empty gray hallway.*

I was screaming and crying, bawling hot tears sliding into an open mouth, backing up against the pillow on the headboard of the bed, backing away from what I didn't want to hear, know, accept. How could Arnie die?

Anger, fear, terrible regret, loss. Arnie, whom I had loved and feared most in my life.

Relief that I wasn't with him when he had the heart attack because I know it would have been my fault. I would have killed him. I would not have been able to go on. *Thank God*, I thought, *he was with her, whoever she was, and not me. I was here on 83rd Street.* Arnie had endured so much, too much, and I'd loved him, feared and loved him. Both fill me, now, fear and love. Arnie Manoff . . . and then: *He can't take Dinah now.*

I felt the strangeness and the expectations of old friends filling the apartment, the kindness of them bringing cake, making coffee, imposing the role of wife on me whether I wanted it or not. They took the arrangements out of my hands altogether. I don't think either the boys or Eva came to my house. The shock, the horror of sudden death swept me away. I was afraid Arnie would punish me; I couldn't believe his power left that suddenly. I thought I would always be proving to Arnie that I was good enough and smart enough, or even trusted enough.

At the funeral, Dinah, then eight, sat with Eva. I was the mourning wife. I was terrified. I had been pushed alone into the room where Arnie's body was lying in his coffin. It seemed as though I was looking up at him. He was beautiful, his eyelashes resting on his cheeks. Mouth full, skin tan and smooth. I thought he moved. I ran from the room. I ran.

All that winter as I rode the bus, I would look out the window and see him moving in the crowds on the sidewalk—appear and disappear. I would lean back sharply in my seat so he wouldn't see me.

The Public Theater
and Peyton Place

This was the time, 1964–1965, when Joe Papp succeeded in his vision. The Public Theater's Shakespeare in the Park was now a reality. Joe Papp. Papirofsky. Joe. Diminutive in size. Handsome. So handsome. Brown hair falling over one eye. Dynamite. He had asked some actors to meet him at Mayor Wagner's office at City Hall. I was walking down the hall to the last office when I heard Joe's voice—loud. He was yelling at Mayor Wagner, jumping up and down. He was demanding a theater and a cultural park for the people of New York, and he was literally throwing his weight around, jumping, stomping, punching his fist on the desk, to force the mayor to give it to him. And Joe got it.

In 1964 I finally got to work with him. He would open the season with *Hamlet*; he asked me to read for the following play, *Electra*. I got the part. Joe set me up with a breathing and speech teacher.

Electra is for a woman what *Hamlet* is for a man. She has lost her father, hates her mother, and longs for her soldier brother to return. It is, of course, Greek tragedy and to me the key to the tragedies of my own life. My training was there for me to use, fully. There wasn't one line that I had as Electra that I hadn't written an equivalent of for myself, that took me deep and deeper into Electra and into myself. We were, in that period, a perfect fit.

I had so much bitterness, rage, and anguish bottled up inside me, from my marriage to Arnie and my loss of the boys to my long battle with the government, the FBI, and other groups I had fought and abhorred for twelve years. Electra was the first part that allowed me to release everything I'd held inside for so long.

The series debut, *Hamlet*, had been televised and sent out to millions of American homes. It was a disaster; it ruined the career of a very good actor, Alfred Ryder, who had a very bad night. (Alfred's sister, Olive Deering, was famous in those years for her sentiments during her filming of the endless DeMille epic *The Ten Commandments*: "Who do I have to fuck to get off this picture?")

Electra was supposed to be televised but wasn't because of Alfred's disaster. I was relieved. I knew that the work I did would have compromised me; for me, the camera was an intruder.

In those days, we performed seven days a week. I was exhausted, and the doctor from the first floor on 83rd Street was giving me B_{12} shots. I was literally crawling onstage. The designer had built a ramp from the lake in the park to the twenty-foot-high grotto I pushed through to make my entrance. In my mind it was the dungeon of my past Electra was kept in, crawling out to open the gates. "Thou holy light, thou sky that art earth's canopy" was my Electra, yearning for freedom from the dark, the past, and her bottled-up need to take revenge on those who had submerged her and kept their heels on her neck for so long. Electra was not a charmer; she was primal, that animal part of me bursting to get out.

Once during *Electra*, it was still light at eight at night—or it could have been a matinee in those days—and it started to pour. I wore a heavy, blood-colored dress designed by Theoni Aldredge, and the bottom was soaked through. With the cold rain pouring down, I splashed around the wet stage, dragged my soaked skirt with my hands. Olympia Dukakis, who played my sister, came on. She stood facing the audience, declaring her lines, while I stood with my back to them, hissing, "Get me off this fucking stage. Tell them to stop the show. It's raining too hard to move."

Her eyes widened in alarm, but her lines went on.

"Tell them," I hissed.

I turned to face the audience. No one had moved, but a sea of newspapers floated over their heads. Troupers. A little thing like the rain wasn't going to stop Joe's audience, Joe's people. I learned my lesson from him and from them.

I'd reached my apex as an actor in *Electra*. My Method training, the breath and speech work, and my own life collided and exploded. It was as close to my best work and passion as I would ever reach in the theater.

It was also the only time I took the challenge of carrying the play. Everything depended on me.

Many times since I was offered great roles, real challenges.

I was afraid.

Resistant.

Electra was the only true risk. If I'd stayed with Joe Papp, I think my talent would have grown and grown. I had no fear with him leading us.

There's a life-string that began the next season at the Public and has taken me to the present, today. It was the summer after *Electra*. I was rehearsing another play for Shakespeare in the Park. It was a wonderful, hot New York day. I was standing onstage, facing Central Park West. I'd become one of the Joe Papp actors. It was a good time. Dinah was in third grade in a public school a block from our building on West End Avenue. She walked to school. Phyllis Raab called me at rehearsal. She was hysterical.

"I've taken a job for you. I've signed the contract. Don't you dare say no. You have a child to support and no money." Her voice continued to rise. "And don't you yell at me. You're leaving for L.A. next week."

"I can't. I'm opening *As You Like It* in a week."

I left for L.A. The job was *Peyton Place*, the most-watched show in America. I completely fucked over the man I was most grateful to.

Joe Papp didn't speak to me for years, but I had to go.

Phyllis knew I had no money. I was thirty-four. I felt I had only till forty, six more years, to work in television and film before my age and looks caught up with me. In theater I was accepted. But the theater could never pay the bills. Hollywood was where I had been barred. It was where the blacklist began for my artist friends. I was off the blacklist. Whatever success I might have, there would also be a kind of revenge. For me, for all of us. Actors. Writers. When my character, Stella Chernak, was introduced, *Peyton Place* was on television three nights a week. Three new stories a week. Mia Farrow, Ryan O'Neal, Barbara Parkins, Dorothy Malone. They were gods and goddesses and members of the audience's family.

Phyllis was right. She grabbed it, grabbed me, and threw me right into the big world, big exposure, and for me, big, steady money. Getting back at the blacklist. Showing them took over my life.

I don't know what good angel led me to the great Pool House I rented in the Malibu Colony. The Colony was a gated, exclusive community, separated from the Pacific Coast Highway by a wall. A Bank of

America was just over the Colony wall, its sign reflected in my pool. That first day I threw myself, clothes and all, into the watery Bank of America, splashed the *B*, kicked the *A*, lay back on the whole damn thing and looked up at the blue, blue California sky. Dinah and I were not only safe; this was fun, freedom—a new world.

The New York Times printed a letter from Robert Brustein, who at the time was the dean of the Yale Drama School. I'd been asked to do a piece in the Entertainment section about transitioning to L.A. I'd written what I've written here about Malibu. The dean called me a sellout; he was in a fury against those of us whom he accused of abandoning the theater. It was so gloves-off academia, so far from the reality of an actor's life that it made me smile. Ah, yes—a sellout at last!

Three TV shows in New York, one in London. An independent movie filmed in my apartment, summer in Central Park doing *Electra* with Joe Papp, and then suddenly a magic ride that spun out of control and landed me on *Peyton Place*. There must be some mistake. The heavy past I'd been carrying seemed to be slipping away. Now, hand in hand with twenty-five-year-old Joey, I was the youngest midthirties woman in Malibu. Old paranoia, caution, disbelief, clutched me—was I really getting away with this? But it dissolved into sheer, blind bliss. I was safe.

I ran on the beach, arms out, and ran and ran until I ran myself out. Hands on knees, panting, my feet in the ocean—this was a miracle.

M y first time on the set of *Peyton Place* was a night shoot. It was with Don Quine, the actor who played my troublemaker brother, Joe. The scene went fast—everything went fast, they had a half-hour show to film. They had built a new set on the Twentieth Century lot. A waterfront—with water. The Chernak family's home base, on the wrong side of town.

When I watched the show, my name wasn't listed in the credits. I called my agent at William Morris and asked for an appointment with Paul Monash, the show producer.

I went into Paul's office by myself. Just the two of us. He was a good guy or he wouldn't have hired me. I knew that. I asked him why my name wasn't listed with the rest of the cast at the end of the show. Paul said he was going to ease it in; he was waiting to see if there was a reaction to casting me after the blacklist.

I told him, "If my name's not listed with the other actors, I won't work. Replace me. I've fought too hard to use my name. I want to be listed with the other actors. Be brave and take a chance. Audiences don't look at credits, anyway."

He understood. From then on, my name was there with the other actors'.

The other thing I needed to raise with him was how I looked on-screen. This was an issue that would both free me and cripple me as an actress in the years to come. I looked terrible in the waterfront scene. I knew I wouldn't work in Hollywood if I didn't look good, and I was up against great natural young beauties like Mia Farrow and Barbara Parkins.

"The waterfront set was lit," I told Paul, "but not me, certainly not with the care that's taken with the other women on the show."

Dorothy Malone, who was older, was not easy to light, but great care was taken. He understood this was a practical question. I had a new career to protect, and looking beautiful was a simple employment issue. Nobody on TV or watching TV cared about your quality as an actress or your talent. Talent was my secret weapon. But to survive in Hollywood, I had to physically fit the town's requirements for a young woman. I had to be pretty, and I had to be cute and funny on set. No trouble at all. I understood that. I was fortunate. Ted Post, from my Actors Studio days, was one of three directors, and I worked with a DP who surpassed all dreams I might have had. He knew about lights I'd never even heard of. A master.

I loved, loved my job. I was the only bad-girl character, so I reaped the cream of the drama three days a week. My character's father was sick and dying, my brother was in trouble all the time; now he was fighting with Ryan O'Neal. I was having a secret on-screen romance with the doctor, Ed Nelson. Omigod! I was having such a good time and got to cry on camera at least once a week.

While I was on *Peyton Place*, Oscar Levant started calling me. Joey handed me the phone one afternoon. "It's Oscar Levant," he hissed.

"Really?"

So began a long-term phone affair between Oscar and Stella Chernak from *Peyton Place*. Oscar would interrupt himself in the middle of his monologue, hearing his wife's footsteps. "Uh-oh, June's coming," he'd rasp, and quickly hang up.

"I want to meet June," I interrupted on one of those calls, though I knew the fun of it for him was cheating with Stella.

I loved his calls.

"Listen to this, listen to this," and he'd tell me hoarsely about bad reviews of plays that opened on Broadway a half a century ago, like Judith Anderson's terrible reviews for *Hamlet* and Sarah Bernhardt's reviews as a one-legged man—all about women playing men. He'd chuckle over each bad review as if the plays had opened on Broadway the night before.

I felt privileged sitting on the floor of the sun-drenched living room. Hidden behind a big yellow plaid armchair, I would sink to the thick carpet and listen to bits and pieces of whatever was on his curious mind. I would listen sometimes for an hour before Oscar hurriedly hung up as he heard his wife's footsteps.

After we'd moved to the Red House I insisted that Oscar visit with June. So the wife and the faux mistress hugged as co-conspirators. Oscar's phone affair ended, and June invited Joey and me to dinner at their house in Beverly Hills.

To me, Oscar was a real celebrity—he was George Gershwin's best friend, for God's sake. I heard him play "Rhapsody in Blue" in an open-air amphitheater one warm New York summer when I was thirteen, my freshman year at Music & Art. There are pieces of music that dig into your soul when you're a teenager. "Rhapsody" was music to faint by—romance, loss, spring rain on pavement, longing. And here now was the artist who awakened all that in me. Oscar Levant, my new friend.

We were introduced to Oscar's longtime friend Goddard Lieberson, president of Columbia Records, and his beautiful wife, the ballerina Vera Zorina.

Someone, Vera Zorina maybe, said, "Play for us, Oscar."

"No, no," he said. "The piano isn't tuned," mumble, mumble. "The Steinway people spy on me."

"Oh please, Oscar," I pleaded, "please, please play Chopin, play Chopin for us." Right out of some bad MGM movie. I was his muse, Hepburn-like, leading the fading artist back to his glory.

We all moved to the music room. The others sat around while I, center stage, stood by the piano, encouraging him with my smile.

Oscar plunged into Chopin fiercely, attacking the piano, his face flushed with music and focus. His hand hit dead keys.

Half of the keys didn't work.

Goddard moved forward in his chair, puzzled and concerned.

The finale's powerful chords were punctuated by farts escaping with each effort; with each passionate chord Oscar rose from the piano bench accompanied by farts, whilst I, the muse, stood by him at the piano, my smile frozen on my face.

Everyone was quiet as I stole to a chair and sat.

"For God's sake, Oscar," Goddard said, "get the piano fixed. You can't play that."

"No, no," Oscar said, "the Steinway people will take it from me, they gave me the piano, and I haven't done a concert in years."

"Get it tuned."

"No, the tuner is a spy for Steinway."

Not long afterward, Oscar went into an upscale mental facility for treatment of obsessive-compulsive disorder. He called from there often with gossip about his fellow patients.

The houses on the beach side of the Colony opened right onto the white sand and the blue ocean. Lana Turner lived there, Jimmy Dunn from *A Tree Grows in Brooklyn*. Lots of big film people: Hal Ashby, my friend Susan Strasberg, Lee's daughter, and Susan's daughter, Jenny, by that wild actor Christopher Jones. Jenny, born with a defective heart. Ryan O'Neal lived on the beach and still does. Dorothy Malone lived on the beach side of the Colony, too. She had cast parties there all the time. Dorothy was a really nice, good lady. She had a long, mostly B-picture career and was a sun worshipper from the era when tall, blond, and tan won the guys.

Barbara Parkins was a nice girl and a nice actress. She had small features and dark hair that somehow blended into great beauty in front of the camera, like a miracle. Her close-ups literally took your breath away.

"Who is that?" I'd say.

Family portraits of my mother with her siblings and parents, soon after they arrived in the States from Odessa. My mother is on the left in the first picture, and wearing the white hat in the second.

Mom, left, with Fremo, while she was pregnant with me.

Mom and me.

Abner and me.

Dad and me at Pocono Camp Club.

Practicing my ballet on 148th Street, at age five.

I loved to dance.

My mother and me,
photographed while
getting passport
pictures for our
trip to France.

My father.
This photograph hung on
the wall of his office at the Y.

LEFT: My mother, modeling for Ipana toothpaste.

BELOW: My Aunt Fremo.

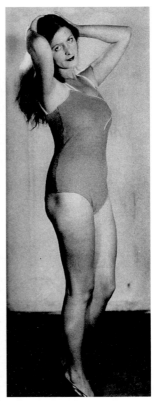

Posing for the camera.

Early days on the stage—my first summer job in stock at
Tamiment, during the Neighborhood Playhouse years.

Performing in more stock at Tamiment.

Signing autographs after a show for the troops.

Dancing on the set of *Detective Story*.

Detective Story, 1951.

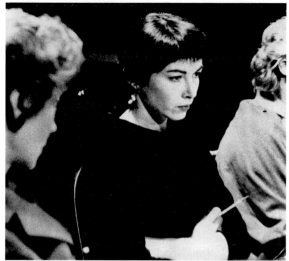

In rehearsal for
A Hole in the Head,
1957, the year I was
called to testify before
the House Un-American
Activities Committee.

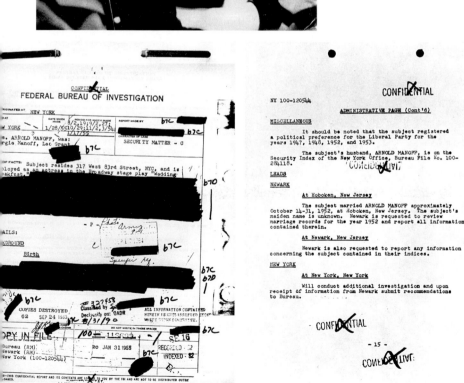

Classified, highly redacted documents from my FBI file.

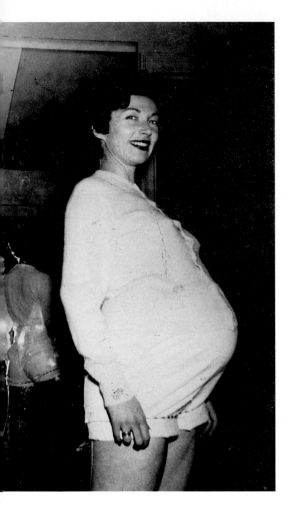

ABOVE: Pregnant with Dinah, 1958.

RIGHT: With Dinah, age two.

LEFT: Replacing Anne Bancroft in *Two for the Seesaw* in 1959.

RIGHT: With Burt Lancaster on the set of *The Young Savages*.

Arnie around the time we met.

Arnie's two boys, Tommy and Mikey.

In *Terror in the City* (1964),
co-starring Sylvia Miles and
directed by Allen Baron.

Me and Joey
in the sixties.

Joey.

Joey and me in the sixties, Malibu.

LEFT: With Shelley Winters on the set of *Buona Sera, Mrs. Campbell* in 1968.

BELOW RIGHT: With Sidney Poitier and Rod Steiger.

ABOVE LEFT: With Sidney Poitier in *In the Heat of the Night*, 1967.

RIGHT: With Sharon Tate in *Valley of the Dolls*, 1967.

LEFT: Telesnaps from the set of *Festival* in 1964. The episode was called "The Respectful Prostitute."

Playing croquet with Beau Bridges
in *The Landlord*, 1970.

With Peter Falk in *The Prisoner of
Second Avenue*.

Applying stage makeup
before a performance of
*The Prisoner of Second
Avenue* in 1973.

LEFT: In *Plaza Suite* with Walter Matthau, 1971.

BELOW LEFT: On the set of *Shampoo* with Jack Warden in 1974.

BELOW RIGHT: With Elizabeth Taylor and Dinah Shore.

Sitting on Warren Beatty's lap in L.A., with Jack Nicholson in the background.

ABOVE: With Warren Beatty on the *Shampoo* set.

LEFT: A marquee for *Shampoo*—I had top billing over Warren!

Accepting my Academy Award from Joel Grey
for Best Supporting Actress, for my performance in *Shampoo*.

ABOVE: Our Green House, which Joey built.

RIGHT: With Dinah, our first year in Malibu.

BELOW: With Belinda and Joey at the Red House.

With Jack Lemmon.

Me in the seventies.

With William Holden before
shooting *Damien: Omen II* in Malibu, 1978.

RIGHT: With Burgess Meredith at the
Red House in Malibu, late seventies.

BELOW: Directing *Tell Me a Riddle*,
1980, with Lila Kedrova, left, and Fred
Murphy, a great cinematographer,
behind the camera.

With friends and actors from my documentaries.
CLOCKWISE FROM TOP: Lauren Bacall, Gregory Peck, with Milton Justice and Joey,
winning the Oscar for Best Documentary for HBO's *Down and Out in America*,
Goldie Hawn, Vanessa Redgrave, and Mary Beth Yarrow.

With Dinah.

With Belinda.

Joey, photographed
by Roddy McDowall.

Me in *When You Comin' Back, Red Ryder?* (1979).

"It's that nice Barbara Parkins."

Mia was a puzzle. She looked like Alice in Wonderland when I came on the show—an odd, lovely waif, there and not there at the same time.

"Was I good?" she asked once after a scene.

"How do I know?" I answered. "I was in the scene, not watching you."

She was curious. Her agent kept telling her how great she was, and she wanted to know if he was right, if other people agreed. She brought her big deaf white cat to the makeup trailer. It was stifling inside because she insisted that the doors be closed so that the cat wouldn't escape. But she also insisted that the cat not be on a leash or in a cage. Cats should be free, so the humans having their makeup and hair done with sweat streaming down their backs had to adjust. Soon after, Mia cut off all that lovely Alice in Wonderland hair. She showed up in the makeup trailer, like a beautiful haunted boy/girl, backing away into the corners because she'd made the front page.

"Allison cuts her hair off."

This was the hot topic in every American household. And what did Frank think? Mia was engaged to Frank Sinatra at the time. *Peyton Place* not only survived the hair-cutting but made out on it. Pictures of the pale, shorn Mia with her fragile neck standing next to Frank Sinatra on his yacht appeared in every tabloid.

Mia, as I later came to find out, had polio when she was a child, in the years when it was regarded as "the plague." All her siblings fled the house in Beverly Hills; her father, a well-known director, left. She was very sick, isolated in her home with her mother for almost a year. Mia's adoption of multiple children, some blind or crippled, and her loving them into independent, kind adolescents came out of that period of isolation.

Her ambition had been to become a doctor. She went into acting to help support her family after her father died. The impulse to cut her hair off, like Jo in *Little Women*, came from that core need to be herself, independent and strong, and break the image of Mia as Allison, the gentle romantic little girl from *Peyton Place*. And she did.

After my first season on *Peyton Place*, I was nominated for an Emmy. Entering the banquet hall, I was terrified a hand from the FBI would touch my shoulder, turn me in.

False identification, posing as a what? I remember walking across my first red carpet, wearing my first formal dress since high school, heart pounding with fear of being exposed: "This woman is an imposter; the real Lee Grant is un-American, blah, blah, blah."

As I was standing backstage shaking, Frank Sinatra walked over to me. He was there with Mia. His eyes were a steady blue. He took my ice-cold hand in his warm one. He knew. Everything. And was on my side, and was saying *Cool it* without a word.

I'm so astonished these moments are still inside of me.

And I won. I won. From three nights a week *Peyton Place* could have gone to five. The line between the audience and the characters on the show was so fine. My character's father died on a Friday. Saturday afternoon I drove into Santa Monica to buy shoes. I was trying them on when the clerk who was waiting on a lady nearby crept over to me.

"Excuse me," he said. "That lady wants to know, isn't today your father's funeral?"

"Tell her," I said, "that's why I'm buying the shoes. I'm going to the cemetery right after I leave here."

The lady, the clerk, and I nodded conspiratorially at one another and I left.

All those smart Hollywood people who knew all about me never spoke about it, but opened up homes, hearts, work, till *Shampoo* pushed me over the top. After three Oscar nominations I took home the gold and another nomination to follow. Twelve good years, following the twelve bad ones.

Even so, I was becoming my own worst enemy as an actor, traumatized onstage and fixated on staying young so I could keep working in film.

A woman of a certain age does not play in movies or TV; we're kicked to the side or out. And I was a woman of a certain age, terrified I'd be found out and unemployed again. Not by HUAC, but by plain old Hollywood standards for women on-screen. Plain old reality, too old.

Driving my Bentley down the Pacific Coast Highway, I heard on the radio: ". . . and today is the birthday of blah, blah, and Lee Grant." I pulled over, breathing hard. They could find out my age! I drove home and told Joey. As a birthday gift that year, Joey called my publicist, Dale Olsen, and arranged to have my name and birth date removed from the celebrity birthday roster.

The Jump

There was a break in the *Peyton Place* schedule, and I was offered a prestigious TV show back in New York: three one-act plays, three couples, written by Murray Schisgal, an outrageous comedy writer and playwright. Stanley Prager, an ex-blacklisted friend, was directing. Alan King, a terrific comic, was costarring. It was being shot in New York. I couldn't wait to go back.

I showed up at the address given for the shoot. It wasn't a studio, it was an apartment building on West 14th Street. The assistant director met me in the lobby, and we took the elevator up to the top floor, a penthouse, large, with three-sided views.

The play was set in a penthouse, but an actor rarely gets to work on location. It was both unnerving and exciting. I have a fear of heights that makes me dizzy even as I write this.

Alan was already there. I don't remember if we arrived in makeup or if they had a makeup room in the apartment, but there was a "Let's get a move on and shoot this thing" kind of energy that was coming from Alan and the two young producers.

We rehearsed two or three times with our director, old friend

Stanley Prager. He turned to the producers. They nodded; he said, "Okay, let's shoot it."

The scene was a bitter, funny argument between us on the terrace of our penthouse, where I, the wife, threaten to jump off if my husband doesn't do what I want. The dialogue ends with something like:

> *Me:* "If you don't stop, I'll jump off this penthouse terrace!"
> *He:* "You think you're scaring me? Go ahead, jump!"
> *Me:* "I mean it, I'm jumping off this roof—"
> *He:* "I dare you—go ahead—"
> *Me:* "I will!"

When I got to the point where my character actually jumps, I looked at my director and asked, "Where's the studio?"

Stanley looked at the young producers, who walked toward me.

Producer 1: "There's no studio, Lee, we've set up the jump here."

Me: "Where?"

Producer 1: "Here. You jump to the terrace right below. You see, there's a stagehand lying there as a protection between you and the street, and we've set up a mattress so you won't hurt yourself landing."

I looked over the side where they had set up the jump. The traffic on 14th Street swam below me. There was a large concrete balcony one floor down with a broken balustrade. A stagehand was stretched across the balustrade facing out, his long arms holding the base, his boots hooked into an opening on the other end. His chest and belly stretched across the space open to the sky and the curious birds. He turned his head to look at me. His eyes implored, *Be careful, my life is in your hands.*

I looked back at the smiling producers, unbelieving. Stanley had his head averted from the balustrade; he, too, had a fear of heights.

"Look, Lee, be a good sport. Let's get this shot, so we can all go home, okay? You don't want to put all these people out of work, do you?" Gesturing to the crew.

I looked at the crew. They looked back at me.

I looked at Alan, an old pro, the question in his eyes: *So?*

I would later film *Plaza Suite*, in which Walter Matthau crawled out a window and walked on a ledge outside. You don't think Walter crawled out of the real Plaza, do you? This is done in a studio.

Me: "What if I hit that man and he falls? What if I fall?"

Producer 2: "Lee, we don't have the budget to shoot in a studio. We're television. There is no studio."

I felt trapped.

"Set up the shot," I said.

I climbed on the ledge, anger replacing fear, looked down at the distant cars moving on the street below, clear, not dizzy. I glanced at the stagehand, his knuckles white on the balustrade, his head buried in his arms.

Stanley whispered, "Action." He couldn't look. I turned to Alan for the cue.

"I really mean it," I said.

"Go ahead, jump," he said.

I focused on the mattresses way below and jumped.

The crew pulled me back up to the penthouse. They handled me with care. I waited. Grim.

"We could use another take, Lee."

I felt so shut down and bitter and betrayed that I didn't care. Two more times I jumped, carefully measuring the distance away from the stagehand, his neck red with strain. Both of us alone together.

It was a fuck-you jump. They pulled me back up and I left.

I took the next plane out, back to the safe sets of *Peyton Place*.

Monaco

kind of elegant ex-actor, mixer in social scenes approached
me about doing an hour-long TV program on Princess Grace
in Monaco. Budd Schulberg was writing. Interesting. Budd
had given names to the committee. He'd also written *On the Waterfront*, the great film Kazan directed. This was the project Kazan and
Arthur Miller had shopped in Hollywood and been turned down because it seemed to favor the unions—and the studios were trying to
strangle them.

Budd was a charming, worn-out guy. Very simpatico. We met on
the way to the airport—we looked in each other's eyes, saw the worlds
apart in them, and kept our thoughts to ourselves.

I visited the castle, went through all the formalities. Castles are
dreary old places. One thinks, *The upkeep, the upkeep*. We were taken
to the royal living quarters—a comfy living room. Grace was welcoming, charming, stressed, and nervous—I asked her the questions Budd
had written. The answers were formulaic and pleasant. Her posture
was that of a girl whose mother had told her to sit straight.

After the first set of questions, while the camera was reloading, I
spoke to her as one woman to another, one actress to another. Before

this choice to be princess, Grace had gone with my first theater boyfriend, Gene Lyons. Gene and I were together for two years; Grace and Gene were together for two years—and he was madly in love with her. She was a rich girl from Philly. Taking away the trappings, I said to her, "Why are you so cowered? What are you afraid of? Here's a chance to talk about your life, your children, your husband—be open. You're so closed off; the things you're saying sound scripted. It's boring." She started to cry. The producer, who had been her friend in an earlier life, stepped in. "Am I boring?" she asked. "Am I boring? I don't want to be." I watched and wished the camera were rolling. There she was, our Grace, so vulnerable and appealing. The producer was furious.

On camera she relaxed more, was very charming, but revealed nothing. She saved the reality for the periods when the camera reloaded, and then she would really talk. She had no friends in Monaco, and the women in the royal families, those who were in the court, were very critical of her free and easy American style. She, at the time, was surrounded by sharp, mean critics. So she had to watch what she said at all times. Her husband, Prince Rainier? He had a lot of other interests, and she missed him. And he was sending her off that year to live in Paris by herself, because Stéphanie was going to start school there, and he felt the child needed her mother's guiding hand. I said, "Well, Paris—you'll be away from here, at least!" She said, "I spent time in Paris. I was never invited to dinner. I was never invited to anyone's house, their home. The only time anyone asked me anywhere was to some big function, where they wanted me with the ribbon across my chest!"

While I was getting to know and care for Grace, Joey and Larry Hauben joined me in Monaco. I miss Larry Hauben more than any other of my dead friends. He was so fucking unique and smart. Talented and a total druggie. Larry won the Oscar for the screenplay of *One Flew Over the Cuckoo's Nest.*

Larry and Joey took off for Rome, where Joey's friend Cerro was the biggest and cuddliest coke dealer in town. They all stayed up at the Spanish Steps at the Hotel De La Ville, which had been my favorite hotel, and then went through literally mounds of white powder piled up on the coffee table. Joey and Larry understood Italian perfectly, though they didn't speak a word of it, and had hours of heated discussions with Cerro and his friends. Larry slept upright in a closet, and they were both thrown out of the Vatican for lying on the marble floor in order to better view the Sistine Chapel. A boy's life. All the while I stayed behind in Monaco.

The producer never spoke to me ever again.

Buona Sera,
Mrs. Campbell

While we were living at the Pool House, I was offered a film in Italy called *Buona Sera, Mrs. Campbell*. It starred Gina Lollobrigida and was directed by Mel Frank.

"Cunt?" asked Eddie Bondi, my agent at William Morris, his term of endearment for his female clients. "Do you want to do this?"

"Yes, yes," I said.

Joey and I sat in our big sunny living room in the Pool House on the yellow plaid sofa and took Italian lessons from a French friend. We flew to Rome with twelve-year-old Dinah and a dog and a cat. It was almost unbelievable sometimes, this second life of mine was so rich and sweet and charming.

The cat yowled all the way to the Hotel De La Ville. Joey, Dinah, and I threw ourselves onto the bed, exhausted. Our room faced the Spanish Steps. The noise outside was deafening—the *clop clop* of horses and carriages, the yells of revelers, the hum of traffic, were all with us in the room even when we closed the balcony doors. Inside the cat paced and complained, the dog whined. We threw open the doors to the life in Rome at two in the morning and ran down the wide marble staircase into the roaring nightlife outside, where Joey hailed a horse and carriage and he and Dinah rode off into the Roman night.

The next morning Joey tried to order breakfast in our newly acquired Italian and became so frightened by the rapidity of speech on the other end of the phone that he slammed it down, totally intimidated.

We looked for and found a great apartment near the bridges. A nice lady of royal descent from Jordan rented us her wonderful flat, filled with antiques. I desperately kept her attention on me as I signed the lease, while behind her my cat defecated on her Persian rug.

My cat knew very well where his cat box was. It was a test of wills; he wanted to be sent back to Malibu. Dinah was set up in the American school. Fremo arrived. Easels were set up; the living room became an artists' studio. Joey and Fremo took out the oils. Dinah sat for a painting. We were home.

There was a cat, Louie, around the corner from us. Louie was an experienced professional beggar. Half of his body lay in the gutter, half on the curb. Black and scrawny, he looked like a dying accident victim, his meow a soft, sensitive plea for help. We'd pass him, Dinah and me, on our way to our favorite trattoria. The first time, I pulled her away sharply. "Don't look," I said, "he's dying. There's nothing we can do." On subsequent visits to the trattoria, I realized that he kept dying in the same spot all day. Older women would leave their kitchens and bring Louie whatever they'd been cooking, murmuring nice things in Italian. They'd set their offerings on the curb so that they wouldn't disturb his twisted body position.

When Fremo arrived, Fremo having collected cats all her life, the first thing she did was rush up from the street and say, "There's a cat on the street. I've got to help him. Please let me bring him here." We formed a common front. No, no, no. Fremo joined the women who brought him food every day. One night, a young female cat sauntered down our street, and Fremo saw Louie rise from the curb, straighten out his twisted body, shake his fur, and take off after the lady like a young stud.

Far from being discouraged, Fremo decided to feed all the needy cats in the Colosseum. There were hundreds. She brought shopping bags to the Colosseum every day, made new friends, animals and human.

In the meantime, I was being introduced to Italian cinema. We shot at Cinecittà. It was there in the cafeteria that a wagon of steamed artichokes rolled by and I saw a look of sexual yearning in Joey's eyes I'd never seen before. His eyelids closed, the better to inhale the steam. His head turned, and I realized that though I was ten years older than he, my real competition was his appetite for beautiful food. Yes, there would be a woman or two, but basically, food and I would fill Joey's need for passion. Except for one excruciatingly painful time, that's been true.

Cinecittà Studios has all kinds of secrets for making their actors beautiful. They used lots of hairpieces and wigs, because under them were transparent lifts that attached to your ears and pulled your face up so that it was perfect and smooth. Sometimes they braided your hair at your temples so your eyes slanted up at the sides.

I was sent to a small store on a side street where three elderly ladies patted my breasts, took careful measurements, and made beautiful brassieres just for me, giving me that plump cleavage so necessary for Italian movie stars.

Of course, my nemesis Shelley Winters was in *Buona Sera*. As the cast ate lunch outdoors for the first time, at a wooden table in the warm Italian sun, Shelley turned to me and said, "The reason you didn't work wasn't because you were blacklisted. You didn't work because you don't have what it takes to be a star!" It was all downhill from there. Shelley was like a huge dinosaur, its tail thrashing someone out of the way while its head was nodding up and down.

Buona Sera, Mrs. Campbell was the sixties version of *Mamma Mia!*, the exact story the musical was based on. There was the young girl raised by her single mother, Gina. Shelley and I were the wives accompanying the husbands who had slept with Gina when the Americans fought in Rome during World War II. Gina was gorgeous and funny, though she learned her English lines phonetically. I was making an entrance with her when she picked up a razor blade and shaved under her arms. Just the blade, scrape, scrape, and made her entrance.

Telly Savalas played my husband. He was easy and fun. His young cousin was his assistant. Before a scene, Telly would walk around the set singing Sinatra songs. "Fly me to the . . ." He'd snap his fingers, his assistant would fill in "moon," and Telly would go on with the song. "I'd sacrifice anything come what may for the"—finger snap—"sake of having you near," the cousin would jump in, on his toes. And so on. Maybe it was Telly's way of preparing for a scene. He was a crooner. He loved performing a song, loved being Sinatra. Peter Lawford was the other husband. A charming guy with a deep need to please, not to rock the boat.

As time went on, Shelley and I started to hang out a little. She was so much fun—when she wasn't throwing her weight around. The two of us were sitting at a table for ten talking. Peter passed by and started to sit down. Aside from Shelley and me, the seats were empty. "Somebody's sitting there!" she barked at Peter.

He looked confused.

"The table's empty," I said to him. "Sit."

"I'm saving that chair for a friend!" Shelley barked again.

And Peter, instead of sitting down and saying "Fuck you, Shelley," slunk away, hurt. It was odd.

Mel Frank was directing. Suddenly Mel burst onto the set. Shelley had broken a tooth, he said, her front tooth, and was insisting on going to New York to see her dentist. It meant holding up shooting for a whole week. Since there were dentists in Rome—and the actors there had beautifully cared-for teeth—neither the studio nor apparently the insurance company would cover the costs.

Later that day we were filming in the church of a village outside Rome. When we drove over the cobblestones up the hill leading to the town square, there were broom makers sitting in the doorways of small cottages, putting straw together, and fresh-faced children in school uniforms trooping down the hill to go to school, all ironed. The air made you breathe deeper, the smell of straw was so sweet. In the town square, older men in caps and belted trousers were comfortably talking at outdoor tables at the café. We set up camera inside the church.

I sat on a front bench sketching, in costume. I wasn't in the first scene. On the other side of the church near the door I saw Shelley. She was trying to get my attention and she was laughing. She pointed to her smile, and there was a black gap where her front tooth should have been. Then she pointed to the statue of the saint she was standing next to. The saint was slightly elevated above Shelley, her eyes cast upward, appealing to God, and in her outstretched hand she held an ancient tooth. Apparently this saint had her teeth extracted as punishment for her Christian beliefs, and just when Shelley needed a tooth, this saint happened to have one.

I laughed out loud, was shushed by the AD, and tiptoed over to Shelley and the saint. I had to hug her. Twenty years later, she told me the temporary tooth she got in Rome was still in her mouth.

. . .

As a parting present, one of the actors gave Joey a block of hashish for us to get stoned on. Tinfoil over a glass with water in it. Set it smoking with a match. Inhale. Black out. Drowning in heat; the least touch sent liquid through the body. We lay on the red coverlet for hours, able to feel, unable to move. *No wonder people have so many partners on drugs,* I thought. *Just feel me, touch me, lick me, I don't care, I'm floating, gone.*

The next day we had almost a whole block of hashish left, and we were feverishly trying to figure out how to get it back to Malibu. Malibu was home to grass and cocaine. Only in Rome was hashish available. Joey's eyes settled on my velvet diaphragm case. "No, no, no," I said. "Are you crazy? I've just started to work again. You want 'ex-commie caught with illegal drugs' to throw me out of work this time?" Frantically Joey looked at every piece of luggage, his painting stuff. He finally decided to open the lining of his jacket and sew it in there. Fine. On the plane, about an hour outside of LAX, he started to sweat. If there was one thing that scared him, it was jail. He went to the toilet a couple of times to rip up his jacket and throw it in, but he couldn't do it.

I spotted Senator Javits on the plane, Jake Javits from my wonderful weekend with Billy Rose.

"Introduce me," Joey hissed.

I did. Standing in the aisle. "Um, Senator, if someone brought in, um, a substance—something that wasn't allowed, um . . ." I said.

"You mean drugs?"

"Yes," Joey jumped in. "Yes, something like that."

"Very harsh," the senator replied.

"Jail time?"

"Yes."

Joey said, "I have a friend with that problem—"

The pilot's voice: "Take your seats . . ." We were landing.

By now Joey was sweating. The beads of sweat on his upper lip had been joined by small streams from under his hair, which was plastered to his forehead, and trickling by his ears onto his neck. He strapped himself in, doomed and covered with flop sweat.

He also acted transparently guilty.

We both quietly prayed as we went through customs. Our dog was delivered in his crate. As I let him out, he had an attack of diarrhea, which splattered over the whole area. The smell was so offensive and so sickening, everyone nearby ran for fresh air, and the customs officer screamed at us to take our luggage and get the hell out of there. As I was trying to mop up the poop with two Kleenex, apologizing, Joey grabbed my arm, grabbed Dinah, clasped the leash on the dog, and rolled the luggage out the airport door, leaving an attendant's soapy mop to clean up behind us.

The Pool House

Dinah changed from New York Chekhov to laughing beach child. The grayness and coldness of the blacklist days, of my years with Arnie, seemed totally disconnected from this new reality. I was supporting my family. I was a breadwinner. I was proud of myself and getting stronger every day.

This Pool House, so far from my old life. It was not a part of my parents' home, not a part of Arnie's home, not a husband's home. I never wanted a husband again. This was my home. My house. My bills. My everything. My child. My boyfriend. Joey.

We had no plans. We had both landed together in Wonderland. We played each day as it came. Friends, Monopoly games, cards, fireplace blazing at the Pool House. Making love, not making love, but loving each other. Sunny, careless, easy, funny love.

The age difference released both of us from all preconceived notions of what a relationship should be. Joey would be himself: Outrageous? So much the better. We both were passionate, not just for each other, but for adventure. Me to make up for time lost—work was adventure. Ah, how passionate I was about acting. I ate, I drank, I taught, I experienced, I fought. And Joey was turning, exploring everything—his senses, drink, drugs, me, fatherhood, food, cops, a happy rebellion, and a search, without any fear, for his place in this new world. There is something in his Italian genes that makes Joey unstoppable. He will have what he wants, and that's it. He has no problem either being the boss or crawling on his knees to get what he wants. No shame.

When we were first in Malibu Colony, there was a beach party. Warren Stevens, who played the young lead on Broadway in *Detective Story*, was there. Joey, who was barely twenty-four at the time, stared at Warren, steadily, threateningly, while I enjoyed this fun reunion. Talking, hugging, reminiscing. I looked over at this kid that I had allowed to come to Malibu from New York. His eyes were shooting warnings at Warren, but his tie was in his drink. Joey had a gift for being ridiculous. Even he had to laugh. It was a gift that saved our relationship time and again.

Why Joey? Because Upper West Side Jewish girls like bad boys, crazy bad boys, especially crazy, bad, working-class boys, and I secretly admired his chutzpah. I wished I had it. And secretly gasped when he screamed at the cops and stomped in the middle of the Pacific Coast Highway, sometimes twice in one night.

I loved Malibu. I loved the informality, and the beautiful fruits and vegetables in my Malibu market. The easiness folks had with one another. The old shorts and shoes and the bare feet. The Colony was a small town where everyone kind of knew one another. There were no rules to break there.

Dinah was riding her bike up and down the Colony. I had bought a tiny white poodle from a makeup lady on *Peyton Place*. Dinah had him in her basket. Such freedom was shaping her seven-year-old psyche. The New York City kid was becoming a Malibu beach girl.

She had two new friends, Katie and Tootie. Katie had lost her mother. Her father was a successful composer. They talked long into the night. Tootie lived at a beach house Dinah could walk to. Dinah, Tootie, and Katie were in the same class at the wonderful, safe public school in Malibu. In fifth grade, one little girl in Dinah's class, whom Dinah had befriended, turned on her. She and her little friend made Dinah's first school year in California frightening and miserable. These girls were popular and held so much power in their class that they made everyone sign a paper saying they hated Dinah. They called her a dirty Jew. In Malibu there were not many Jewish children. These girls were so scary they frightened everyone away from Dinah.

Every morning before she went to school that first year, Dinah and I would talk about how to deal with those two girls. What to do, where to eat lunch, what to say ("Yell back," I said: "Nazis, Jew haters."), how to cope. I, of course, had gone to speak to the principal. I demanded she punish the girls. And stop them. And protect my daughter. And throw them out of school. She said she felt actions like that would exacerbate and prolong the situation. She said, "Do nothing."

So those two kids continued to show up at our house after school. They would get on their knees and scream for Dinah through a window. They weren't intimidated by me. Finally I got their parents' phone numbers and called them. It stopped. But Dinah got an education that first year she never forgot. She learned to cope. She became a master coper, brave and resourceful. And has kept every meaningful friend in her life, including Tootie and Katie, who also learned a lesson about themselves and friendship.

I started getting migraines while we were living in the Pool House. Naomi Caryl, a new friend, came to the Pool House with her artist boyfriend. Her dad was the Mr. Hirshhorn who built a great art museum in Washington, D.C.: The Hirshhorn Museum.

My good friend Gladys was staying with us, her long romance with Waldo Salt continuing in L.A., where Waldo was writing one great screenplay after another, *Midnight Cowboy, Serpico*, his work cup overflowing. Gladys was doing wonderful watercolors and working with Joey, who was open and hungry for painting. Gladys was a generous, involved teacher. They spent days doing oils and watercolors.

Naomi had discovered a new way to lose weight in exactly the places I wanted to lose it: huge shots of pregnant mare's urine! Yes! She explained the philosophy behind it: In Italy during World War II, pregnant Italian women sometimes became emaciated from lack of food, but their babies came out plump because they made use of their mothers' fat—or something like that.

"Oh me too! Me too!" I cried. "I want to lose fat in my thighs, just there."

"It will happen," Naomi predicted, hugging her monkey.

So I went to the doctor's office just on the other side of the Colony wall and he gave me huge shots of mare's urine—hormones, basically. I lost the fat in my thighs, and for a short time strutted around my pool in a bikini. Then the headaches started. The influx of pregnant mare hormones had thrown my own hormones off balance and led to my first migraines, which were to become the bane and curse of my life.

Caresse Crosby's dictum "Say yes to everything," which I had adopted as a life philosophy, had led me in this case to a few days of paralyzing pain every month. It hit me hard as an actor.

I remember riding to the studio to shoot a two-hour pilot stretched out on the floor of the limo. Whenever I had to work through a migraine, I asked that a pail be placed within reach so I could have something to throw up in. I never, never missed a day's work. And now, when I watch the scenes that I shot with a migraine, I like them the best. There's no "acting."

Years later, when I was filming *The Landlord*, Hal Ashby's first film, I was so sick and in such pain, they hired a nurse to sleep with me in my hotel room, a German lady with braids coiled around her head. Back then, there was no medication for migraines; you just had to tough it out. The German nurse put on her nightgown, took down her braids, and promptly fell asleep in the double bed, a foot away from mine. Flat on her back, her braids arranged on her chest, her hands folded, she fell asleep immediately and began to snore.

I was up all night, maddened with pain and resentment of this noisy stranger who had taken over my private place and was peacefully sleeping while I stayed awake through the night. I couldn't wait for daylight to get rid of her. After, I remember getting made up and costumed, then kneeling and hitting my head on a rock before starting the scene where Beau Bridges, who played my son, and I careened across a green lawn in a golf cart. It was a wonderful scene, and the pain gave me a perfect edge.

Playing *The Prisoner of Second Avenue* onstage five or so years later, I'd bang my head on the wall of the dressing room, and somehow the pounding blood would go somewhere else in my body until I stepped offstage. I don't remember missing a day of work because of migraines, either acting or directing. Just once I missed a matinee of *The Prisoner of Second Avenue*, but it was because of laryngitis. Charlie Chaplin, one of my heroes, was in the audience. A real regret. The doctor came and gave me a shot in my vocal cords and I was back that night.

I don't remember anyone telling theater people that an actor cannot be late or miss a performance. I just know none of us did—no matter what.

Say YES to Everything

L.A. at the time was flooded with talent, and Lee Strasberg, who loved talent, and especially stars with talent, was going to spend three months at a new branch of the Actors Studio on the West Coast. I was assigned to win over Mayor Sam Yorty so he would give us a home in L.A. We had two dinner dates and my mission was accomplished. The Actors Studio was given a home in perpetuity in West Hollywood, rent-free, on De Longpre Avenue, a gift that exists to this day. A more personal gift to me from the mayor was having him use his influence to take five years off my age on my driver's license.

"Please correct a terrible mistake on my driver's license."

"Sure."

I breathed, relieved. *If I can only get ten years off my official birth date, I'll be safe. I can work ten more years.*

I went to the newly formed Actors Studio production of *The Threepenny Opera*, playing at a small theater, under a hundred seats. The work was embarrassing. Actors sitting behind me—non–Actors Studio actors—were making nasty comments all through the play.

"This is supposed to be good acting? This is the Studio?" And they were right. The play hadn't officially opened yet.

I marched onto the stage, told everyone they were terrible, and offered a day and night of free labor if they would let me fix it. Then the director, who was there, could take over again.

I felt the reputation of the newly established L.A. Actors Studio was at stake. I could save it.

The first thing that happened was my beloved Burgess Meredith quit. He had been playing his non-gay character gay and goosing the other players. Another favorite actress of mine was playing with herself while singing "Pirate Jenny," the great song Lotte Lenya made famous in Berlin. One actress couldn't carry a tune, so I had her talk the song instead. The orchestra was put back onstage where it traditionally belonged. Midafternoon of my first day rescuing the play, Lee Strasberg stopped me outside the theater. He was snorting, a clear sign he was very angry. "What do you know about Brecht?" he yelled. "What do you know about German theater? What do you know about Germany in that period? The history? The music? What do you know?" He was furious and indignant.

"I don't know anything about Brecht," I yelled back. "I only know what works!" Suddenly, he smiled. He laughed at me and nodded. I nodded back and went to the theater. The sad end of the story has a "Beware what you wish for" moral. The rescue worked so well that when Jimmy Doolittle saw it, he decided to bring the show to his big L.A. theater.

I had reworked the show for a day and night in a comfy, small space. Suddenly I was facing a responsibility I knew I was totally unprepared and unequipped for. The original director had fled. I asked everyone I knew to take over the direction. I begged Lee, who said no; Burgess, no. There was no money for sets. I knew nothing about lighting. And I was suddenly faced with snarling actors demanding that they not be replaced for the move to the Doolittle, that they get their "big chance." The actor who replaced Burgess walked back and forth in the theater. "I know things about people in this organization that I won't hesitate to use if you try to put someone in my part . . ." Ugly, ugly, ugly.

Camaraderie disappeared. The whole atmosphere changed. *The Threepenny Opera* is a famous musical. The only real singing pros in *Threepenny* were Lesley Ann Warren and Pat Carroll. Opening at a small off-Broadway theater was one thing. But the Doolittle was the Broadway equivalent in L.A. I was stuck and I was sick.

I wandered up and down the Red House in Malibu, praying for the original director to return. He didn't. We were waiting for word whether it would be a go. I was praying for a no. Then Jon Peters, the hairdresser/producer who was going with or was married to Lesley Ann at the time, said, "I don't want the little girl to be sitting on the curb wearing her toe shoes. I'm putting some money in for her."

When I got the call that Jon had financed the play, I leaned over to pick up my travel bag and couldn't get up. I ended up directing at the Doolittle from an electric wheelchair. It buzzed up and down the aisles. We had a week, maybe two weeks to adjust to a Broadway-size space. "Speak up, sing out," I shouted from my wheelchair. The stage was bare. Opening night, the curtain parted. Someone had decided to dress the stage with a tall piece of wood, a phallic wooden sculpture that stretched from the stage to the top lights. A senseless symbol of the whole project. Lesley Ann had the quality of Snow White in this gritty musical. It was a motley crew—brave, but motley. My wheelchair protected me from the hard critique I richly deserved. Lee Strasberg was there. At intermission our eyes connected. He smiled and nodded.

Allen Garfield, a very passionate actor, placed himself on the steps in the theater lobby during intermission and screamed, "This is not Actors Studio work. This work is not the work of the Actors Studio! This does not represent us." He got star billing in one of the reviews. Actually, the reviews were tolerant and kind compared to what we would have gotten in New York. Some of the reviewers from *Variety* and the *Hollywood Reporter* were friends. I'd done so many interviews with them over the years. But by the time we opened, I was in love with the show, which is what always happens. We need to fool ourselves. I was crippled and delusional.

In the Heat of
the Night

I got a call to meet with Norman Jewison about *In the Heat of the Night*. When I read the script, I knew why he'd sent for me. It was about a businessman who is murdered while on a short trip to the deep South. You never meet the businessman, but the wife, me, is given the news of his death. Sidney Poitier is a Philadelphia detective, held as a suspect because he is black and a Northerner. Rod Steiger is the Southern sheriff.

In his office, I sat across from Norman, who introduced me to Hal Ashby, his longtime friend and the editor on the film. At that point Hal had not directed anything, and he still had a wife in Idaho. We looked at each other across the desk and connected in a hundred ways without exchanging a word. I knew about losing a husband, which was what the role was about, and I let myself go there, sitting across from them. By the time I left, they knew everything they needed to know about me and had found what they were looking for.

That was the beginning of a long friendship with both men, but especially with Hal. While Norman was on location shooting, he assigned Hal the job of overseeing my wardrobe. There were no fashion consultants or overseers, just Hal and me shopping for a week in L.A. department stores, talking and getting to be really relaxed with each other. Hal had this laid-back, long-haired hippie persona to begin with. I never saw him ruffled or upset till many years later, long after he had directed me in *The Landlord* and *Shampoo*.

A day before I left for the Midwest, where *Heat* was filming, I'd done a day's work in Norman Lear and Bud Yorkin's *Divorce American Style*. I went from fun and silly to deep and dark as I entered the set.

I had pretty much cocooned myself preparing for the part, had done a lot of remembering and breaking down behind locked bathroom doors. All I wanted was to keep myself in that wounded place through the filming. Rod and Sidney were both my friends, and they went out of their way to greet and hug me, but I needed to keep my concentration internal and in character to play that part.

When Sidney's character finally gave me the news of my husband's death, I reacted the way I had in life. I thought if I didn't hear it, I could turn back the clock and it wouldn't have happened. My throat closes with pain still as I write.

I kept saying "No, no, no" to block out the reality. Sidney's sensitivity in that scene was true and unscripted, and he was there for me every step of the way. Sidney's eyes, concerned, sensitive, his body—I can't see him as an actor, he was that good. He was so talented, I forgot he was acting. Norman Jewison encouraged this fresh exploration to happen and take its course. Haskell Wexler, the director of photography, was doing handheld, and wherever we went as actors he followed with his camera.

I don't think there is a better film about race in America than *In the Heat of the Night*. Rod Steiger's journey as the Southern sheriff reluctantly brought to enlightenment is so remarkable, and Sidney is so damned beautiful and strong inside and out.

We were still at the Pool House when the script of *In the Heat of the Night* came in. I realize as I write that I was the only blacklisted female actor to have reclaimed the visibility and height of her previous career before it was yanked away. The actor John Randolph did a lot of films and had a good career in character parts. Ossie Davis, too, but I seemed to have been discovered anew—as if my other life had never existed. As if that old Lee Grant, the blacklisted one, was still teaching at HB Studio in New York, and this new Lee Grant, the new hot girl in town, was a completely different person. The fact that I'd joined the fight in my early twenties had a lot to do with it. I was just starting out in New York, with only one big picture behind me, while most of the actors, writers, and directors who were blacklisted were in their thirties, forties, and fifties, already successful and prominent in their fields when they were hit—artistically and financially broken, deprived of their right to earn a living and speak their minds.

Rod Steiger once described success for him like being a fighter in the ring. You go the rounds, you're beaten up and bleeding, then suddenly you score a knockout, the referee counts the other fighter out and holds up your arm. The winner! Then suddenly the bell goes off again. The fighting never stops, the slugging it out, no matter how many times you win. This after he'd won the Oscar for *In the Heat of the Night.*

Twenty-four when I was blacklisted, thirty-six when it ended.

My ingenue years gone, and my leading lady years almost over.

Facing forty, I was beginning again, having to hide everything. The heaviness of the past. The producer wants a hot, funny, schmoozy, flirty young actress who can get along with everyone and be there on time. I knew this. I would be this.

The other fear, starting over at thirty-six: Someone could find out my age and I would lose all the parts for twenty-six-year-olds that the agents and casting people were looking for. The beginning of a career in Hollywood, not the end. The fear that my age would be disclosed became the neurotic focus of my life.

Today, with the Internet, I'd be finished. In the sixties and seventies, I could easily lie and maneuver and get away with it. And no one connected the fresh-faced young woman/girl with the eight-year-old daughter and cute Italian boyfriend with the dark political world of the fifties.

The face-lift I'd demanded, rushed into, pure intuition, turned out to be a solid practical necessity—and with this fresh face erasing the downward pull around my mouth, my eyes, I believe it saved my career. My earning power. Even my love life, I guess.

I could look thirty.

When I went out on the road with *The Captains and the Kings*, the play I took when I left Arnie, I had a little romance with a handsome young actor. A flirtation really.

"How old are you?" he asked over cocktails in a San Francisco bar.

I said, "Thirty."

"Oh," he said, crestfallen. "I thought you were twenty-six!"

He was attracted to a twenty-something, not a thirty-something. On this, my first venture away from Arnie, out in the world, I was learning. What to show. What to hide.

In this next venture I was to make through Hollywood, I had both the excitement and the fear of the imposter. I had been a citizen of the New York fifties, the land of my birth and education in life, marriage, motherhood, and politics. I presented myself in L.A. as a girl with no past. I landed here because I was offered a job. That's when life began.

Nobody knew.

Nobody would.

In the Heat of the Night was the breakthrough film of its time; Sidney Poitier was irresistible, and I was in it.

The Red House

renda Vaccaro and I both created houses that everyone gravitated to. Mine was the Red House, which Joan Didion wrote about in *The Year of Magical Thinking*, and Brenda's house was in Benedict Canyon. My house was across from Zuma Beach. It had been built by a well-known California architect for two older sisters—twin houses, each a long barnlike floor-through that we joined together to make one long, charming house. One side faced the Pacific Ocean, the other a big grassy lawn surrounded by woods. When Joey and I drove up the winding road and saw the houses for the first time, the earth in front of us was moving. The place had become a rabbit habitat, every square inch of grass covered by quivering bunny bodies. It was ten minutes up the Pacific Coast Highway from the Colony.

I had no images where men were concerned. All I knew was, I was driving the bus in our life. Earning a living for all of us was my main concern, and it had to be Joey's main concern, too. There was no discussion or disagreement. Joey was madly in love; all he wanted to do was to please me, help me, be family. We were meeting all our new friends together, in a new place. Every job brought new friends; opening the Actors Studio in L.A. brought friends for life.

I never thought we'd be together forever. I didn't think about it at all. There was too much to do. I was cooking, working, acting, teaching, entertaining, mommying. Every weekend, the Red House was mobbed with friends. I'd make sautéed chicken or leg of lamb, or buy Stouffer's frozen lobster over rice, a flank steak with soy sauce and brown sugar, bake a huge custard, then sit around and talk and talk through the afternoon and early evening since everyone had to be up early the next day to work or go up for a job.

I was now living without tension, or fear, or a sense of inadequacy. Joey thought I could do anything, and I could. Because we expected nothing of each other, we were free of expectations. The only condition I ever put to him was that he had to earn a living or leave. So he received a terrible rejection as a gas station attendant and made it as a big commercial producer. I felt this relationship was new, open territory, and I was taking it a week at a time. The only careers Joey had had before were installing plumbing in new buildings, like his father, and as a classically trained ballet dancer, and he was still a kid. I was watching him grow and unfold, even as I was in a new life myself.

He acted in a scene with Ron Rifkin and was accepted into the Actors Studio. I'm sure his being my guy influenced the decision, but it was Lee Strasberg himself who praised his work. With Joey I was living with my best friend, my protector, the most fun person I wanted to be with, in bed and out, and at the same time we were both growing. I'm avoiding the word *love*, because *love* is too trite, too catchall, and too vast.

I had said early on, as he began to travel with the commercials he was filming, "Have your flings. If you're in a strange city and you're attracted to someone, do what you want. Fuck her, have a good time, but don't tell me about it. Keep your secrets, and I'll keep mine." I'd seen how couples tortured each other with their conquests. What I didn't know wouldn't hurt me. What Joey didn't know wouldn't hurt him.

Valley of the Dolls

I had an offer to play the leading man's hovering, tightly wound sister in *Valley of the Dolls*. It had been a huge success as a book, as *Peyton Place* had been in its time. It made its writer, Jacqueline Susann, the most ubiquitous guest on TV interview shows of the day. The setting was Hollywood, steaming and corrupt; the "dolls" were the pills, shortly before drugs and cocaine became the norm. This was Patty Duke's big career break as a grown-up after *The Miracle Worker*. She was to play the nice, innocent song and dance girl who swallows too many dolls and becomes an unbearable, relationship-wrecking, spoiled bitch, who literally ends up in the gutter after a night in a bar in San Francisco. Gay Heaven!

Just before filming was scheduled to start, I realized I'd missed a period, then two. Shooting was only a few weeks away, and I needed the money. I didn't know where to go or who to ask about an abortion. Joey said one of his friends in Delaware knew a doctor. Afterward I'd fly back to Malibu, rest, and go to work. Dinah stayed with her friend Tootie.

Joey and I flew to Philadelphia, rented a car, and drove to the doctor's house. I remember standing in a converted kitchen. A long padded table was in front of me, the wall paint was old, yellow, the linoleum on the floor cracking, and the foot-pedaled garbage tin was overflowing. I felt liquid begin to trickle down the inside of my thigh. It was pee or blood. I sat nervously on the padded table while the doctor looked. It was blood. A protective pour, as it turned out. I had a New York physician check me into a nice sterile hospital to be cleaned out. I was not pregnant. The hospital doctor thought it was the hormone shots I'd been getting that screwed up the cycle. I stared at my skinny legs hanging over the hospital bed and thought about how lucky I was, and how interesting my body's reaction, protecting itself immediately in response to my fear and horror of that room and that doctor.

The story of *Valley of the Dolls* skidding downhill to win the laughingstock prize of 1967 is legendary. It was an unbelievable, laugh-out-loud disaster. I remember coming back from my New York trip and watching the very young, very talented Patty Duke cavorting on the green lawn at Warner Bros. with Marty Mull, her love interest in the film, and my sweet girlfriend from *Peyton Place*, Barbara Parkins, actresses breathing the golden breath of success and impending superstardom, as if to say, *This is it, this is it. Don't you wish you were me?*

No. I was never that brave. Especially in Hollywood, I never wanted the leaden, overwhelming responsibility of carrying a film, or a budget.

How long is the life of a star? How long is the life of an actor? Longer. Longer is all I wanted. I wanted protection against the short life of Hollywood stardom. I was thirty-four when I landed back there, more than a decade after *Detective Story*. By Hollywood standards I was already over the hill. I was neurotic enough about this new life, post-blacklist, instinctively waiting for the hand on my shoulder telling me it was over, it had all been a bureaucratic mistake.

Or that I was no longer young enough or pretty enough for my next job. I was hungry to act, hungry to work, as hungry as a rabid dog.

Most of my scenes were with Sharon Tate—this was three years before her young life was cut down by the Manson family and her death became a grim part of Hollywood history. She was lovely in the part, the only one I really believed on-screen, including myself. She was shockingly beautiful, but she also had an element of victimhood that was right for the part. She sank like a woman drowning in her role. I never saw Roman Polanski; he was away working. Her companion and confidant during the film was Jay Sebring, on whom Warren Beatty's character in *Shampoo* would be based years later.

The director of the film was Mark Robson, who was basically an editor. There is a scene, if I remember correctly, where I'm given the news that my brother's sickness, Huntington's chorea, is recurring. It meant his wife, Sharon, and I would lose him forever. He would have to live the rest of his life in a mental institution. I prepared for the scene and did it. The director tiptoed over to me with his stopwatch.

"You did that in three minutes, forty-two seconds. Do you think you can do it in two minutes and thirty seconds?"

"You want it shorter and faster?" I asked.

"Yes, I'm editing as we go along, and that's the time I gave this scene."

"Oh."

One morning I did a scene with Sharon on a Monday that was a pickup of a scene we'd half finished on Friday. It was a scene that had called for emotion on Friday night, and it had to be carried over to Monday morning with the same feeling. After we'd filmed the scene, the director said he wanted to talk to me. He led me through the whole lot, past sets, trailers, till we climbed the stairs to his trailer.

"How did you do that?" he asked.

"What?"

"You know, carry over that feeling from Friday and bring that same feeling on Monday?"

"Well," I said, "it wasn't a big deal. I'd found something real for me, and I could leave it Friday and find it again when I came back into the situation."

"Yeah, but how?"

I looked at him to see if he meant it.

"It's called acting," I said. We left the trailer together and walked silently back to the set.

Years later I was invited to a fair-sized theater production of *Valley of the Dolls*. Everyone in it was gay. The lines were absolutely the same as in the film, and everyone played it straight, the way we did. It was foot-stompingly funny; as farce, it really worked. The whole audience knew every line. Maybe if John Waters, the writer-director of *Hairspray*, had had a shot at it . . . Who knows, but then it wouldn't have been Jacqueline Susann's *Valley of the Dolls*.

The Landlord

Norman Jewison made my friend Hal Ashby a gift of *The Landlord*. He purchased it for Hal as his first directing job. I read it. I loved it. I wanted to be in it. No, Hal and Norman told me, I was too young for the part I wanted, which was already cast in their minds. Jessica Tandy would be perfect. I kept on reading it and realized I would be even better for it than I first thought. I knew this character. I was raised by this character. She was a perfect combination of my mother and my Aunt Fremo. With all the delicious self-delusion they shared. I found an old honey-colored mink hat somewhere and plopped it on my head for hair color. "Just let me read," I begged Hal. "You don't have to hire me." When I arrived at Norman's office, I pulled them into the hall and put myself and the mink hat under the fluorescent lights. "See, with a top light and yellow hair I can make the age." And then I read the part and they got it. I brought my mother and Fremo to them in a character they'd never met before—fresh and different and ridiculous, and just right for this Long Island doyenne, mother to Beau Bridges.

Bridges is the landlord, who lives in his wealthy mother's mansion on Long Island. He decides to buy a brownstone in Harlem, throw out the black tenants, and redo it into his new home. Pearl Bailey lives on the second floor, Diana Sands on the third floor. Beau falls in love with a young black woman in the neighborhood and the tenants won't move out.

My favorite and best scene was with Pearlie. My character arrives in a chauffeured limo to the brownstone, carrying rolls of curtain material to help her son, Beau, decorate his new place. I end up drunk in Pearl's second-floor apartment. It's a great scene. My favorite. Pearlie and I are the original odd couple. She gets me drunk, loaded, I confide in her, and when I finally leave her apartment, I pick up a coveted pork chop from her supper table and throw it into my handbag. Great? Outrageous?

Except. When we filmed the scene, before I could reach for the pork chop, Pearl had it. And she threw it into my purse. "Here you go, dahling, a little something for the ride home." Scene completely stolen.

"Ha-a-a-a-l," I bleated, like a kindergartner.

Hal wagged his finger at Pearl. I threw my own pork chop into my own bag. But she almost got away with it. Smiling, sparkling at her own daring.

After filming was finished, I invited everyone to a cast party. What I really wanted was to have a good sit-down visit with Hal all to myself. He had a new wife who was abnormally possessive and overwrought.

I had rented Walter Bernstein's big old apartment on the Upper West Side. I decided to fry chicken legs and wings for the party. Hundreds of legs and wings, it seemed, as I threw them in to fry in the big dark kitchen. I had hired two Spanish-speaking women to help me. The oil splattered our faces and arms. I cut holes out of three paper bags, and we put them over our heads and lunged back and forth between stove and table for an hour, sweating inside the bags. We were a

Diane Arbus photograph. In the end it was a dud. Most of the cast had returned to L.A. already. Diana Sands and I sat on the couch and talked. The phone rang. It was Hal. "I can't come."

I could hear his new wife screaming in the background. "Hal, please, please."

"She won't let me."

"What?"

"She's going through something."

I heard her sobs. "Bye."

"Bye."

Diana and I talked some more. We agreed that we hated Hal's new wife and that she was a neurotic jealous bitch. Then we ate the awful fried chicken.

Dinah

Before Dinah went off to Lazy J Ranch in Malibu, she pulled me into the bathroom at the Red House.

"Mommy," she sniffled, "when I am going to get breasts?"

"Oh my baby!" I hugged my thirteen-year-old little girl to my body and we swayed back and forth. "Soon, soon."

She kissed me and held me and clung to me. Dinah was my grail, my constant; nothing and no one could get between us. Dinah and my need to support her financially, morally, viscerally, and my rage at those who had taken twelve working, acting years from my life, were what motivated me.

Summer ended and Dinah, my lovely child, was back from Lazy J Ranch camp, which had nourished her lifelong love of horses—and her breasts. She returned from camp with two big round mounds and a preference for the company of studly Malibu boys and young men, instead of her mother. Also a predilection for drugs, and a full-blown case of adolescent rebellion that would continue for fifteen years. Yes, my Dinah morphed into a Malibu teen. It hit me hard. When other parents had said, "Wait till adolescence, just wait," I felt sorry for them. That could never happen to me. Not to my Dinah.

The example I had set for her with Joey was hardly exemplary. In 37A, the Colony house, we were given our first grass by Bobby Walker and his wife, Elly. Bobby was Jennifer Jones's son with Robert Walker. The bodies were piled high at their beach house. Everyone ate hash brownies. The dogs ate hash brownies—and dropped where they stood. It was mellow. They were beautiful and fun. The first time we smoked grass we lay on the couches in the living room of the Pool House. It was late afternoon. Dinah was eight and sleeping over at her friend Katie's house. Joey said, "Give me a word to spell." "Criminal." He spelled it. "Exemplary." He spelled it. "Fortitude." He spelled it, and on into the evening. The thing was, Joey was and is dyslexic. He could not spell. Cannot spell. His brain does not compute letters. Which is fine. Except that afternoon, for two or three hours, something in his brain computed. His brain took a leap of faith and something miraculous— for Joey it certainly was—something really happened. Grass was beneficial. Not being a person who does things by halves, Joey threw himself wholeheartedly into weed, then as it became an ordinary party drug, cocaine, and to wash it all down, why not a little brandy? So it was not exactly a surprise that Dinah followed her parents' cool example.

How often had she huddled against me as a child in the backseat of the Bentley, crying, as Joey was stopped on the Pacific Coast Highway by the Malibu cops for speeding or driving erratically? They knew the car by sight; they'd given Joey so many tickets that our Malibu judge would say, "C'mon, Joey—what did they get you on now?" Goodnaturedly. So no, we were not exactly a shining example.

Those were mostly scary nights for me. I did my widow's walk up and down the length of the Red House, angry, furious at Joey for not calling, fearing him dead at the bottom of Benedict Canyon. And of course the Bentley, maroon on top, black on the bottom, and in the old square classic style, was a moving target for the cops on the Pacific

Coast Highway. "Let's get Joey!" And true to form, he would jump out of the car stomping and waving his arms like a crazy man refusing to say the alphabet, which with his dyslexia he couldn't say right. Once he told them he had diabetes. They took him to the Malibu hospital and he was almost given a shot of insulin. That night he called and said, "I'm in jail for the night."

I said, "Thank God," and I slept soundly.

D inah was a suntanned, bikini-clad, post-hippie Malibu girl. She and her girlfriends all had horses. They rode together on the beach. They rode their horses across the Pacific Coast Highway and up to the village market, where they tied them to hitching posts and hung out. They were all having sex with their high school boyfriends. They partied.

"What's wrong with that, Mom? Huh, Mom?"

We had awful, screaming, crying fights all the time. Between the two of us. Between Dinah and Joey.

Joey and I were equally inept trying to cope with Dinah's adolescence. We were all three at war—she rebelling in totally scary ways, we shocked and angry. The experience turned Joey into Eddie Carbone, the Italian longshoreman at the center of Arthur Miller's play *A View from the Bridge*. Carbone is so protective of his orphaned niece that his hackles are raised when any other man is attracted to her physically. Joey had this innate Italian gorilla thing with all the boys that Dinah brought around who were hot for her. Joey could barely control himself from fighting them as they sat at the dining room table.

"Why's your neck so thick?" he'd ask, watching as the boy would turn red. "No, tell me, why is your neck so thick?"

In all honesty, he had the same possessiveness with all his women:

his twin sister, Phyllis, me, then Dinah. I remember sitting around the table on 6th and Lincoln, the house in Wilmington where they were raised. Rachel, their mother, ran an open house—friends dropped in and hung out at any hour, any day. Phyllis's date was there. Joey couldn't sit still. His hackles rose like the hair on a wolf's back.

"Where do you live? What do you do?"

Like the head of the house interrogating a street bum who's turned up to ask for Phyllis's hand. He was so over-the-top that it would make me laugh, and everybody else would yell at him. You know those dogs with the low growls at whom everyone shouts, "Stop it!" But Joey's low growl didn't stop. We three women were his possessions.

Dinah had moved out of her bedroom to the attic opposite the front door. All of a sudden skuzzy, revolting men, not boys, were driving up to the Red House bringing drugs to Dinah's attic. I screamed them off the property, chasing them down the hill like a banshee, like the Wicked Witch of the West's monkeys. "No, Dinah!" I screamed.

"They're my friends!" she screamed back.

"Then leave!" I threatened. "Leave!"

And she did. She moved in with her high school boyfriend Richard's mother, who worked in the principal's office. Richard was a dear boy who spoke with the pure, slow, child-of-Malibu accent. His mother was a lovely down-to-earth woman. It was such a relief. Dinah and I were killing each other, inflicting real wounds. She was trying to rebirth herself, to break away from a powerful, needy, panicked mother. I was trying to pack her back inside me.

One night, while Joey and I were having dinner at Frank Pierson's house, I got a phone call. Our Mercedes had been in a head-on collision. Dinah and two passengers were in the Malibu Medical Center. We left Frank's house and drove down the Pacific Coast Highway. As we neared the medical center, I recognized our Mercedes as it passed by, dangling above the tow truck. It had been totaled. I don't need to describe my panic. We were very lucky. Dinah had a broken wrist and ankle, so broken she had to be homeschooled for the rest of the year by a teacher sent out by the school system, but she was alive. The face of the boy who'd been sitting in the passenger seat was a bloody pulp, full of glass. I don't remember whether it was her sophomore or senior year in high school. So many of the children Dinah grew up with lost their lives in car accidents on the Pacific Coast Highway. Dinah was stoned, of course. If she hadn't been driving our Mercedes, we would have lost her. The Mercedes was a tank.

Because of my migraines, I rarely did more than a token toot or drag of grass, and I never drank. But for some reason, I totally accepted that Joey was just one of the boys. And he was. There were guys that did less than he did and there were guys and girls that did much, much more.

Every A-list actor and director hung out at Brenda Vaccaro and Michael Douglas's house in Benedict Canyon. You got stoned just opening the door. But great work was still being done. This was the seventies, the decade the best, the freshest, and the most daring and original American movies were ever made. Major studios took a backseat as entrepreneurial filmmakers, writers, and directors made history, and lots of money, too. And I was coming into my own.

The Neon Ceiling

Carol Sobieski brought *The Neon Ceiling* to the Red House for me to read. The writing was beautiful. I thought of it as the first indie movie written for TV. I identified deeply with the woman she'd explored, a housewife with a twelve-year-old daughter, married to a dentist for whom she could do nothing right. Couldn't look right, think right, talk right. I knew her cold. Frank Pierson was set to direct. Frank was a golden Hollywood writer: *Dog Day Afternoon, Cool Hand Luke, Presumed Innocent*. He was also a neighbor, in Trancas, one beach up from us in Malibu. He dropped off his rewrite of *Neon Ceiling* two nights before we were to start shooting. I read it. I didn't sleep. I stayed up until agents stirred and I called mine, Jack Gilardi. I told him to come to the Red House. I couldn't do the script. He called Frank, and they arrived together.

I told Frank, "I won't play this woman. You've killed her."

"What do you mean?"

"I don't recognize the character Carol wrote. I don't recognize the marriage. In your draft the dentist is married to a spoiled neurotic who makes his life impossible—and is a rotten mother to boot! The whole insight into that relationship is blown! Who is that character?"

Frank: "Well, she's based on my sister-in-law."

"And you hate her?"

"Yes."

"Okay, get some other actor to play your impossible bitchy sister-in-law, who makes life hell for her poor dentist husband!"

I felt that whatever bad times Frank had had with women had been completely imposed on a character written by a talented woman, containing revelations about her own life. Her insight didn't come from observation; she'd been there, had lived it.

At some point I saw this awareness register in Frank's eyes. "Okay," he said. "I got it. Wrong script for my sister-in-law." I breathed. He breathed. It was Frank's first directing job. He could not have been more discerning or sensitive and was a true friend, for life.

We filmed *Neon Ceiling* deep in the desert. The scene when I, as an always inadequate wife and mother, take my wise twelve-year-old daughter and run away from home and husband was liberating.

It was, of course, the story of my life with Arnie and Dinah, which was why I fought so hard for Carol's vision of her script. As I, as the character, drive away from home, a Bach chorus comes on the car radio, and my daughter and I sing along triumphantly as we head out on a new life, as unprepared as I had actually been when I left Arnie. We drive for hours into the desert. At the end of the day we spot a gas station. The gas station owner is Gig Young, who kindly gives a hungry, faint mother and her child a place to spend the night.

Gig, an elusive, charming Hollywood guy, a natural actor, was born for the part. The character, a loner who has this home-slash-gas station-slash-diner deep in nowhere, has created a fantastical ceiling out of all the old neon signs that used to exist: cocktails bubbling in different colors, motel signs flashing on and off. When it's dark out and the regular lights are turned off and the neon lights are turned on, it's his vision of magic, the world he wants to live in. Gig and I, both of us hiders, hidden people, find a common soul in each other—much to the devastation of my twelve-year-old daughter, who's developed her first romantic crush on Gig. Lovely?

I, as the character, spend my days in his rocker on the back porch, looking at hot desert. Sand and sky, nothing more. As happens with some film or theater experiences, the desert went from city-dweller boring, incomprehensible, to seductive, fresh. The scent of the sand, of dry heat, the shimmer, the light, the calm entered me. My eyes opened to the way artists saw this endless, changing, subtle, powerful life-scape.

At lunchtime, a group of thirty or forty dark shapes stood on the dunes against the sky, watching us eat. They were Sioux Indians. Their leader, a fortyish woman, Louise, came to our caterer and asked that the tribe be given our leftovers to take back to their families. She was firm. She did not want garbage, but food that was untouched, food the cast and crew could not stuff into themselves, food that had not yet been put on plates. Virgin food. Our producer agreed, and so it was that the Sioux became a part of our new lives in Pearblossom, California.

Louise became a friend. It's been so long, I've forgotten how that group of Sioux ended up in the desert, but it was clear that life for them there was hard and unsustaining. I had dinners with Louise and her husband in their cabin. She was elegant and proud; when shooting was over, she gave me one of her poodle's pups. Nusski, she told me to call him, Sioux for something. Noble? Dog with Soul? Nusski was all that.

I took him into the limo that would drive us home, his warm, plump, silver-haired body lying on my chest all the way to the Red House in Malibu, inhaling his sweet puppy smell.

Nusski was a great, great friend till he died, twelve years later, after we'd moved back to New York. Like the Sioux woman who gave him to me, kind, loving, full of valor. I cherish his memory and miss him always.

And Gig Young, a decade after *The Neon Ceiling*, killed his twenty-one-year-old wife and himself. Despair, I thought. That great sadness of Gig himself, which he covered with such great charm in *Neon Ceiling*. Despair and desperation.

Portnoy's Complaint

I have heard that Ernie Lehman wrote in his autobiography that Lee Grant threw him off his own set. Yes. While directing his own script of *Portnoy's Complaint*, Ernie turned into a cross between Cecil B. DeMille and Caligula.

The first clue came when I met him about the part of Portnoy's mother. Portnoy was played by Dick Benjamin. I learned at the time that my rival for the part was Elaine May, my remarkably talented friend. I know she would have handled the situation differently, particularly since the first words out of Ernie's mouth as we crossed a soundstage were, "I've got things on Mike Nichols, locked up in my safe."

Huh? "But *Virginia Woolf* was brilliant!" I replied. "Your screenplay, his direction, the performances?"

"Never mind, I'll get him if it's the last thing I do!"

Mike had directed me in *Plaza Suite* and become a friend. His talent was legendary, and he needed no defending from anyone.

As a matter of fact, Ernie's talent was pretty up there also. He'd written *North by Northwest* for Hitchcock and many other first-rate films. But the man I was meeting for the first time was an angry, small man with his neck pushed forward.

He showed up on the first day of shooting, on his first director's job, dressed in pale linen, dark glasses, and an ascot. When he called "Action!" he would fall to his knees and demand that padding be slid under his knees as he fell. Since he never fell in the same place twice, as the scenes progressed, the unhappy wretch with the padding would be gliding around trying to guess where Ernie would land next. If Ernie landed on his linen-covered knees, the poor stagehand wouldn't hear the indignant end of it. So, from the first day of shooting we all understood the main drama was going to be behind the camera, not in front of it.

In a dinner scene, the glasses placed in front of us were filled with red wine. We toasted—to God, or something—but the glasses at our places were water glasses, tall water glasses. Dick Benjamin suggested we exchange them for wineglasses, like real people drink from. Ernie walked back and forth, thinking about it, then asked for the story-board on the scene. The storyboard artist had indicated "water glasses on the table."

"No, these are the right glasses," Ernie said. "They're right here on the storyboard."

Dick and I looked at each other and sipped wine from our water glasses.

Later in the scene, I toasted my son, my eyes full of tears.

"Cut! Cut!"

We turned to our director.

"Lee, your voice sounded funny. You know, thick . . ."

"I was moved, Ernie," I said.

"Moved?"

"Never mind, Ernie. Let's do it again, my voice will be clear."

The last week of the shoot had an important hospital scene. I, Mrs. Portnoy, would age from forty to eighty, the character was now old and sick, sharing a room with another woman patient. My son comes to visit me; I'm lying in bed in my hospital gown. To convey my age and condition, I'd worn a lot of padding and wigs throughout the film, and for this scene, I'd chosen a big brassiere and filled it with birdseed, so it seemed like my breasts were falling on either side of me, like I'd seen on older, heavy-breasted women. The other woman in the room was played by an experienced Actors Studio actress, who had one line to say to me before my son entered the room. I don't remember her line, but it was something like "So, your son's coming to visit you. I'll bet you can't wait—blah, blah." Innocuous. Ernie, now standing, no longer falling to his knees, had found his target. The actress read the line this way and that way.

"Cut! Cut!" he'd scream. "Can't you do anything right?"

He screamed at her until she could no longer put the words together; they made no sense to her. This went on for an hour, leaving the big scene between me and my son dangling.

"Action!" he screamed every two minutes, pointing at her.

Suddenly I jumped out of my bed, in my hospital gown, my long birdseed breasts flopping against my ribs, my panty-hosed backside exposed.

"Stop it, stop it," I screamed at Ernie. "You're torturing her to death, you little shit. She's a good actress! Look what you've done to her!"

The actress had tears running down her face. She literally could not put two words together by then.

"Get out of here!" I shrieked. "Go to the camera trailer and direct from there. Dick and I will do the scene without her line!"

Ernie looked around at the crew. They were silent.

"Go!" I pointed to the door, like an old Eloise.

He left. Dick and I filmed the scene, and Ernie stayed in the camera truck that day.

Everyone in this business knows that a problem with a line on set can be fixed in postproduction. Ernie Lehman was playing Erich von Stroheim, reveling in sudden power. Viewing *Portnoy's Complaint* in the theater for the first (and last) time made me shrink back in horror. It was not a good reflection of Jewish family life. Maybe Ernie's rage at Mike Nichols made him treat actors exactly opposite of how Mike does.

One more side note to *Portnoy*. Karen Black played the Monkey in the film—the crazy-beautiful model Dick Benjamin has an affair with. Karen had already done *Five Easy Pieces* and many more first-rate films. She was a big talent. We were going to the same parties around that time. Karen had a baby, a little boy, almost a toddler, whom she breast-fed at the parties. She wore satin nightgowny dresses, very glamorous, very alluring. She would lower one satin shoulder strap to reveal a charming breast, which in due time she would bring to the baby's mouth. Her conversation had nothing to do with the breast or baby, it had to do with the universe, philosophy, things on a higher plane. I had totally missed the whole hippie thing, but I thought, *What an innocent but provocative way to be really sexy and stand out in a crowd at a big party.*

George Schlatter

There were good angels all over L.A. who were giving me work in every other thing they produced or directed. Norman Lear and Bud Yorkin, who created *All in the Family* and *Maude*; George Schlatter, the creator of *Laugh-In*. We became dinner party friends. Joey and I would drive in from Malibu to Norman's or to Bud's and George would be there, a larger-than-life, over-the-top laugher with a big heart and a beautiful wife.

So, George Schlatter called. We were in the Red House; I was reading a script on the bed.

"Lee, I'm putting an all-woman comedy show on TV: Joan Rivers, Lynn Redgrave, Brenda Vaccaro, songs, sketches. You want to join us?"

"Sure, are you kidding? Great."

"And I want you to direct it."

I sat up in bed.

"I have someone to do camera, but I need you to work on staging the sketches."

A little pang of fear went through me.

"Jeez, George. I've never directed anything. This is a big deal. I don't feel up to it."

I felt intimidated, in a hole, trying to live up to a professional position that I had no experience or talent for. I'd acted in comedy sketches on TV directed by Bud Yorkin and Norman Lear with Dick Van Dyke. Those guys knew what they were doing, and they were fast, on top of everything. This was way too big for me to handle.

George had me go into the office to meet the writers, hear the material, and meet my codirector, Carolyn Raskin, the woman who would direct the multiple cameras from the control room the day of the shoot. George Schlatter is the warmest, funniest fast-talker, pushing all my "But George's" aside and, without ever saying yes, I found myself directing a huge TV comedy special, *The Shape of Things*, with all women in 1973. George is a feminist.

I expressed my nervousness to a friend, a very good actress at the Actors Studio, and she recommended her psychiatrist, who was terrific with her "fears and doubts," she said. I made an appointment.

It was the period of the Nixon break-in. The whole liberal community was suddenly free to make fun of a hidden Nixonian plot to subvert the justice system. A lot of the sketches were related to that, as in *Laugh-In*. George is a great rule-breaker, in the best way.

So that was fun. We had something like a two-week rehearsal schedule and a long day's shoot, as I remember, in which the camera director, Carolyn, took over. Lynn Redgrave, Brenda Vaccaro, Phyllis Diller, and I sang a song in little Dutch Girl costumes: a grand Watergate number from the viewpoint of Mrs. Haldeman, Mrs. Ehrlichman, Mrs. Mitchell, and Mrs. Dean. Funny. Joan Rivers had her own material.

The whole show was a very important experience for me. The real Nixon presidency had been giving me Cassandra tremors of misfortune to come for years, that funny old "Can't anybody but me see that

Nixon is subverting the justice system?" feeling. The openness of the whole event, easily combining politics and entertainment and directed at the wide TV audience, was very reassuring politically, relaxed a lot of my instinct to hide, to protect myself.

Brenda Vaccaro took it upon herself to veer from our candyish white formal dresses, went to her own designer, and wore a clingy violet half-naked number. She sang a solo to a huge athlete in her husky voice and won herself an Emmy.

During lunch hour, I was running to my new psychiatrist to express the fears and conflicts I had about this new responsibility. To get to his office on time, I had to skip lunch and drive from the studio in the Valley to his office in Beverly Hills, a drive of ten to fifteen minutes depending on the traffic. The doctor had a small, dark waiting room that contained only one person at a time. The door to the doctor's office was locked. He would have to open it to admit you to his large windowed room.

The first half hour of our session was always spent with him remonstrating over my lack of respect for him, and me apologizing for being late, explaining once again that I was working a new job as a director that didn't permit me to take off early, and that's why I was meeting with him—because I was insecure in that job.

We developed a routine in which he always found me disrespectful and I was always trying to please him. I realize writing this that it carries echoes of my first marriage. My actual image of his office is him sitting in his big armchair, me sitting on his footstool, explaining, explaining, to his offended face.

So the problem became not about my insecurity at work, but my inability to ever please this shrink.

One lunch hour I arrived at his office, sat in his waiting room for half an hour, tried the locked door to his office, knocked on the door, no sound inside, knocked again, listened. I knew the office was empty.

I ran downstairs and called him at home from the drugstore. He picked up the phone right away. "This is what you get when you're late—la la la." I found my car, climbed in, and burst into tears, loud kid sobs, openmouthed, snotty, spitty, deep-throated.

Later, he sent me a bill for the hour.

How was the show? Good, I think.

Did I pay the bill? You've got to be kidding!

Plaza Suite *and* The Prisoner of Second Avenue

The first Neil Simon play I ever did was *Plaza Suite* in 1969 at the Doolittle in Los Angeles. Mike Nichols was the director, and rehearsals for the L.A. run were held in New York, where Maureen Stapleton and George C. Scott were playing it on Broadway. Neil Simon was absolutely vehement that every word of his play be accurate—from the beginning. As an actress, I always ended up delivering the playwright's words as written, but allowed myself to fill in lines as needed in early rehearsal, to improvise my character's intentions, till I knew the lines and had had a chance to study them. Mike was watching me from the front row. Neil Simon—"Doc"—was sitting in the middle of the theater someplace. I was rehearsing the first of the three wife characters in *Plaza Suite*, the fiftyish wife who discovers her husband is having an affair.

The phone in the suite was ringing as I ran into the room from the hallway with a bellboy. I picked it up, out of breath. I forget what the point of the phone call was, but suddenly I heard Mike speaking in an unfamiliar staccato, like a music teacher accompanying his words with waves of a baton: "If, But, Which, Can, Do!" "What?" I said. Mike leaned back with his arms extended across the seats on either side of him. "Those are the words you left out," he said. "Come in again." I went offstage and ran around to make myself breathless a second time. The bellboy opened the door; the phone was ringing. I picked it up. "If but which can do!" I said, stunned. The words were engraved in my brain. It frightened me. An actor's sensitivity to suggestion onstage and in film is so acute that it can override her basic intelligence. Mike may have been bored to death—he has a low threshold for boredom—or Doc may have come down front and said something to him, but its effect shocked me. Those meaningless connector words took over my head. How vulnerable we are. I'd always had stage fright, always had rituals—penny in my shoe, say "Good luck" to me three times, exercises—but that was the first time in my life that I became afraid of forgetting my lines.

N ow it was 1973, and I'd had a huge career in Hollywood— wonderful nonstop roles, another Oscar nomination for *The Landlord*. I'd come back to Broadway to do Neil Simon's *The Prisoner of Second Avenue*. Once again, the director was Mike Nichols. I'd committed myself to a year's run in New York, rented out the Red House, and found an apartment on Riverside Drive and a private school for Dinah to attend. Joey was out on the road doing commercials.

Mike was especially sensitive in his preparation, molding me, without my even knowing it, for what was essentially a two-character play, Peter Falk and me. After our first reading, Mike turned to me: "You're the gardener, he's the flower." The blood drained out of me. I had not rented the Red House for a year, I had not moved to a strange apartment, I had not put Dinah in the New Lincoln School to come to Broadway as the gardener.

I was familiar with being a gardener, as were all the wives at 444 Central Park West.

We'd been good gardeners. Truly concerned with our husbands. Endlessly worried and wordless. Money, bills, rent, our husbands' states of mind.

But I was a leading lady now. I'd dreamed I'd return to Broadway in a smash hit and be rediscovered and celebrated. I had come to be the flower.

But in a split instant, I recognized my fate and accepted it. Two actors cannot have nervous breakdowns on the same stage. Peter was the flower. I had no choice but to be his loving gardener. And I was.

In rehearsal, Mike Nichols had us lie on a cot together in the dark backstage and go over and over our lines with a girl prompter sitting on a chair at the head of the bed.

It was wonderful direction. Peter and I breathing our lines to each other became comfortable lying so close together. Relaxing into each other like old friends. Like husband and wife. Mike forced us to trust each other totally. The prompter kept us from getting self-conscious about our bodies and intimacy.

Peter breathed in and I breathed out.

It was the last week of the run for both of us. The play had been a huge hit, 798 performances and four previews.

Compulsive superstition is part of my baggage as an actor. The more religious among us can pray, cross themselves, legitimize the need for help from their god, before opening night and every night thereafter. (Matinees come with a free pass from anxiety, unless we know someone important to us is in the audience. That's why I like to go to matinees; the actors are less guarded, more relaxed.)

The person we depend on to send us safely off to the stage is usually our dresser—the one to put the penny in my left shoe, to whisper "Good luck" three times before sending me out the door. To knock wood and light candles before we take our great leap into the void. Donald, my young, handsome, gay dresser for *The Prisoner of Second Avenue*, was with me every step of the way, hand in hand, every performance. Breathe on intake, ready for crisis.

It was lonely for me without Joey. Dinah was in private school, hanging out with a bunch of stoned, bearded, Deadhead classmates whom I abhorred, sitting cross-legged on the floor of our sublet apartment. It was time to discuss birth control. She was sixteen and had been kidnapped by trolls.

I begged Joey to come to New York for a week, ten days, to fill my empty bed. His commercial business was taking him all over the country.

"I'll be a nun for you," I promised. "You can fuck a nun—" desperate, "Sister Anastasia."

I had Donald rent me a nun's habit. When I turned the knob of my dressing room door a week later, it was locked. I could hear something inside. I had my suspicions.

"Donald?" I called. "Open up."

"Just a minute."

"No—now. Now, Donald!"

The latch clicked, the doorknob turned, and there was sweet little "Sister Donald," with eyes downcast. Caught.

"I only put it on to see where the pieces go. It's complicated!"

The habit hung like a ghost in my closet on Riverside Drive till Joey arrived. While he lay in bed, watching television, still in the clothes he flew to New York in, I hurriedly added layer after layer of Bad Nun, then silently appeared by the side of the bed.

Joey flew into the air like a cartoon cat, backing across the room against the wall, sliding away from me.

"Come to me, my boy," I intoned. "Come to Sister Anastasia."

He pointed to me. "Take off the rosary, take it off . . ."

You can take the boy out of Catholic school, but you can't take Catholic school out of the boy.

Every time we've gone into a church, for weddings, memorials, funerals, particularly in St. Anthony's parish in Wilmington, beads of sweat appear on Joey's upper lip. He's a guilty eight-year-old kid all over again.

"I don't think I can do that," he hisses to his sister, Phyllis, as a line for Communion forms.

"Yeah, you can," she says as she joins the line.

His ears sticking out, his neck stiff with guilt, he joins her. He knows God's gonna strike him dead. Particularly as he's there with me, the only Jew in church.

So to do a sacrilegious act with me, wearing Sister's holy garb, was not the turn-on I'd hoped for.

I thought I had a cold all winter, when what I'd actually done was overdose on Neo-Synephrine. I had three inhalers stashed onstage so when my nose stopped up, I could clear it. Joey knew I was hooked and made our doctor, Lou Cooper, intervene. When I gave up Neo-Synephrine, I couldn't breathe through my nose for a week. Also, I'm sure I damaged my brain, the memory part, with heavy-duty sleeping pills and Irish whiskey chasers. Sleep was eluding me. I was getting up later and later. New York days are short in winter; it starts to get dark at three in the afternoon. I was lonely without Joey and my friends in

L.A. Isolated. Just Peter Falk and me, except for one scene in the second act with Peter's character's family.

I think it is Neil Simon's best play. Terrible and funny.

In a week, Peter and I would go back to our real spouses in California, and other actors would take our places in the hit play.

It was during a Wednesday matinee that my mind went into its first subconscious slip. I think it had to do with the rent we were paying, Peter and I, in the play. I said, "Two thousand, five hundred dollars," which was my weekly salary in my first film, *Detective Story*—so much money that I never forgot it. It came out of some subconscious place onstage. A totally inappropriate amount. I think the correct line was seven hundred. I said, "Two thousand five hundred." Peter's head swiveled. He looked at me hard.

A few hours later, the Wednesday night performance, second act. Peter's lost his job, he's sitting in our apartment in his pajamas, and I come in the door. I'm now the breadwinner. The second act is my hit song, my solo turn, my big moment. Three straight pages of Doc Simon dialogue, backed by Mike Nichols's brilliant staging. It's a brilliant tour de force—like doing forty-eight turns en pointe in ballet. I come home from work to make lunch for Peter. I take off my coat and boots, unpack the big paper bag of groceries, pour him tomato juice, make him a grilled cheese sandwich for lunch in the toaster oven, put out the silverware and napkins, serve him, and tell him about my day while he eats. Without stopping for a breath. I've done back-to-back matinee and evening shows every Wednesday, eight shows a week, for a year.

That Wednesday night, my last week in the run, while I was pouring the tomato juice, I went up. My mind had gone completely blank. I had no idea what to say next. It struck me as almost funny, because, thank God, Peter would save me. As actors do. Actors go up all the time. And always save each other. Disaster recovery is part of theater lore.

I went up.

I said, "Here's your tomato juice." The ball was in his court.

Every actor has forgotten his or her lines in theater. Theater is a war zone. You're in the trenches with your fellow actors. Actors love each other. It's an adventure.

Not this time.

Peter was staring at my apologetically smiling face as I placed the tomato juice in front of him.

"Here's your tomato juice," I said again.

Suddenly he turned to the audience and gestured to me with his thumb. I felt cold. In my mind, he'd named me. The audience laughed. They were complicit.

I ran into the wings and looked at the script. The words meant nothing; there was a buzz in my head. I had entered the actor's nightmare. I was alone. I was out of it. I could feel the blood draining from my head. Peter and the audience were looking at me. He was still pointing. I put the TV dinner into the toaster oven upstage and called out to the stage manager: "What's the next line? What's the next line?"

The stage manager came out from wherever he was schmoozing, his face an O of panic, scrambling to find where we were in the script. He couldn't find it. Peter was walking up and down the stage, gesturing to the audience. The stage manager found the page. I looked at it. The words were as alien as the lyrics of an ancient musical. Dead. No connection to the stream of life and action I brought onstage.

"Pull the curtain," I said. "We'll start after the monologue."

They pulled the curtain.

Peter was white as a sheet. I was cold and grim. I felt I'd been turned in by a former friend to the Un-American Activities Committee with a flick of his thumb. We were all shaken as we quickly discussed where to pick up the play. They had pulled down the curtain. We would start after the monologue. The curtain went up. I smiled at the audience, sharing what we've all been through. Suddenly, an ovation.

An ovation! The audience was saying, "Thank you for sharing. Thank you for letting us see pain and confusion in real life."

They wouldn't stop till I bowed, smiled, and held up my hands for them. At curtain it was the same. The audience felt so privileged to be included that Wednesday night. That's the lesson I never appreciated enough: Let them into the play.

B ut it was my last night as a glorious theater artist. I could no longer count on my talent or my instincts. I was wounded. My wonderful superstitions weren't strong enough to save me. I didn't trust them anymore.

I called the jolly little Catholic priest from the Actors' Chapel, a few blocks away. He'd stopped by a couple of times a week during the run, just sat in the dressing room, relaxing in an armchair, to make cozy small talk for fifteen or twenty minutes. He'd always ask if I knew Penny Singleton—she'd played Blondie in the Blondie and Dagwood movies in the thirties, forties, and fifties. I'd always tell him, "No, I never met her."

"Oh, you should have known Penny," he'd say. "Wonderful, wonderful girl." And, I expect, a good Catholic.

I asked the priest to come and sit in the dressing room every night before the show. I knelt obediently for his blessing before I went down to my cot backstage, from where I made my entrance. His gentle holy Catholic hand patted my sick Jewish head, and I finished the run.

Some mysterious component in my brain had now played the same trick on me it had when I had blurted out the names of two women in front of the HUAC lawyers in Washington years earlier. From that day on, I forgot the last name of every one of my friends when it came time to introduce them. Blank.

"Introduce yourselves," I'd say.

Now the Greek god of punishment had made off with my lines and my security. My circle of talent, which had seemed infinite, was shrinking to a small circle of light in the corner of the room.

I'd found unexpected strength when it came time to fight the outside world, but I had no resources to fight my inside world. When you see a performance on the stage or in film, where something is happening that lifts a lid on something fresher and more truthful than truth, when an actor is living dangerously through a part, taking private chances in public, exposing himself or herself in a way that makes you, watching it, say, "Oh, I see," makes your heart beat faster, or makes you laugh or cry or feel something in a new way—then they've done their job as an actor. That was my job—reckless endangerment. And it all worked, up to this point.

At the Neighborhood Playhouse, one of the elements of concentration I was taught was the fourth wall. The wall between the actor and the audience. Privacy in public.

In theater, I was good at fourth walls. The laughs, the coughs, the late entrances, the matinee chatter, all absorbed in a comforting way, as "the neighbors," a kind, supportive group who all laughed at the same lines and, at the curtain call, suddenly appeared, clapping, loving, homogeneous. Not unlike Fremo and my mother.

I wasn't a performer. I had no need to seduce, or astound, to impress in any way. The Method was taught by Sandy, to create the world of the play. To plug up any holes and believe in my new life and its situations totally.

So (in addition to my feeling of being turned in to the HUAC) when Peter looked at the audience and gestured to me with his thumb, his thumb also broke my fourth wall; the conceit, the scrim, the protection came tumbling down, and all these strangers were staring at me, hundreds. I was caught with one boot off in the former privacy of my own living room.

In the last four performances of *The Prisoner of Second Avenue*, I'd lost the magic.

Lost my freedom to fail onstage.

Lost.

An actor's wiring is too peculiar and sensitive to figure out. I knew I had to get up on the horse again after I finished *The Prisoner of Second Avenue*.

B ack in Malibu, it seemed one week I was telling Joey to get a job or go back home and the next week he opened a TV commercial company with Dick Chambers, which took off like gangbusters. He changed his name to Feury when his clients couldn't pronounce Fioretti.

What did he know about the commercial business? He'd been an apprentice plumber and a ballet dancer. Suddenly, he raised the money for two low-budget films and produced and sold them that year, this before he was thirty. He made it happen because he learned fast. Emergency fast. Hyper-fast. Down-the-road-before-I-get-my-foot-out-of-the-car fast. Dangerous fast, sometimes. Dangerous. That's the overused word I was looking for. The Italian non-Jew I wanted in my life. I'd experienced the Jewish intellectual. This experience was healthier for me, but came with its own risks. This man was ridiculous. This man was unexpected. He was lovable, loving, eruptive, and talented. He was a great, great protector and friend. A pain in the ass. Mine.

It was in that period that Joey started talking about having a baby. I wanted a baby for Joey. He should have his own child. But Joey was terrified for me to get pregnant. His mother almost died of purpura hemorrhagica when his younger brother was born. But I was in my forties then, and it turned out that I couldn't conceive anyway.

Still, he wanted a baby, and it fed into my sudden and urgent need to adopt a little girl, fueled, I'm sure, by losing Dinah to the Malibu circus. Don't we all have a problem when our beautiful, dependent babies, our mommy-adoring children, mommy-needing children, who want only mommy to lie in bed with them at night, cross that cruel line into adolescence? That was me.

We went to a lawyer about adopting a baby. Back then, you couldn't adopt without a marriage certificate. I had no desire to marry again, but I made an appointment for late on a Sunday afternoon with the minister at the little Malibu Church off the Pacific Coast Highway. We invited two couples over to play poker. I told them we had to pick up stuff at the market, and we went to the church. I wrote our names on a piece of notepaper and handed them to the minister. We could see a calm ocean through the big church windows. It was nice. We were getting married only so we could adopt a child, but I had scribbled our vows on a piece of paper ahead of time and brought it with me. This is what I wrote:

> Will you please continue to be my dearest friend—to be there when I am afraid, or lonely, or unwanted—as you always have been? To help me grow, even when growing separates us, and will you continue to acknowledge my freedom and solitary rights, as I must acknowledge your freedom and solitary rights?
>
> Answer: I will try.

We both said "I will try," not "I do," thanked the confused young minister, went to the market, and went back to our friends, who remained totally ignorant of the fact that they had missed a wedding.

A few weeks later I received a yellow store receipt from the state saying our marriage was official, and we started looking at pictures of children.

Adoption

A dopting a child opens a door to a new complicated world.

We contacted a lawyer who dealt in adoptions. The first baby he told us about was one born in Florida to a waitress. We learned the mother was perennially pregnant by God knows who, turned the babies over at birth, and made a good living from it. A one-woman baby mill.

Joey and I were interviewed by some state adoption people at our home. We acted very parental, but never heard back. At the time it was hard to adopt in the United States. I don't remember why.

Then our lawyer showed us pictures of a pair of twins, three-year-old girls. *They'll have each other*, I thought, thinking of the trauma displaced children have to deal with.

The lawyer put us in touch with Dr. Stephen Youngberg, a Baptist minister based in Bangkok who arranged introductions to adoptable children, several of whom lived with him at one time or another from birth on.

I didn't want a baby. I wanted a child whose eyes I could look into and see the person. I realized this was going to be a long, complicated relationship.

The child we found would have had a life before us; her new parents would feel like kidnappers to her. On the other hand, children whose fathers were American servicemen paid a terrible penalty.

There was an American base in Thailand and many houses to sexually accommodate them, many Madame Butterflies available for housekeeping arrangements. The girls had their babies, and the American boys returned to the States after their tours were over.

The penalty fell on the mixed-race children born of these relationships. They were not allowed to live in the mainstream, not allowed an education; both sexes were channeled into prostitution.

That was the new daughter I wanted to save.

Just before we were to go to Thailand, I had a really flimsy film to do in London, *The Internecine Project*. The script was no more than a sixteen-page outline, but the money was good and my costar was James Coburn, an actor I admired and wanted to play with. After filming, Joey and I planned to fly to Bangkok to meet with Dr. Youngberg and his children, all of whom had been given to him by their Thai mothers, who had other children to care for, wanted their new babies to have a better life, or needed the money that came with adoption.

Lufthansa lost our luggage, so I left freezing London and landed in steaming ninety-degree Bangkok in a fur coat and rain boots, a stranger from another planet.

It was still morning when we taxied to the Dusit Thani Hotel, a modern Western-style building with big air-conditioned rooms and a balcony that looked out onto a huge live elephant, the hotel's signature pet. I ran down to the hotel's dress shop to find something to wear while Joey called Dr. Youngberg. I changed out of my soaked cashmere sweater and jeans and into a long light Thai dress and weightless sandals. The doorbell rang, and a shortish man stood in the doorway with what looked like a two-year-old boy and a two-year-old girl, one under each arm.

Joey checked them out and said, "We'll take her. Let's have lunch!"

We had met our daughter.

She was a slip of a thing in an oversize dress, no panties, a boy's haircut, and large, wary, lived-in brown eyes.

We went up to the roof garden for lunch. The little girl, whose name was Lindah, ate everything she could get her small hands on. The little boy, James, roamed the restaurant. He was two and a half, she was two—not brother and sister, more like twinned casualties. We ended up keeping both children with us in the hotel room for the two weeks it took to finalize the adoption.

I took care of them at night, Joey in the morning, and we shared the afternoon. After lunch Joey called the desk for the bellboy. "Thai sticks," he yelled. "Thai sticks."

"How many?" the bellboy asked.

I was indeed a stranger in a strange land. One night at the Dusit Thani, our very international hotel, I reached in the dark for my glass of red wine to wash down my sleeping pill, but I couldn't get the wineglass to my mouth. I quietly climbed out of bed and took it to the bathroom. There, standing in my wineglass, was a water bug as long as a finger, its feelers waving at me. I screamed and screamed till Joey came. I could only point and scream.

We drove through the empty countryside to small communities where many other children were up for adoption. The houses were basically open-air platforms raised about two or three feet above the ground. The first one we saw had about eight or nine children laughing on the platform, including five-year-old twin girls who regarded us with a cool distant gaze. It was a photograph of these two girls that first drew us to Thailand. Sitting on a chair with them was a large woman in a sari whose teeth and gums were red with betel juice. Other platforms had straw walls and roofs. There was no furniture. Every home had a framed picture of the king.

The offices we visited to legalize the adoption were crammed with desks and people; stacks of papers were balanced all the way from floor to ceiling. They were records, but of what? How does someone remove one paper without bringing down the whole stack? Each desk had a roll of toilet paper, presumably to take with you to the bathroom. All bathrooms, except in modern buildings and hotels, were deep holes dug in dark, damp earth.

We had to meet Lindah's mother in order to get her signature on our adoption papers. We then brought those papers to these offices behind the many desks.

The little girl's mother met us in a park near the hotel, bringing two fair-haired, fair-skinned sons with her. They looked to be about eight and ten. The mother had had several children, but Lindah was the only one she ever offered for adoption. I asked her, "Why this little girl?" She said she'd had very little contact with Lindah since she was born. Her grandma had raised her. I asked her about Lindah's father. "I don't know," she said. "I don't remember." She was pleasant and ordinary and matter-of-fact. We gave her five hundred dollars; she gave me Lindah.

I had wanted to name Lindah something Russian, since that was my mother's background. As she lay in her crib next to my bed, I would whisper to her, "Natalia, Natasha, Ninushka." She would sit there, as self-possessed as a cat, staring at me with big, dark, wary eyes, her spine curved to protect herself against me. I would set her small weightless body on the toilet. "Please love me," I would plead as she peed, watching me.

One night during the search for the right name, I threw up my arms and said, "Oh, be Lindah! Be Linda, Belinda." She blinked. That was enough for me. Belinda.

Just before we left Bangkok, I was invited to lunch with the American ambassador. As we were leaving the embassy living room, heading for the garden where lunch was set up, my brand-new soles slipped on the carpeted stairs and I fell. Joey's hand reached for me, my hand reached for his, and in slow motion I seemed to sail right over a flight of stairs, landing hard at the bottom. I was shaken up, dizzy, and embarrassed. I had been talking party talk a second before, and now all these faces were staring down at me. "No, no, no, I'm fine," I assured them. My head was buzzing, my legs wobbly.

As Joey steered me across the lawn to the white gazebo, a duck nipped at my heel. I was seated next to the ambassador, and cold soup was served. I tried but could not get the soupspoon to stop shaking on the way to my mouth. I knew I would not be invited to any more parties in Bangkok. "Sir," I said, "Mr. Ambassador. I'm in the process of adopting a Thai child. What can be done about the G.I.s who are serving over here taking responsibility for the children they spawn and leave behind? Huh? Don't you think they should help to raise their babies somehow? Money? Support? Anything?"

The ambassador smiled at me. "Oh, Lee. You can't stop the boys from having a little hanky-panky, can you?"

The morning before we left, Joey took James and Belinda to the hotel coffee shop. He ordered food. When the big breakfast arrived, Belinda made sounds like words. Joey called the waitress over. "What is she saying?" he asked. Belinda made more sounds.

The waitress said, "She said, 'We don't have the money to pay for the food.' "

Her first words. Joey emptied his pockets and gave her the change.

When we flew home to the Red House, we bought her a little chest and filled it with money. It was her favorite toy.

Some months later, I registered Belinda at the nursery school across the Pacific Coast Highway. As I was leaving, I saw one of the girls who had tormented Dinah in the third grade. Our eyes met. I went out the door and drove back home. There was no way I could send my new daughter to a school where that girl would be caring for her. The question was, did I sit down with the owner and tell her why, about that girl's history with Dinah? The phone rang. It was the girl. Could she come to my house now and talk to me?

In ten minutes she was sitting across from me. An unexceptional young woman. "I loved Dinah," she said. "I loved her. I don't know why I did what I did. It's haunted me ever since. Please, please, let me make it up to you. I will take care of Belinda the way I should have been a friend to Dinah. I need to."

By this time, Belinda was three and a half. She spoke not a word of English, only Thai. Until we took her home with us, she had lived with an old grandmother, who raised her and adored her. In Belinda's mind, in a three-and-a-half-year-old's mind, I'm sure Joey and I were two big white kidnappers who stole her away from her beloved grandma.

I looked at the blond girl sitting across from me in the living room of the Red House. "Please," she said. "I promise you won't be sorry. Let me look after her."

"Okay, we'll try it out."

"You won't be sorry," she said.

I wasn't sorry. Dinah's nemesis became Belinda's angel. She baby-sat for her. She made her Halloween costumes for two years. She protected her at nursery school. She gave her the attention a strange child in a strange land with strange new parents needed.

Belinda adored Joey, and he was a great and magical daddy for her. He hugged her, threw her in the air, covered her with kisses, tickled her, blew in her face. He wore down her resistance, much as he had worn down mine when we first met. She took right away to Joey's mother, Rachel, as well—the best, warmest Italian grandmother, lion, boss of the block in Wilmington, Delaware. Later, when we hired Trini as our housekeeper, Belinda would be spoiled to death by both women. She resisted giving me her heart.

For the first year she slept on the long window seat in our bedroom. There was a stone fireplace in the room. It was bright and cozy and safe. She wanted a baby bottle filled with juice at night, but it was turning her teeth gray, and the dentist told me to wean her off it. In a few months her teeth were white. She still bent her back, but she let me rub it gently. The doctor said she had no spinal problem, but it wasn't until I took her to gymnastics that it straightened entirely.

She held out on me emotionally. I knew in some way she felt abducted and it was my fault and no one else's. She wouldn't kiss me, though I was allowed to kiss her cheek. She let me lie with her and sing to her at bedtime. Once she told me that the Peter, Paul, and Mary song "Leaving on a Jet Plane" reminded her of me. I knew she cared about me, but also knew that by withholding she could manipulate me and hurt me.

Soon after we brought Belinda home from Thailand, our friends Len and Jenny Friedlander, who had no children, adopted James. The Friedlanders also lived in Malibu, so James and Belinda had each other still and saw each other all the time.

When Joey's mother first plopped Belinda in her big warm lap, Belinda got her grandmother back. Not me. Me she kept at a distance, making me work for every smile, for every sign of approval, holding on to the reserve she needed, a private place away from me. Her real mother was in Thailand, not in Malibu. I understood it was going to take a long time and knew that the only way for Belinda to really, really accept me as her mother was to go back to Thailand and spend time with her birth mother and grandmother when she was older.

After Belinda finished high school, I hired a detective to track down her mother in Thailand. She was making silk from silkworms on a farm outside Bangkok. Dinah accompanied Belinda with a movie camera. She and Belinda had a huge fight at the hotel. When they returned home, Belinda wouldn't talk to Dinah for a year. Belinda wouldn't talk about her mother for a long time, but I knew at long last that the longing-for-the-mother-in-Thailand myth was busted. She was mine, but at what price?

In Thailand she met new brothers and sisters and old brothers she had never known. Her father had been a U.S. serviceman, stationed in Bangkok; her mother couldn't remember his name. She'd had many children, with many fathers. Belinda was the only one she gave away for adoption. On the ride back to the Thai airport, Belinda finally asked her mother, "Why me? Why did you give me away? Why not them? Why me?"

Her aunt told her, "The fortune-teller told us to give you away, because you were sick and might die."

Her mother didn't say anything. Belinda finally broke down and bawled hot tears of rejection, while her little bent granny patted her hand and her mother looked out the window at the passing wet green countryside.

My turn finally came when Belinda graduated from college. She made a drawing, a pencil drawing of flowers, and on the side she wrote, also in pencil:

Dear Mom,

No one works like you do, no one makes people happy like you do, no one makes people angry like you do, no one understands how I can stand living with you when you are not here. But I do. Because when you are here you make it all up. And that is why I love you. For the things you do. No one can love like you.

Unsigned

On the Set of Shampoo

Warren Beatty was Mike Nichols's friend. Mike had a wonderful-looking assistant, a tall young girl built like a tall young boy. Mike was offering this jewel to Warren, but Warren was interested in me.

"I have a movie for you," he said.

The movie turned out to be *Shampoo*, which he wrote with Bob Towne. Goldie Hawn was in *Shampoo*, and so was Julie Christie, both of whom Warren had had romances with. With Julie, long; with Goldie, movie-length.

I found that good danger zone again in *Shampoo*. And I found depth and an absence of depth in the narrow life of my character, Felicia. Costumer Anthea Sylbert designed the clothes. She'd done them for *The Prisoner of Second Avenue* and I knew her well. She had my character's name embroidered in the lining of her mink coat. I'm glad I did the role before my fear of failing spread to films.

The first scene we shot, Warren and I, was the scene when I return to my Beverly Hills mansion with my hair in rollers under a scarf. Warren the hairdresser is there waiting for me, ostensibly to comb out my hair, but really to meet my ravenous sexual needs. As I write this, my heart thumps in remembered anticipation, my sense memory of it is so strong.

The hairdresser Warren plays in the film has just fucked my daughter, played by Carrie Fisher. I open the door to her room, see him there, and say something like, "Come upstairs and comb me out."

Before we ever did the scene, Warren sat me down at a little glass table and proceeded to tell me what my character, Felicia, was thinking in the script. I was stunned. Hal Ashby, my friend and favorite director, was directing *Shampoo*. He would never say anything but "Surprise me" to me. And here was Warren, who I was supposed to relate to as my hairdresser, sitting me down before I went on camera, telling me what my character thought.

"Listen," he said. "A friend of mine had someone going down on him under a desk. His girlfriend walked in, walked out again. She never saw it. Didn't choose to know. She blocked it out."

"Maybe she knows that's what comes along with the territory," I said.

"No, no," said Warren, "I really know this, women just don't see what they don't want to see!"

I went home that night with a raging migraine. I couldn't sleep. I went to the set the next day. The migraine was so bad, I couldn't see straight. It was the scene where Felicia takes the hairdresser up to her bedroom to have sex with him. I kept on my mink coat, my head scarf, and my boots, pulled down my panties, and got on top of him. Behind the camera, Hal hissed, "Open your mouth, open your mouth, use your tongue!"

"I can't," I hissed back. "I'm sick. I'll throw up."

The next day I came onto the set after thinking all night. The migraine was gone and I wasn't working that day. I went up to Hal.

"I'm quitting," I said. "I can't work with an actor who gives me direction."

Hal had a movie to shoot.

"Okay," he said.

Hal was mellow. I asked Warren to give me a minute when he was free. I sat on the iron ladder steps, watching the action, at peace. Warren lunged up the iron steps, clanging, and sat on the step below me.

"I'm quitting," I said. "I can't work with an actor I'm playing with directing me."

"What?"

"It's making me sick. It's not how I work."

"Whaddaya mean?"

"You're my hairdresser. My hairdresser doesn't tell me how to think. And you're not my director. Hal would never tell me what I think about anything."

"Listen—"

"No, this is not going to work. Get someone else to play the part."

"Willya listen a minute? What do I know? Huh? This is my sixth movie. Do what you want. I'm crazy about you, you know that?"

Huh? Huh? "You mean it? You'll stop pushing your dumb theories about women on me?"

"Sure."

Pause. "Okay."

That's when I became Warren's romance for the movie. The air was so thick with heat that the hairdressers had hot dreams. I, as frustrated Felicia, sex-starved Felicia, was in such a constant state of heat that I wanted to pull truck drivers out of their cabs. No one was safe. Of course Joey got more and better sex than he'd dreamed of, but my point was, I/Felicia knew immediately that my hairdresser made love to my/her daughter. I/Felicia was so crazed with need when I/she caught them that all I/she cared about was getting laid, then! Right away! Now! Now!

The analyst I drove to like a maniac when I was doing *Shampoo* told me he hadn't a clue as to whom he was treating, Lee or Felicia. I came in with all her problems and I worked them out. I left my movie husband, beloved Jack Warden.

Warren loved women. Loved them with a ravenous appetite, the way my husband, Joey, yearned for food. The way Fremo and Gladys had love for painting. That Waldo Salt had for writing screenplays, that Jimmy Breslin has for writing, that I had for acting. An appetite, an appreciation, an involvement that is obsessive, fascinated. Warren had a speech in *Shampoo*, addressed to Goldie's character when she caught him having sex with Julie Christie. Something like, "I love women. I love their look, their smell. When I go into an elevator, I see a woman and I just want her legs around me." I'm quoting my recollection, not what the exact lines were. Warren wrote the lines.

When he shot that scene with Goldie, I was halfway across the soundstage from where they were shooting. I heard Warren say those lines with a passion and exposure I'd never heard from him before. I ran back to the set.

"That's it, Warren," I said. "Don't do any more." I was so moved.

While he appreciated my reaction, he went on to do a hundred or more takes, until the exposed Warren was tamer, more acceptable to him.

Goldie, who had to do the scene with him for a hundred takes, went outside and threw up when the scene was over.

For a consummate filmmaker, Warren plunged into the boy part of himself as an actor. His hairdresser is an innocent.

To act in a film he both produced and co-wrote is a big jump. Maybe that's why he needed all those takes.

The Chateau Marmont was a second home when I was working and had to be ready on set at eight a.m. The drive from Malibu was too far.

I occupied the suite on the fourth floor with the long balcony. It once looked out over Sunset onto a huge billboard of the Marlboro Man, which was then a permanent fixture of the landscape. It was where I stayed when I filmed *Shampoo*.

The morning after we completed the movie, I was in that suite at the Chateau, packed up and ready for the ride back to my life in Malibu. The phone rang. It was a girlfriend, Joanne, with a long story to tell about an incident in a diner the night before. As I listened to her complain, the doorbell rang. It was Warren. Standing in the doorway. We kissed and kissed and walked/staggered to the window kissing, me listening all the while to my friend Joanne.

"Uh-huh," I'd say breathlessly. "What did you do then? And what did he say?"

Felicia had taken over my body. She finally said good-bye to her hairdresser for the last time.

Joanne was still talking as I stood at the door, watching Warren walk down the carpeted hallway to the stairs, waving good-bye with his back to me. All that energy, lightly, jauntily, taking the stairs. It was still morning, after all. He had the whole day and night ahead of him. I heard the phone squeaking in my hand.

"I'm still here," I said.

We had never kissed in the film, just been naked in bed together for a few uncomfortable days, with me simulating fucking and sucking, the crew around our bed, our director, Hal, sitting close by. "Suck harder," he instructed me as I knelt beneath a blanket somewhere between Warren's legs.

So the visit to the Chateau was a lovely, tender farewell. Romantic and passionate and clandestine, kissing took on a whole new meaning, one that left Felicia and the hairdresser behind and let Lee and Warren say good-bye, in the most delicious way.

. . .

There is a postscript to this idyllic ending.

About a week after we'd finished shooting, Warren called. I'd been getting ready to have a big cast party at the Red House. I thought he wanted to add a few more people as guests.

His voice was low, seductive. "Why don't you drive down to Brenda's tonight?"

"Mmmm—I don't know."

"C'mon, c'mon, c'mon."

The truth was I missed him. I loved the guy. I missed being teased, too. I thought . . . Never mind what I thought.

When I arrived at Brenda's house, Warren was there. And Jack Nicholson, and Kenny Solms, Michael Douglas was home, the usual crowd. In that period, Michael was very serious about marrying Brenda. He'd come to the *Shampoo* set one day, sat in my trailer, and talked about his conflicts. Brenda was, in those days, gorgeous and, as in these days, unique. They broke the mold with her. Hilarious, original, a daredevil, always.

Anyway, Warren was giving me his deep focus, his "let's get away from all these people and go somewhere, just us" focus. And I was eating it up, heating up in his sun, loving the attention, being the girl of the moment in front of all my cool friends, when I saw Warren's eyes attach themselves to something in the distance. I turned around and saw in the next room, the dining room, Dolly Parton, quietly sitting at the table, alone, scribbling on a pad.

In an instant, I could feel myself dropped as this new yummy dish was making Warren's mouth water. He actually licked his lips as he left me on the couch and sat down next to her at the table.

I followed him like a jilted wife, jealous, clumsy.

I needn't have bothered; Dolly was immune.

Warren tried the whole deck of cards. Dolly concentrated on her numbers, adding, subtracting, and smiling adorably at his attempts.

Watching her, I couldn't blame him for trying. It was 1975. Dolly was all cream and roses, just astonishing and nice.

I rose from the table; Warren was relieved. I said my good-byes and drove back to the Red House, humming to myself.

W e were packing up to leave the Red House the week of the Oscars. I had been nominated for Best Supporting Actress in *Shampoo*. A film crew was covering all the nominees. Lily Tomlin and Ronee Blakley from Bob Altman's great, great classic *Nashville*, my friend Brenda Vaccaro, and Sylvia Miles. I had never won an Oscar. I had never been a bride. My first marriage had been in Hoboken, dressed in Fremo's jacket. I married Joey wearing jeans just before stopping at the market. *Shampoo* was my third nomination for Best Supporting Actress. I yearned to be the bride this time around, not a bridesmaid yet again.

I went to my costumer, Burton Miller, who showed me the charming antique white lace dress that said "Take me, take me!" I loved her. I rented her. Burton found me shoes, a light blue satin sash, and a little comb with white satin flowers for my hair. I was ready for my secret wedding. I was marrying my past and leaving it behind.

When you walk down the red carpet as an Oscar nominee, all the fans and the paparazzi scream your name.

"Lee! Lee!"

"Camera's over here, Lee."

"Look here!" Flash, flash, roar of the crowds, like the Roman Colosseum.

Oh my God. How important am I? They love me, they love me!

Then, when you lose, those same adoring camera people are elbowing you, stampeding you out of the way to get a shot of the winner. It's good for one's humility to lose a couple of times. But the truth is everyone wants to win.

There's an apocryphal story of Tony Quinn and Marlon Brando meeting in the parking lot after they'd both just lost the award to another actor. "I'll read my speech to you if you read me yours," Tony said.

Sitting in my seat in that enormous red and gold theater, grim, sinking in my bridal dress, I heard "And the award goes to Lily Tomlin." I leaned forward to congratulate Lily, who was sitting right in front of me, a big silver crown shining on her head.

"Lee," she said, "they said your name!"

I didn't want to make a fool of myself. A lot of people were looking at me now. Someone was pulling me out of my seat and pushing me into the aisle. As I walked with rubber legs and a roar in my ears ten yards to the stage, it was an out-of-body experience. I don't know what I said, but I know it meant "I do." *I do know at this minute I am loved. I do know no one in this vast audience is out to get me.* I'd been nominated for my first Academy Award in 1952 for *Detective Story*—I won in 1976 for *Shampoo*. Twenty-four years later, exactly my age at the time of the first nomination. Twelve years after the Blacklist ended for me in 1964.

I had an historic sense as I stood there onstage alone, my mouth thanking people, looking out at a vast audience, bobbing faces, balcony full. I felt on top of the wave. My heart rested. Peace.

Whatever that decade, the seventies, had been, it was a good decade; artistically in film, a great decade. Those people at that moment adored me almost as much as my mother did. I could celebrate the work and leave behind the torment. And probably my need to prove myself was over.

Fay

I was playing the title role in a really fun TV series called *Fay*. *Fay* was a smart show, a series, written by a comedy writer, Susan Harris. Tony Thomas, Danny Thomas's son, and Paul Junger Witt produced. (A few years later, they would produce a great series that Dinah would star in, *Empty Nest*.) The character, Fay, was a newly divorced woman with a grown daughter who enters the workplace for the first time in her forties.

Pretty ahead of its time.

Gloria Steinem was then the editor of *Ms.* magazine, and because of *Fay* she wanted me for the cover. Wow! Big-time. Gloria came to the Red House to interview me, along with a photographer to take the cover photo.

The essence of Gloria's inquiry was how much tougher the standards were for actresses than those for actors in the film business. I disagreed. "They're tough for everyone," I said. "Okay," she said, "you write it. Say whatever you want."

The last sentence of my article for *Ms.* said, "I've been married to a Communist and a Fascist, and neither one of them ever took out the garbage." Gloria used that line at the end of interviews for years and years. "As my friend Lee Grant put it . . ."

Unfortunately the show was scheduled in what was called "the family hour," a time reserved for families with children. So, even though the numbers were high, after we'd taped about nine episodes, NBC canceled the show. But neglected to tell me.

I showed up at the NBC studios for rehearsal, and *Fay*'s furniture was out in the street. Like I hadn't paid the rent, like I'd been evicted! I called Paul Witt, the executive producer. "What happened?" I asked.

"We were canceled."

The Tonight Show with Johnny Carson was on the NBC lot also. I'd been scheduled to appear on his show to publicize *Fay* that same day. I drove across the lot to their studio, and Johnny came out.

"We were canceled," I said. "I have nothing to talk about."

I was sad. Johnny took pity. "C'mon," he said. "Talk about getting canceled."

He was dear, and what an outlet for me. To rail against the family hour and the man who canceled us. I gave him the finger, which they blacked out on-screen. So thanks to Johnny, I had a very public triumph, instead of driving home and pulling over to the side of the Pacific Coast Highway to cry. After we were canceled, I was nominated for an Emmy, Outstanding Lead in a Comedy Series.

The Stronger

One sunny Malibu afternoon in 1975, the phone rang. I sat down at my little desk. It was the American Film Institute. They were forming their first-ever women's directing workshop and wanted to know if I had any names to suggest. I did. Then I stopped for a moment. "Me," I said.

There were about twelve women, including my friend Dyan Cannon, Lynne Littman, an editor, and another actress. "Do whatever you want to," they said. "It will be on tape; we'll supply you with a producer and a crew. A half hour in length." I looked around. We were meeting in a room at the old American Film Institute in Westwood. Black and white marble floors, a curved marble staircase, lush, 1800s-style green grounds with secluded seating areas, even ponds and willows. I thought, *What period piece could I use this place for?* I remembered seeing Anne Bancroft and Viveca Lindfors's *The Stronger*, a Strindberg piece, at the Studio.

The play is a very rich, complex piece about two actresses meeting by chance in the Christmas season. I looked around me. I would turn the main room into a restaurant, filled with diners in 1800s costumes. Two musicians would be playing; two young women on violin and cello. The staff would be running around, eager to please the diners coming and going. There would be a velvet settee in the lobby where one of the actresses would wait for someone. She would smoke. With the help of the AFI producers, my afternoon imaginings came to life.

One actress is celebrating her success onstage and reveling in her producer husband and adorable children. She talks incessantly. The other actress listens and smiles, she never speaks. She has a secret. Who is the stronger?

Joey called Andy Davis for camera. Andy has since made a huge name for himself as a director. I cast Susan Strasberg as my elegant and successful actress and Dolores Dorn, another Actors Studio actor, as my woman with a secret. They were both brilliant. I drew on all my Actors Studio actors for the maître d', waitresses, and extras playing diners in this, my first entrance into directing.

The AFI awarded money to film in color. When Joey put out a call for crew, all the crew guys from the commercials he'd made volunteered. I had dolly pushers, crane and lighting guys; Burton Miller costumed, and the costume houses gave us all those grand period costumes for nothing. Everyone gave and gave. I even had Susan drive up to the establishment in a horse and carriage, with snow falling and a chorus of children singing old Christmas carols, before she made her entrance up the great restaurant's marble staircase. I cast my dear friend director Clyde Ventura as the elegant maître d', running up the staircase to greet Susan, playing a great theater artiste. An intimate scene took place in the mirrored powder room, with interruptions from strange ladies (of the period) entering and leaving.

It was magical.

Most of all, I could do it. I could dream something, take four typewritten pages of dialogue from a play, and create a world for actors to inhabit for a twenty-five-minute film.

A door was opening. If I walked through that door I might not

have to "depend on the kindness of strangers." Not have to wait for
some studio or network to call my agents, who would then call me. Not
wait, as all actors do, for the telephone to ring. Of course I knew *The
Stronger* was a one-time thing, shot over a weekend. Everyone wants to
be a part of someone's first step, first movie, and they help push you
over the top. Joey produced. He didn't know it then, but it would be
the first in a long run of our working together. He producing, I directing, fighting over everything.

Voyage of the Damned

Stu Rosenberg called. Stu was the director of the *Defenders* TV show, who had cast me in the series when I first got off the blacklist. Now he was directing a big film, *Voyage of the Damned*, with an international cast—Faye Dunaway, Orson Welles, Ben Gazzara, Maria Schell, Malcolm McDowell, on and on, all wonderful, global actors. It was the story of the *St. Louis*, a ship that sailed out of Hamburg in 1939 carrying a thousand German Jews fleeing the death camps. The ship was refused admittance first in Havana, then in the United States by order of FDR, and was sent back to Germany, where most of the passengers perished. It's a true story.

There was no script yet, but Stu said, "Take it—I promise you an Academy Award nomination." "Well, okay!" I decided to get a permanent, since women in the 1930s had that look. What I didn't know was that permanent solution, when applied to hair with bleach and dye in it, shrivels the hair into a frizzy mess. I was off on the wrong foot. My concentration went to how I looked through the whole film, making life for the director a burden he didn't need, and for the cinematographer a pain in the ass.

The perks were Spain! Barcelona! The hotel! We brought everyone with us. Milton Justice and I went first. Milton had come into our lives when I was doing *The Little Foxes*, starting as my assistant and remaining along for the ride as long as it lasted.

We were booked into the Ritz Hotel. The first night, Milton and I stayed in the king of Spain's suite, running through the rooms like mad children. When Joey, the girls, and Sammy Reese arrived, we settled into a more sensible but still grand set of rooms that opened into one another.

We were in and out of one another's rooms all the time. Sammy was an actor from the deep South who had written a wonderful terror movie that we were developing, and for which we had start-up money from a backer. I remember young Steven Spielberg reading the script in the kitchen of the Red House and looking up at me with puzzlement in his eyes. "Why? Why would you want to do this?" Waldo had the same reaction. I loved the script and I still do, bizarre, disturbing, and funny as it was, and is. I could see it come to life.

My make-believe family on *Voyage* consisted of Sam Wanamaker, who played my husband, and Lynne Frederick as my sixteen-year-old daughter.

When I landed at Barcelona Airport, I spotted a figure hiding behind a pillar. It was a blond woman, her head covered with a black scarf.

"Lee!" she whispered from her hiding place. It was Jan Sterling.

"What are you doing here? Why are you hiding?"

"Sam's meeting me here. I just don't know if his wife came with him!"

Jan and Sam Wanamaker had been lovers for years, and she had taken an apartment in Barcelona to be near him. By the end of filming, Lynne, the pretty young English girl who played our daughter, the girl every man on the film tried to get into bed, including our director, succumbed. To whom? Daddy. Sam Wanamaker.

The voyage takes place on an ocean liner. All of our filming took place aboard this big ship, in its casinos, ballrooms, four stories high. It was in dock most of the time, but for Sam's attempted suicide scene, where he jumps the railing into the ocean, we sailed farther out. All of our dressing rooms were cabins on the boat. It was a self-contained world.

I hate being on water.

I'm trying to figure out why I became such an insecure diva on *Voyage of the Damned*. I remember buying a mood ring in Barcelona. I put it on before a scene to test myself. The ring turned black in response to my ice-cold hand. By the scene's end the ring was bright blue in response to the heat that changed in my body as I worked.

Faye Dunaway was, at that time in her career, beyond beautiful. This was the film she made right before *Network*, for which she won an Academy Award. She was flawlessly beautiful. I was flawed. Put a flashlight on Faye and she'd look amazing. Not me. I needed the cameraman to look at me and light me.

I asked the DP, an Englishman named Billy Williams, with whom I would work many years later as a director, to meet me in the hotel restaurant on our day off. "I'm not beautiful," I said to him. "I need some adjustment to the lights, an eye light, something that works for me, not for Faye."

Billy was taken aback. I was playing a German Jewish woman running from the Nazis. My character wouldn't give a damn what she looked like. But Lee Grant knew Hollywood. "Yeah, she's a good actress, but she's getting too old." "Too old for the part." And Lee was protecting herself. I would act the part, no problem, but if I wanted the next picture, I had to stay young—younger, anyway.

There is a scene in *Voyage* where my character sits in front of her makeup mirror and grimly, silently begins to cut her hair off down to the scalp. I've lost my husband to suicide. In my mind, cutting my hair off is an act of Orthodox Jewish protocol before killing myself. I think the scene takes place after America has turned our boat away and we're heading back to Germany. Faye enters, her character sees that I've lost my senses, and she does everything she can to bring me back from the edge.

Previously, when we'd read through the scene, I could hardly talk for the tears. Now, with the camera rolling, there were no tears, nothing. I was dry, grim, empty, cried out. Faye stood behind me and placed her hand on my shoulder. She was very still, but so intense that I could feel her heartbeat through my back—thump, thump—and the heat of her body. It stunned me. I looked at her reflection in the mirror. Nothing. Yet inside she was pulsating, giving off heat and heart. It meant a lot to me. She cared, and her performance took the scene in a different direction.

All of us ate together, played together—German, English, American actors reveling in one another. At lunch I sat between Faye and Maria Schell. At night my whole gang went out with the film company. Günter Meisner, a German actor, became our friend. He would carry Belinda everywhere on his shoulders. Sammy, Dinah, and I climbed all the way to the top of the stairs of the Gaudí cathedral and we walked everywhere. All of Barcelona was in the piazza at two a.m., even children and babies. It was a partier's paradise. One night, Joey and Michael Constantine, another American actor, got so loaded that they just lay down on the sidewalk leading to the hotel. They were so far gone, they couldn't move. Dinah and I walked right over them and went back to our rooms. I had to work early the next day. I was in bed, churning, furious, when Joey burst into the room—"Blah, blah, blah." Dinah and I put him in the shower with his clothes on—"Blah, blah,

blah." He finally passed out. I was dying to push him off the bed. I showed up for work on three hours' sleep.

Maria Schell was waiting for me in the ship's dining room. "Lee," she said, "I saw the dailies. You are right, you didn't look too good!" I gasped and ran crying past the diners sitting at their tables. Past all the actors and our director. Stu caught up to me as I threw myself on my bed in the cabin. "What is it?" he said with genuine concern. "What happened?" As I sobbed out my anguish over my lighting, I could see his expression change. I could see myself in the mirror of his eyes, and I was ashamed.

Our last night in Barcelona, firecrackers began going off, and people ran shouting through the halls, laughing and singing. "What is it? What is it?" we asked. Franco had died, and we were all there to share in the celebration of a dictator's end.

The cast and crew moved to London for the last few weeks of filming. We rented a cheery house in St. John's Wood and stayed through Thanksgiving. There were eight of us for dinner—Luther Adler, Sammy, Milton, Dinah, Belinda, Joey, me, and another guest, the backer for Sammy's movie. A really nice guy, with money, who announced while we were eating our turkey that he was pulling out. Sorry. No money for our movie. Really sorry. Our hearts fell to our bellies, where they joined the food. We all made polite conversation. We couldn't look at one another. Sammy and I were sad.

Complicating my misery was the fact that I'd had several conversations with Kim Stanley about playing the lead in the film. Kim was an old friend and a truly great actress. She'd read the script and agreed to do it. We were all set for a great shoot. We had the money. The talent. Shortly after the backer pulled out, I got a call from Lucy Kroll. She was Kim's agent, and had been mine briefly in the blacklist years. She was a good and smart lady. She said, "Lee, you can't use Kim. You have to call and tell her so."

"Why?"

"She's an alcoholic, Lee. She's just gone on the wagon. If she acts, she'll drink again." This from an agent who only benefits when her client works. We talked back and forth, me trying to reason with her, dissuade her, anything to work with Kim. I'd take her drunk or sober. Any way she wanted. I felt I could still save the film and find the money.

So now I called Kim. "We lost our backer, Kim." She was teaching in Oregon somewhere. She was cool. "The minute we get the money to do this thing, I'll call you." Cool. She knew I'd spoken to Lucy. I felt terrible.

We spent our nights in London at the White Elephant, hanging out with the elegant West End actors. But the party was over. We all went home. Our luggage was a small mountain.

Just as Stu Rosenberg said, I was nominated for my fourth Academy Award as Best Supporting Actress for *Voyage of the Damned*. I figured it was for shaving part of my head. It was the sympathy vote.

I lost interest in acting almost the minute I realized I'd outlived my enemies. And when the fight went out of me, fear leaped back in. Fight or fear. I had always had a tendency to sabotage myself, to shoot myself in the foot and the head. Sometime after *Voyage of the Damned*, the fear of forgetting my lines started to interfere with my film work for the first time.

Up until then, the fear had limited itself to the stage. Now suddenly—and illogically, since everyone knows you can do another take if you go up, it's no big deal—I became consumed by my fear. I didn't tell Joey. I didn't tell anyone. I knew I was dealing with illogic, or should I say ill-logic; the same old fear with a different face. Nameless Fear was back.

I was getting ready to do Neil Simon's Chekhovian play *The Good Doctor*, a Broadway play he had adapted for TV. There was a good cast: Marsha Mason, who was married to Neil at the time; Richard Chamberlain, who would leave for London shortly afterward and make a name for himself playing Hamlet; and wonderful direction by Jack O'Brien, a talented theater guy who had directed great pieces on Broadway.

I was the haughty lady of the house. Marsha Mason was my servant, and I never stopped talking, demanding things from her. I loved the play and the part. I had all the lines. I hired a girl to go over lines with me for a week during rehearsal. With her, of course I knew them all; on set, the panic button would go off. There were no takes. The plays were being filmed in their entirety.

I asked for a diary and wrote out all my lines. I'd cleverly established the diary as my character's account book for bills. The costume designer gave me a lorgnette on a silver chain that had belonged to his grandmother as a gift, which I used both the better to see the lines and as a perfect character device. Feeling protected, I even enjoyed myself.

But I knew that something was painting me into a corner, limiting my activity more and more. It wasn't coming from the enemy outside; it was the enemy inside. Was I feeling guilty? Was it that I had said the names of those two women in front of the lawyers from the Committee? How could I stop the enemy inside me?

Everyone in L.A. got loaded. It was cool. The more out of it you were, the cooler. Look at Dennis Hopper. After *Easy Rider* he was King of Cool. Crazy was even better. Close to the edge. I told you about the friends of Dinah who died on the Pacific Coast Highway, driving stoned at seventy miles an hour. Dinah wrote this in her diary:

DINAH

> My friend
>
> Who knows me
>
> And still doesn't mind
>
> And likes my
>
> Bad side
>
> And prefers it to
>
> Someone else's
>
> Good side
>
> Even

I tore this coffee-stained page out of Dinah's diary when she was about fifteen, maybe fourteen. It's in a small silver frame in front of me, where I see it every day. It's the truest barometer of friendship I've ever read, and the criteria for all my relationships, including with Dinah. I admire and respect and am in awe of Dinah, more than anyone else I know.

In adolescence, she didn't show much aptitude for any salary-earning career. She got by in school with the minimum effort, as all the Malibu kids did. She and her girlfriends all had horses, which they would trot across the Pacific Coast Highway and tie up at the small Point Dume shopping center—Dinah wearing a colorful knit string bikini. At around fourteen, I lost my baby girl, my heart and soul. Everything I did was connected to caring for and raising my daughter, the one constant in my life. Sometimes you get lucky, and sometimes your luck disappears for a while. My baby always made me laugh, and at every age she fascinated me and clung to me, until adolescence. The new adolescent Dinah was teary and rebellious and had access to drugs I had no real idea of—until she grew up and told me. Cloris Leachman's handsome and charming son Bryan was one of her partners in romance and drugs early on. They made a charismatic couple and, I later discovered, stole my sleeping pills. This wonderful boy died of an overdose.

Around eighteen, Dinah suddenly became interested in acting. I worked with her on *This Property Is Condemned*, a Tennessee Williams one-act, for her audition for the Actors Studio. Then came Marty Maraschino in *Grease*, then a running part in *Soap*, a hot TV series. Then the lead in Neil Simon's play *I Ought to Be in Pictures*. She was accepted by the Studio and quickly hired by Robert Redford as the girl in *Ordinary People* who commits suicide.

She was going with an Italian boy, Greg Antonacci, while *I Ought to Be in Pictures* was trying out in L.A., prior to moving to New York. They were in love, but Greg set one condition for marriage: that she give up acting in general and the Neil Simon play in particular. Joey and I liked Greg. When Dinah told us she was thinking of leaving the play, in which she had the lead, in which she was the "I" of *I Ought to Be in Pictures*, we were both stunned. Joey and I talked to her for hours. "You can't back out of this, only once in a lifetime do you get this opportunity"—something I knew only too well. Hadn't I left her father when he'd given me the same ultimatum, "If you take this play we're through"?

Greg had a strong hold on her. Joey and I set up a meeting with Dinah and Greg. Greg was easy and charming, laid-back. He agreed with everything we said, but he was unmovable on the question. If Dinah opened the play in New York, they were through. "Call me chauvinistic, call me backward, call me anything you want. That's my condition."

"Greg, do you love her?"

"Yes."

"Then—?"

"Sorry, that's it," he said, leaning back with his arms over the chair, totally relaxed. Dinah, sitting back, listening to her life being squeezed into one young man's concept of how she should live as a wife, as a woman, got it. It freed her. Greg, not long after, married a nice girl and had a family.

Dinah opened the play in New York. I was in the audience, open-mouthed. It was an out-of-body experience. I had never seen an actor so relaxed, so comfortable onstage. It was her home, her living room. No nerves, not like me. On opening night she gave a delicious performance, lovable and quirky and original. She won a Tony. Her first time onstage. Isn't that something? Her date for the Tonys was Bruce Willis—you know, the then-bartender of a popular joint, Café Central, on Columbus Avenue.

W e'd lived in the Red House for eight years. Oh my God, the discussions, the people, the soul, the fun—we were the center of the world.

The view was gorgeous at the Red House, because it sat high on a ridge, facing the Pacific Ocean, with green grass all around. The sunset happened over the water, shifting from crayon-yellow to orange to pink to purple to ink panoramically.

The work I was doing at the time was beautiful, the talent I was moderating at the Actors Studio, my own wonderful, endless challenges as an actor and then as a director. We were greedy, sexy, happy, stoned on ourselves and on one another. Gobbling everything and one another up.

Warren, Jack, Brenda, Michael, Goldie, Julie, Waldo, Ron and Iva Rifkin, Lee Strasberg, John Schlesinger, Hal, Oscar Levant, our kids, their Malibu friends, their moms and dads, Easter egg hunts organized by Peter Yarrow, Halloweens, July Fourth sunsets on the beach. Heaven.

Airport '77

I'd been nominated for an Oscar three times, I'd finally won one, and the next picture I was offered was *Airport '77*, a formula disaster movie. Who was in it? Jack Lemmon, for one, and Olivia de Havilland and Joseph Cotten and Jimmy Stewart. We all knew the score. One for the money, two for the show. This one was definitely for the money. A big, scary, special-effects airplane movie. I had it written into my contract that when the ocean breaks through the fuselage and pours torrents into the plane, a stunt double would take my place. When it comes to drowning, as Lee Strasberg would say as he stared at the ocean, his feet planted in the sand, "Eh. I don't want to get involved."

My dialogue was so stilted that I hired my good, funny friend Harvey Miller to rewrite my lines, and do it in such a way that it wouldn't interfere with the lines of the other actors. The producer, an old hand with great Greta Garbo stories to tell, said, "Sure, anything you want!"

My character was a brittle rich woman married to Christopher Lee (of *Dracula* fame); she is not someone you want around in an emergency. Olivia de Havilland is traveling with a black female companion (whom she later saves, of course). My old friend George Furth was there, too, playing a cranky person.

I forget if our plane is hit by lightning or what brings it down over the ocean. But the plane slowly sinks to the bottom of the ocean floor, intact, and stays there, the air miraculously still circulating in the cabin.

Everybody's a good sport about it but my character. I'm a real pain in the ass. Nobody can stand me, not even my husband, Christopher Lee. And then I really cross the line. I become hysterical, lose it, and charge the doors that are keeping the ocean from flooding in on us.

The stewardess was none other than Brenda Vaccaro, my great friend in real life. Brenda decks me. I fall to the floor of the plane, out of commission. She's saved the day.

Brenda and I took longer to do our fight scene than any of our other scenes, because we fell down laughing for three takes. The wonderful absurdity of my turning the heavy wheel to open the plane door, her hand on my shoulder, turning me to look at her cute face, then doing our rehearsed one, two, three punches and shoves, just broke us up. My legs were jelly, I was wheezing with laughter—it was the closest I'd gotten to being in a school play. Sympathy for our nervous young director pulled us together just enough to get through it.

The big climax of *Airport '77*, what the audience is squirming in their seats for, is when this plane at the bottom of the ocean is inundated by water. The filming took place on a huge soundstage, with the plane suspended in a big tank of water. Two giant barrels of water were set above the plane. When it was time to be flooded, a stuntman was placed in one of the plane seats, the barrels were pulled over by stagehands, tons of water poured out, and the stunt person was deluged, swimming upward in what had become a foaming ocean of water eight feet high.

I watched from an overhead grid, safe and dry, thinking how clever I was to avoid drowning contractually. I wondered who else had been as wise as I. "All right. Who wants to be first?" said the producer using a bullhorn, taking over from the director. Silence, then, "Oh, me, me!" came a voice from the rafters. Olivia spent her days climbing the rafters, watching the action below, schmoozing with the stage-hands high above. "Me! I want to do it!" My jaw dropped as I watched Olivia, a seventyish daredevil heroine, perched eagerly on her seat in the plane while tons of water arched and fell on her, then shake her little head as she bobbed up to the surface, smiling.

I let a few more actors drown before I went down to the plane and took my seat.

"Lee," the producer yelled, "we have your stunt double ready."

"What stunt double? No, I don't need a stunt double. I'm fine."

He: "You sure? She's right here!"

Me: "No. I want to do this, really. Really."

The DP set up an eye light—an inky, it's called—floating on the water after I drowned so my dead face was lit properly. Even dead I needed to be beautiful. If ever a character deserved to die, it was me. But in the end, at least I died almost as bravely as Olivia de Havilland.

The Green House

One day the owners of the Red House called and said they wanted to double our rent. Of course they did. We were paying something like $750 a month, but the request gave Joey the idea of buying land and building a house. I couldn't understand why. We'd been so happy renting, first the Pool House, then this one. I'd always rented. My parents rented at 706 Riverside Drive.

"It's against my principles to own," I said. "It's an alien idea." I'd never owned anything but Uncle, our ancient Bentley.

When my money manager sided with Joey, I bought a large piece of land that Joey found on Zumeriz Drive, on the ocean side of the Pacific Coast Highway. We rented an interim house while the new house was built, which we called the White House, in the Colony again, on the ocean.

But the true enchantment was gone. The love affair between the Red House and Dinah and Belinda, between the Red House and Joey and me, lost its magic.

Our new house was Joey's baby. Joey found the lot, planted silly tiny sticks to grow into trees, and acted as foreman. I wanted the house from *Meet Me in St. Louis*, a big turn-of-the-century house for a family for all time. I wanted to float a house from San Francisco down the coast to Malibu. The new house would be built on a hill overlooking the ocean. There was an orchard attached. I'd been wrapped up in Strindberg, and I was broke.

While we were in the White House I developed a script from another Strindberg play. I was beginning to shift my thinking to directing, giving myself a new rock to step up to over the rushing waters. Someone, a man, came up with enough money to film it. Most of the action took place at a summer home on the beach. Max Schell, Anjelica Huston, Carol Kane, and Richard Jordan were set. Anything was possible. Didn't I film *The Stronger* over a weekend at the AFI? We were rehearsing when the phone rang. The backer was sorry, but he was putting his money into a road movie. I'll never forget Max Schell's wise eyes as I reluctantly faced my cast, who had given their time, worked for free. "That's all right, Lee," Max said. "It rarely works out, the money. We did good work." Bless Max.

Airport '77, The Swarm, Damien: Omen II, and my mother built my beautiful Green House with the big white porch. Saying yes to everything is in an actor's DNA. "I'm working" is the optimal phrase. To keep making a living, you have to say yes to second-rate films but try your best to do first-rate work, and it's possible. Second-rate films I've acted in were filled with famous employable actors, whose money advisors told them, "Take the money and run."

My parents came for a visit when Joey and the architect were starting to build the new house. My directing project had just fallen through, and I had grabbed *The Swarm* for the money. The story is about killer bees from Africa heading straight for a small town in America. My part is a valiant newswoman who sights them, runs into the town square and warns, "The bees are coming! The bees are coming!" Big names in this movie, too. It was one of Michael Caine's first American films. He played an Army major. When I, the reporter, tried to convince him of the dangers, Michael Caine the actor fell asleep standing up. Just as David Janssen had years before. Our director, Irwin Allen, had me yell, "The BEES are coming! The BEES are COMING!" endlessly. "THE BEES ARE COMING!"

The nursery school on Long Island was doing well, and I asked my father for a loan. When he heard it was for building a new house, he refused. "Folly!" he said. My father loathed Joey. He would not give money to anything Joey was connected with.

For my father, respect was everything. He asked me to contact Mike Wallace; he wanted me to get him on *60 Minutes*. I told him I didn't think I had that kind of power. He insisted.

I lied. "They're booked solid, Dad."

"The values in this country are disintegrating. I think it's important they hear what I have to say."

I could feel his need for a platform. Didn't I want one myself? I hired a camera crew. They filmed him on the big porch of the White House. He itemized the Boy Scout oath. I think there are ten tenets— close to the Ten Commandments. He was passionate and urgent and simplistic. Maybe he thought the Boy Scout ethos would connect with an audience.

In the background, on a white bench in front of the window, sat my mother. Her straight, shiny hair was now white, a self-conscious smile frozen on her face. He exhorted for an hour. She demurred when I asked her to go on camera, sweet.

"Dear, have you heard back from Mike Wallace yet?"

I continued to come up with all the legitimate reasons both Mike and *60 Minutes* were booked up, until months later, when I had to tell my dad they were not open to personal statements.

He was hurt and baffled. He wanted to leave a mark on the world. Longed to leave one.

After they returned to New York, my mother secretly emptied her hidden account and sent me the money. The loan would be paid back to her monthly, in installments. I paid faithfully, knowing how difficult it must have been for her to hide the "mad money" she had hoarded over many years. It was a real sacrifice on her part.

Joey had given up the commercial business to build the new house. He and the great DP Billy Fraker had been partners. Business was good, humming in fact, but it wasn't *Mad Men*; it just paid the bills. But Joey hated the clients. Joey understands money. I never have. With me turning from acting to directing, he felt we needed something to fall back on and that only property would do it: A valuable house on valuable land in Malibu equaled a valuable asset.

Joey turned foreman. He was at the site every morning at six. He oversaw every stick of wood, every stone put into place. Shortly after the house was framed, a series of storms hit Malibu. The ocean rose higher and higher until it swept through the houses on the ocean side of the Colony. We all worked to sandbag the beach in front of us. Students from Pepperdine joined in. Bruce Dern's house was flooded. Nobody could collect insurance for damages because ocean invasion was expected.

Then, out of nowhere, a tornado whipped through Malibu Canyon, aimed right for our property, and picked up the house we were building. Picked the frame of the house right up and blew it sixty feet.

Well, we had tornado insurance! Some obscure paragraph in the policy covered tornadoes, which paid for reframing the house and gave us enough extra to build a porch that encircled the whole house. Just like *Meet Me in St. Louis*.

While I was making *Damien: Omen II* in snowy Wisconsin, I saw the color green I wanted the house painted. Larry Hauben mixed the paint in a mixing ceremony. Joey and I went to Chicago to find old stained glass recovered from turn-of-the-century houses. One huge panel went in the top of the window in the living room. The other was for the front door.

No one made a more beautiful house than Joey did. He had landscaped the grounds. The little tree sticks he planted grew into thirty-foot-high eucalyptus trees that hid the house from our neighbors. The rose garden, filled with lavender roses, was always in bloom. Green grass covered the hill that sloped gently down to the odd little wooden bridge leading to the house. White stairs led up to the wraparound porch. On the ocean side, a big terrace covered in flagstone, with little shoots of grass outlining each one, was bordered by a low stone wall to protect the shrubs and our occasional marijuana plant, a favorite target of the neighborhood teenagers.

I have a black-and-white photo of my gray-haired parents sitting close together on the porch, looking out at the ocean. I remember how I felt when I took the picture and felt a sudden lurch in my heart, realizing for the first time that there was an end to life. To their lives.

I had flown from L.A. to New York to do the television version of Thomas Wolfe's great novel *You Can't Go Home Again*. I was playing Aline Bernstein, the New York woman that Wolfe was having an affair with. She was rich and older than he was. Chris Sarandon was playing Wolfe. Ralph Nelson was directing. On the plane I remembered Aline Bernstein coming to the Neighborhood Playhouse years before to lecture on the theater. I was seventeen. As she walked down 52nd Street toward Fifth Avenue, a fellow student and I deviled her. "Mrs. Bernstein, Mrs. Bernstein, talk about Tom Wolfe." She took her hearing aids out so she couldn't hear us and walked serenely toward Fifth Avenue. Now I was playing her.

Did I tell you that Gladys died? My beautiful spunky girl was eaten up with cancer. She'd married Waldo by then. I took a cab straight from the plane to Gladys's apartment. "I've gone from forgetting names to forgetting my lines," I cried. "My head is like Swiss cheese. I'm painting myself into a corner."

Gladys was pale. "I have a pain in my stomach."

"You always have a pain in your stomach," I snapped. "I'm in a panic, what am I going to do?"—ignoring her complaint, annoyed, in fact.

My darling Gladys, lying white in a white hospital bed, trying to be practical about losing her black curly hair, her long eyelashes. "I know where to get great wigs," I told her. Waldo was massaging her small white feet, warming them. "Here," she said, handing me a pot of yellow crocus. "These will bloom next year. If they bloom next year, so will I." I took the little pot. We looked long and hard at each other.

Waldo died six or seven years later in another hospital room. His daughter Jennifer Salt was with him, all the time. Waldo was never without a joint. I have a huge black-and-white drawing Gladys did of Waldo's hand holding a joint. For years his breath rattled when he talked. His lungs were shot. He wouldn't stop, couldn't stop.

As the Green House was nearing completion, Joey started arguing for adding a stone wall and a gate to the property. If we had to sell the house, he felt, it would guarantee the sale. This meant I had to take a movie in Canada, *Visiting Hours*, which I'd already turned down. It was a B-minus movie, and I was the lead. Michael Ironside, Bill Shatner, and Linda Purl were set to costar. *The Swarm* and *Airport '77* were awful films, but they had huge casts and budgets. There was safety in numbers and anonymity, and everybody paid their bills. This one was a damsel in distress movie. I'm a TV reporter attacked by a crazed man

(Ironside) who chases me through the corridors and cellars of the hospital I've been taken to. My wardrobe was a hospital gown.

I did the movie in Quebec, where everything was French and charming, except I heard on the radio one day that they still had signs in the countryside that said NO DOGS OR JEWS ALLOWED.

I went to the film's opening at the big Loews on Sunset Boulevard. What I realized in that dark Loews theater was that I could no longer get away with looking young and beautiful. The train was coming. I was on the tracks. My age was showing. *Shampoo* was over, *The Swarm* was here, and *Visiting Hours*. If I'd been given any gift from the blacklist, it was a strong sense of reality. My glory days in wonderland were numbered.

And what about my earning days? I knew nothing about money, except that I had to make it to pay for everything. And I made it by acting. But I had to be asked. I had to be wanted. Wanted. Wanted.

I'd been given everything this town, Hollywood, had to offer.

After the AFI, I could see another rock in the rapids I could jump to. Not only could, but wanted to. Needed to. A director was born.

The actor in me had committed some kind of suicide. An actor who cannot retain the writers' lines is unemployable. As unemployable as I was when I was blacklisted.

I took myself out of the picture. I put other actors in the picture, on the screen. Onstage. With the relief that I had a new talent and was safe.

I didn't know how old I was anymore. I'd blocked it out. I didn't want to know. I knew, generally, and didn't like what I knew. I was owed twelve years. On the big screen I was looking my real age. I either had to move to older character parts or concentrate on a new career.

The Willmar 8

In Malibu one day my friend Mary Beth showed me a piece in a Minnesota newspaper about eight women on strike against a bank in Willmar, Minnesota, Mary Beth's hometown. Mary Beth was married to Peter Yarrow of Peter, Paul, and Mary, and he got funds from a group interested in important but overlooked documentary subjects.

It was winter when Mary Beth and I left for Willmar. We left the beach at a sunny eighty-five degrees and landed in Minnesota at twenty degrees below zero.

We drove to Mary Beth's childhood home, a half hour from the airport. Her dad was Dr. Mac McCarthy, brother of Senator Eugene, and her mother was Muriel. Mary Beth's six sisters had scattered, so I had one of their rooms to myself.

I had been dropped into a Midwestern town, totally foreign to a big-city girl. We walked on hard, frozen ground to the bank, where I saw eight people, snow-jacketed, mufflered, and booted, walking up and down past an unimpressive one-story building that had the word BANK printed in gold letters. They carried wooden sticks with placards.

The women had been picketing for a year, winter and summer. Their case would be heard in court at the end of the month.

They ranged in age from their twenties to their fifties. All had been tellers at this bank, some for many years. One of the women, Irene, had realized that the women had trained, one after another, young men hired by the bank president, then watched them go on to become their superiors. Their bosses. With better pay and kinder hours. When Irene confronted the bank president and asked why the women, especially those with seniority, were never promoted, he dismissed her out of hand. "You are only women, after all," he said.

The women went on strike. All of them were married, most with families.

It was a privilege to become friends with them on my first excursion into documentary filmmaking—to film their lives, this crisis, and the people in the town of Willmar.

One day as I walked the snow-covered streets with a microphone and camera crew, I tried asking a question of a passerby, "Whose side are you on, the bank's or the women's?" and my lips froze. I couldn't form the "Who?" to ask the sentence. That's the cold they walked in every day.

By the time we finished, Judy Irola, who was on camera, a real teacher, and I had become an intimate part of the women's lives and understood how important it was to document them. They lost the court case. But they won. They made history.

Nationwide, bankers saw the documentary and changed their policies. Other women were given positions the Willmar women had fought for. The youngest of the eight, Glennis, became a labor organizer in Minneapolis. And I was hooked. I wanted to make documentaries.

This was a politics that went to my heart. Not fair. A woman taken advantage of, put down, bullied. A way I could take sides and still be safe. Not labeled Red, Pink, Mauve.

Now it was not acting but directing that was the new challenge, the new place I was being stopped, where all women were being stopped. The studios and producers who remained so gracious to me as an actress reacted as if I were overripe cheese when I mentioned directing. There were only three active women directing at the time, and they were all from New York, independent filmmakers with no connection to the studio system: Joan Micklin Silver, Martha Coolidge, and Claudia Weil. I had to do it because Hollywood said I couldn't. My cue was always "No, you can't."

Tell Me a Riddle

Tillie Olsen was a San Francisco icon, a writer who put her career on hold for thirty years and then produced a succession of exquisite stories, starting with a collection called *Tell Me a Riddle*. In 1980, three young women who had heard Olsen lecture while they were still in college saw my production of *The Stronger* and decided they wanted me to direct a movie for their company, The Godmothers, based on Olsen's title story.

Their names were Rachel Lyon, Mindy Affrime, and Susan O'Connell. Everything in my life at that time was so magical, so filled with endless possibilities, that I took being chosen to direct *Riddle* for granted. It's only now that I appreciate the sheer miracle of it, that these girls got *Riddle* made and persuaded Saul Zaentz to be the executive producer.

Saul was a great, veteran producer and an interesting, charming guy. At the time, he was building a huge sound studio and editing facility in San Francisco. It was there we edited the film. The only other people working there at the time were Tippi Hedren and her then-husband, Noel Marshall. They had just finished a documentary about their house full of lions. Tippi's fifteen-year-old daughter, Melanie

Griffith, was part of the lion household and was mauled by a lion under the misdirection of her stepfather.

Joyce Eliason, the gifted and sensitive writer who wrote the screenplay, and I bonded while we worked on the script for a year at the Green House, waiting for the Godmother girls to raise the money.

They had shown the script to Melvyn Douglas, the urbane, light leading man who had played opposite Garbo in *Ninotchka*, and who we hoped would play the male lead. Douglas said he wanted to do it, pending a meeting with me, a first-time director. We met for lunch in a small bistro with dark green walls. He was sitting at the table, nervously looking at a menu, as I walked toward him. The charming lover of all those great ladies of film in the forties and fifties was in his seventies now.

I'd known that his wife, Helen Gahagan Douglas, was an actress who was elected to Congress in 1944 and that she'd later lost her seat to Richard Nixon after being brutally smeared as a Red. Now here he was—a gift from the Godmothers.

"Would I have to use an accent in this?" he asked.

"Yes," I said.

"I've never done an accent," he said. "I've never worked on an accent. I don't know whether I can do it."

I looked at him and loved him so much. Such an actor. All those films behind him, and with this one, it was like he'd never worked before—a child actor, insecure, open, perfect.

I had called Germany to try to get Elisabeth Bergner to play opposite Melvyn. I had adored her when I was growing up. She, too, carried a buried child inside. She, too, had to be in her seventies by now. The main story in *Riddle* is the long marriage of two émigrés from Russia. Eva, the wife, is nearly deaf, lost in memories of her youth in Russia, where she had been a revolutionary. She listens to old, stirring music and pores over her photograph albums, which preserve the heroes of her youth. She is happily immured in her house and her yard, her kitchen and her things, turning her hearing aid off when she wants to retreat into her own world. Her husband is too old to care for the house anymore. It's become a burden. He'd been a union house-painter, but now he physically cannot climb the ladder to fix the roof. He wants to move to a senior center, where his friends are, and play cards and enjoy himself. Eva has a fainting spell and is taken to the hospital. She has incurable cancer. Melvyn doesn't tell her. He secretly sells the house and takes Eva on a trip to visit their children, ending up in San Francisco with a grandchild (Brooke Adams), who is a kindred spirit for Eva. In the end, the old spark ignites between Melvyn and Eva; the loss of their house brings them together, and their need and caring, their love for each other is found before he loses her.

When I told this story to Elisabeth Bergner over the phone in Berlin, she sighed. "It's too close, darling," she said. "It's too close. I can't do it."

For me the only other woman who could play the part was Lila Kedrova. Childlike, vulnerable, passionate, a consummate artist. She played opposite Tony Quinn in *Zorba the Greek* and was a revelation.

Melvyn and Lila bonded, as enemies and as lovers. The day we began shooting in San Francisco, Melvyn was trying to climb a ladder to fix his roof in the scene. His arthritis was so bad and so painful in his legs and feet that he couldn't get past the first rung. In frustration he banged into the house. "They're going to hate me," Melvyn worried. "The audience will hate me for treating her like that."

"The audience will see you trying to climb this ladder, Melvyn. You can't climb it; they'll see that. They'll be on your side forever after that."

He nodded, lunged into the character, and never looked back.

Riddle had huge echoes for me, factually and emotionally. It was so my story in a way that I swam in the making of it. Drowned under-

water, part of the time. I felt that Eva and I had made the same journey, she to overthrow the czar, I to overthrow the blacklisters. Eva's
discovery was that the Stalinists, the replacement czars, were killing
and imprisoning the poets and writers and artists she worshipped, the
heroes in her album. They weren't in Tillie Olsen's story. I, as director, put them there, because they were in mine, too—Arnie, Joe
Bromberg, Phil Loeb, John Garfield, Canada Lee, and all the others
who lost their lives and freedom to the McCarthy period.

The journey was a huge and thrilling release for me. I was surrounded by genius, starting with Tillie Olsen, Melvyn and Lila, Fred
Murphy on camera, Patrizia von Brandenstein, production designer,
costume designer, invisible cook running Eva's kitchen. And my own
vision was so clear. I knew what I needed to see. I used my new viewfinder. I was totally, easily in charge. My head and heart in sync, technically and emotionally.

Lila was a French actress, sensitive about her age and her looks. In
real life, she was married to a much younger man, who doted on her.
Tell Me a Riddle was based on the lives of a couple who had emigrated to America in the twenties. Lila had asked if I couldn't make
them emigrate around World War II, so she could be younger. She
would sneak thick black mascara onto her eyelashes. I'd look through
the camera and there they were, her big scandalous eyes. "Rosie," I'd
yell at her makeup lady, by prior agreement. "Rosie, how many times
do I have to tell you? No mascara on Lila." Lila would look sideways at
Rosie, a little smile on her face.

The only problem was that migraines moved in to stay during the
filming, though remarkably, never while I was actually shooting. I
don't know what body changes were taking place inside me, but every
Friday night after work, as soon as I opened the door to my little apartment, one side of my head would start beating, one eye would close,
one pulse in my temple throb. I was stunned by the pain and nausea.

I let ice-cold water beat on my head in the shower, tried ice packs and sleeping pills, and sobbed in frustration.

Doctors in that period were jaw-droppingly ignorant and stupid about migraines. "Warm milk." "Stay calmer." "See a psychiatrist." This was fifteen years at least before Fiorinal, Butalbital. Imitrex was developed by Montefiore Medical Center in the Bronx. I know—I was the first recipient of Imitrex, which, at the time I was given it, around 1990, was a self-administered shot. But that's another story.

Monday mornings, as soon as I started work, something in my body would kick in and keep me going until the next weekend. I don't know how much the combination of migraines, pain medication, and a lifelong regimen of sleeping pills contributed to my forgetting my lines. I do know pain and sleeplessness were at that time in charge of my life, enough to require constant medication in order to do a day's work. I was on a constant balance beam to keep my concentration on track.

Riddle made it all worthwhile. Lila, Melvyn, Brooke Adams.

There is a scene toward the end of the film, on a long staircase leading down to an outside door, where Melvyn finally tells a fleeing Lila that there's no more house for her to go back to; he'd sold it. The two of them were so moving, so remarkable. Sitting on the stairs, she stunned, he crying, regretting. I sat under the camera on the stairs, facing them, bawling, stifling my sobs and trying not to ruin their shot. That scene alone made up for all the migraines, and there were many such scenes.

Watching *Riddle* again last year at a screening Rachel Lyon gave at the college where she was teaching, I groaned at my self-indulgence in the editing room. I hung on to moments at the end of the film, when Eva dies, to the point where it's excruciating. Self-delusion is my forte, and I never recognize it when it's under way.

Melvyn made one more film, the great *Being There* with Peter Sellers, directed by my friend Hal Ashby, which someone recently told me was a box office flop. Lila was struck with early onset Alzheimer's.

O ne bizarre footnote to the audience for *Tell Me a Riddle.* The film opened and closed in New York at an obscure uptown art theater after a run of two weeks. I was in mourning. All that work and brilliance and devotion, finished, gone.

A young gay friend of Milton Justice approached me. He convinced me there were people with lots of money to distribute art films in Tyler, Texas, the Rose Capital of the World. Milton assured me he was connected, so one weekend Milton, Joey, and I flew to Tyler. We drove from the small airport straight to their main big old-fashioned movie theater. Stepping out of the car to enter the theater, the heat was like a hand pushing down on your head.

We entered the coldest air-conditioned, rococo, vast movie theater. Scattered among the old red velvet seats were two dozen people, couples mostly, politely standing to meet me, the director of the movie.

As I approached the smoky silhouettes, they turned into people. Rosy-faced, hearty men in cream-colored suits, no strangers to bourbon. Frail ladies in print dresses. On their permed heads, small hats with little veils.

I knew, unmistakably, I was their first Jew, and they were here at two-thirty on a sizzling Texas afternoon to watch a movie about Jewish immigrants, formerly Communist Jewish immigrants, with an esoteric deaf Jewish heroine, a long, slow film about The Other.

My heart sank.

I wanted to save them.

They scattered in seats in the empty, cold theater and politely sat for almost two interminable hours.

At the film's end they swiveled in their seats and patted their hands together. Some of the ladies patted with white gloves.

Afterward, we drove to someone's modest home for the reception. Outside the car window was sandy desolation. Not one rose in the Rose Capital of the World.

On the way back from the bathroom, I passed a bedroom, the door slightly ajar. There on the carpet sat a luscious woman with short dark hair avidly reading *Women's Wear Daily. Omigod*, I thought, *a paisan.*

I moved on to the parlor and deliberately picked a small green velvet couch to sit on, saving the only other seat for my mysterious ally from the bedroom.

A line formed in front of me. The audience had arrived, and each person who saw the movie was going to personally meet me and have a private conversation.

As the juicy lady from the bedroom entered the parlor, I patted the seat next to me. "Keep me company," I whispered. She smiled adorably and sat.

As limp, gloved hand after hearty, warm man hand shook mine, I heard, "Lovely! Really lovely!" from pale crumpled faces, from red flushed faces. "Fine! Just fine!"

I finally sat on the velvet sofa and turned to my new friend. I searched for the opening words. "I see you read *Women's Wear Daily*, da da da." Then, searching for common ground, she says, "I hate blacks, don't you?" in a real Southern accent.

Of course she did.

I was in Dixieland, USA.

Witia

Death makes me furious, which is a pity because I'm really up there myself, and someone is going to have to deal with my death sooner or later. I know there is no escaping it, but I resent all the holes in my life, the disappearances of those I hold dear. Death is not fair. Just when you get it—when you finally say *aha!*—the game changes.

I was not at the bedsides of those who gave me life when their lives ended. My vulnerable mother, who had thyroid problems, was overdosed with iodine by an arrogant new doctor, which made her so radioactive, she couldn't join us in a house in the snow at Christmas. Indeed, she wasn't allowed downstairs to be with her nursery school children for weeks. Her regular doctor was away, vacationing in Florida. I sat on the steps of the old house and called him. "My mother is radioactive—how could this happen?" Over the next fifteen years the cancer spread to her bones. "What's wrong with me?" she moaned as she wandered the house at night.

I flew to her too late. Too late to hold her, to comfort her, to tell her how much I loved her. I know she expected me to save her. She thought I had all the powers she'd dreamed of when I was in her belly. The powers she infused in me to the point that I, too, believed nothing was impossible. I knew she was waiting for me to save her, and I knew I couldn't save her, and that destroyed me. That she would reach for me, the way I did for her when I was drowning in chloroform on the cot in the Poconos.

The call came our last week of filming *Tell Me a Riddle*. I decided to take the red-eye to New York at midnight so I could finish the day's shoot. I called my best friend Mary Beth back in New York and asked her to go to the hospital, to be there for my mother and my father. On the plane to New York I prayed my mother would still be alive when I got there.

I flashed on a memory of my Uncle Joe lying on a gurney, pushed up against a wall at Long Island Jewish Hospital. He had a blood clot in his leg. As we approached him, my mother and me, he fixed me with his eyes, desperate: "Get me out of here!" I was sixteen. My lawyer uncle was looking to me to save him. Did he think I had the power to save him?

Mary Beth had left Manhattan for Long Island at four in the morning and was sitting in the corner of the room when I ran in. My father sat facing my mother's bed, his back to me. "I didn't know I would miss her this much," he whispered, bewildered, heartsick. My mother was gone, a frown of pain still visible between her eyes. Her lips were slightly apart. *Where is Lyova?* those lips said to me. *Lyova?* Standing in the middle of the room, I screamed and screamed and screamed.

She was laid out in a coffin in a neighborhood funeral parlor near her nursery school, where she had been the beloved of generations of little girls and their mothers for having infused in them a sense of their great talent and beauty.

Fremo was aghast at how the funeral people handled her sister's hair and makeup. They had assumed she was a Long Island matron. She was not. We combed the curls out of her naturally straight white hair. She had always worn her hair in bangs like a schoolgirl. We wet washcloths and rubbed off the pink rouge and lipstick. We powdered her white face. Fremo took out a red lipstick from her purse and carefully smoothed it over my mother's mouth.

Do I think I might have made it in time to my mother's bedside if I hadn't been directing *Tell Me a Riddle* in San Francisco—the story of a dying woman, riddled with cancer? If I hadn't waited to take an overnight plane, after I was done working?

After my mother died, I asked my father to come and live with us. My father nursed a Polish intellectual Jewish contempt for Joey and clung to it fiercely. His sensibility, his intellect was confounded by the Italian working-class in-laws and being displaced as head of the household for the first time. He was a quiet, fierce man. Also, he was losing his eyesight to macular degeneration. We had seen the top eye doctor at Cedars of Lebanon. Nothing could be done. He had lost his wife, the only woman in his whole life, he was losing his eyesight, and he was living in a hated stranger's house in a strange, unfamiliar location, far from home, with his anxious daughter.

Rachel, Joey's mother, was also staying with us. She prepared Abe's soft-boiled egg in the shell, just so, made him oatmeal, toast, jam, and tea every morning. He would walk with his cane down our road to the ocean and sit there on a fallen log with the neighbor's dog. Then he'd walk back up for lunch, nap with his folded handkerchief over his ear, listen to the radio, and sit on the porch, where he and my mother used to sit facing the ocean when they visited.

A month or so later, our accountant read us my mother's will. In it, she forgave the debt I had been paying back, the loan she'd given us for the Green House.

When my father heard this, he insisted that I pay him the rest of the debt. I said, "That's not what Mother wanted." "Yes, she did." And so we battled for years. Stubbornly. We never discussed the debt when I visited him, but it was there like a big hard lump between us. Both of us fighting for my mother, over my mother, each in our own stupid and unforgiving way.

At the same time, Joey was asking for recognition: *Look at me, respect me.* Abe was dismissive. He was punishing me because I was with a man he bristled at. He was only happy when he was with Dinah, who was now in her twenties, living on the Pacific Coast Highway in her own apartment. Dinah adored him. With her, he relaxed and joked, answered her complex philosophical questions. Her grandfather was very proud of her; she was the bright spot in his life. But the situation in the house was becoming intolerable. I couldn't breathe and I felt bad for Joey; he didn't deserve this. "Motel management, that's what you should go into," my father would say to Joey. "Motel management would suit you." It was demeaning and cruel.

I don't remember who discovered the hotel with residents close to my dad's age on Ocean Avenue in Santa Monica, whether it was Dinah or me. I know when I passed it families were visiting on the porch facing the ocean. I went inside and saw the rooms, the common dining room. I drove straight to the Chateau Marmont and checked in. I was alone. I collapsed on the floor in tears, in pain, in guilt, in sorrow, in helplessness—a terrible racking regret.

I asked my own father if he would prefer a hotel to living with Joey and me. He jumped at the chance.

"The Girl"

We were still living in the Green House when Joey became infatuated with another woman. It lasted more than two years, through our move to New York. First he felt protective of her; then he became hooked.

"The girl" was never a threat, which is what made her so threatening to our relationship, Joey's and mine. I'd never had a hang-up about Joey bedding available girls when he traveled for commercials. Like a dog peeing on a lamppost.

That's a mean metaphor. There's also plain old heat, attraction. I had that, too. Occasionally on a film there was either an actor or a grip or a cameraman who flicked a switch in me, and I'd go into heat. I came to expect it as part of the process. It didn't need to be acted on. What was reassuring was how quickly the switch shut off at a film's end.

So his instincts told him not to mention his liaisons to me; mine told me not to mention mine to him. It was our agreement.

"The girl" was not a fling; she was a promise.

"The girl" was my assistant and helper when I worked on *The Willmar 8* and *Tell Me a Riddle*. She came into our lives while we were editing *The Willmar 8* in the editing room we'd set up in our garage at the Green House. At the same time, I was working on the Tillie Olsen script, which we were getting ready to shoot in San Francisco. And I was furious with Joey. He was stoned all the time. He demanded attention. He'd finished the Green House and he'd left the commercial business. His mother, Rachel, was with us, cooking, seeing to his every need, every whim.

Did I tell you this before?

I was explaining something incredibly important to me. It was around one in the morning, in our bedroom. We were both sitting on a bench. I was making my point, I was impassioned, when out of Joey's mouth came a loud "Ma-a-a-a, Ma-a-a-a," a braying sound, a mooing: "Ma-a-a-a." Rachel appeared in the bedroom doorway in her nightgown.

"Wha'?"

"Gimme a sliced steak and cheese on toast!"

"With or without tomato?"

Me: "Are you crazy? Waking your mother in the middle of the night to make you a sandwich? Don't do it, Rachel. Go back to sleep!"

Joey: "With."

Rachel disappeared, padding her way downstairs to the kitchen.

So you see there was a certain inevitability about Joey getting his way most of the time.

"The girl" was breaking up with her boyfriend, who had been lecturing her on her faults; he was overbearing and jealous. She needed a sunny place to restore herself, to recover an image of herself that wasn't stupid or awkward.

She basked in our approval. Joey basked in hers, and basked and basked. He could not stop basking. Whatever approval beams "the girl" gave off became light and breath for him.

Joey and I became her friends and advisors. "Don't do that. Do this." "Leave him, move in with us, we have a spare room!" She, drinking in our warmth, superiority, glamour, worldly experience, did what we told her to do: left the two-year relationship with the jealous boyfriend and moved in with us. Wrong move.

Joey, looking for an occupation after the Green House was built and slightly stoned much of the time, his value continually degraded by my father, turned his head to her, his lips slightly parted as they always are for pasta or steamed artichoke. Her neediness was a new, delicious drug.

One morning I woke up in the Green House, went out on the bedroom balcony, and saw Joey and "the girl" walking toward the beach, she explaining, he nodding, and my stomach fell out from under me.

Later, when he came back, he told me what "the girl" had been upset about. "She feels you're cold to her. She turns to you, you're older, experienced, she feels you've changed. What's she done to deserve it?"

I wanted to kill her.

There was no sex. There was desire. Desire is much deadlier than sex. Constant unrequited desire, day and night. She ate it up. Who wouldn't? Passion without guilt. How Catholic.

We were a threesome; she was a great friend. Young, looking for guidance, depending on this power couple for wisdom. Joey loved being looked up to, being needed, an advisor, not an adversary, not facing a fault-finder.

I was sick with emptiness, jealousy, and loss. Joey was doing his best to please us both, she and I. But I felt old and discarded and didn't know what to do.

I accepted work that took me out of town, to Quebec and Toronto. Joey came to Toronto. The infatuation was over, he said. He didn't want to lose me. I wasn't attracted to him. I couldn't trust him. I walked and walked the gray streets of Toronto. I was totally unprepared for the pain.

I was in so much pain, I couldn't take a deep breath. I was jealous of the two of them, my husband and "the girl." But fatalistic. I had always liked her. I was the outsider; the romance was the real threat. They never slept together, and the tension of not going there made it even more romantic for Joey.

This was not just a Joey involvement. Wasn't "the girl" starving for approval? For the glow that comes with adoration, especially after a cool, critical long-term relationship with her boyfriend? Wasn't she opening and basking in Joey's powerful sunshine? While I was crumply and mean and envious in the cold? Nuh nuh nuh nuh no!

I was bitter and morose and unable to take the knife out of my gut. I was achingly in love with my husband, sick in love, maybe for the first time. It hurt. Joey had a twin sister, Phyllis, whom he was close to, so having two women in orbit around him was normal for him.

Ohio Shuffle

Natalie Cooper had been an acting student of mine at HB Studio in New York when I first started teaching. She was, a fascinating, gifted young gay woman. She'd written a screenplay called *Ohio Shuffle*, a fresh take on the relationship of three unrelated people, each of whom needs to escape a person or a danger. The three—two women and a man, total strangers—run away together. She had sent me her script to direct, and I was moving ahead with it.

Jill Clayburgh, who had just had a huge career breakthrough in *An Unmarried Woman*, had committed to play the lead. Mace Neufeld, a solid, respectable producer, was committed. Holly Hunter seemed the right choice for the other woman. The problem was casting the man, an innocent decent guy, a farmer. Stan Kamen called from William Morris. "Chris Walken," he said. "Cast Chris Walken in the part and I'll guarantee you the money." Chris had just opened in a movie. My friend Mary Beth and I ran to see it. Chris is a monster, murdering people right and left. Big scary close-ups of big scary Chris Walken. Mary Beth and I looked at each other in horror. That guy playing my girls' innocent farmer?

I called Stan. "Stan, no, omigod, he's scary, no, no, all wrong."
"Meet him!"

We arranged a meeting at the Green House. Chris was remote. I couldn't ask him to read; he intimidated me. "Where were you born?"

"Queens." He didn't look at me. He gazed across the room into the distance, narrowing his eyes. I think I bored him. We had a few more awkward exchanges. He left, free at last.

I was relieved. I told Stan.

"Too bad," he said. Wise Stan.

You know the story. I'd been given my chance. Two weeks later, Jill pulled out to do her husband David Rabe's script, *I'm Dancing as Fast as I Can*. I felt abandoned and shocked at her betrayal. Mace Neufeld moved on to other projects. Meanwhile, I had turned down both the money to make the film and the best actor in the world. All right, one of the best actors, fascinating, always original Chris Walken. A year later I saw Chris on something on PBS, playing a character with all the sweetness and candor of my farmer in *Ohio Shuffle*. Did I learn my lesson? I've never learned my lesson. I've made similar mistakes in project after project and lost them because of it.

Charlie Chan and the Curse of the Dragon Queen

I did an awful movie, *Charlie Chan and the Curse of the Dragon Queen*. But do you know who was in it? Peter Ustinov, Roddy McDowall, Rachel Roberts, Angie Dickinson, and the very young ingenue Michelle Pfeiffer. The prettiest, kindest, sweetest girl. At that time she and the young leading man were on a strict vegetarian diet. At lunch I could hear them discuss excitedly the change in their bowel movements.

It was a farce, of course, the highlight of which was getting to know Peter and getting to hang out with my friend Roddy.

Rachel had been married to Rex Harrison. She told a great story about him. He'd been up for his part in *Cleopatra*—the Liz Taylor, Richard Burton classic—and was expecting a call telling him whether he'd gotten the part from the director, Joseph Mankiewicz. He was fretting and walking up and down the room. Talking to himself, to her—"I need this part, I don't need it, screw them all. Do you think I'll get it?"—and on and on, when the phone rang. He picked it up. "Hello? Oh hello there, Joseph, how are you? Good. How's the weather in California? Eh? *Cleopatra?* When are you shooting, old boy? I hope I don't have a conflict. Two months should be fine, yes. Shall I tell my agent to ring you in the morning? Lovely talking to you, Joseph, bye bye." He clapped his hands together in triumph—"Hah!"—then proceeded to walk up and down the room again.

Rachel: "Rex, what's wrong?"

Rex: "I'm not sure Joe Mankiewicz is the right director for this film."

Rachel was madly in love with Rex. He'd left her for a beautiful, tall, fragile model. Rachel was drinking a lot. Inconsolable. It was Roddy who told me she'd committed suicide after the film, six months later.

Roddy had started in film as a child actor in the forties. He was the little frail boy in *How Green Was My Valley*—in black and white then. He grew up on the studio lot with all the other child actors—Elizabeth Taylor, Judy Garland. He asked nothing of anyone at the studios, maintained himself as a portrait photographer. He photographed all the stars in his life, with great insight. There are many photo books of the celebrities in Roddy's life. I'm in one of his albums, an unpretty shot from *Charlie Chan and the Curse of the Dragon Queen.*

One afternoon, in the late nineties, the phone rang. I picked up.

"Lee, it's Roddy."

I started to say "Hi."

Roddy said, "Lee, I'm dying, I have incurable cancer. I'm calling everyone I love to say good-bye."

Silence. "Roddy, who is with you?"

"Stefanie."

"Can I talk to her?"

Stefanie Powers got on the line. "It's true, Lee." I was dizzy and crying. I'm crying as I write this. *Gallant* is the word for Roddy. Gallant.

No one in Hollywood had the cachet that Roddy McDowall had. Roddy lived in a modest charming house in the Valley. Tycoons and talent drove to his house from Beverly Hills, Hollywood, and Malibu for the privilege of sitting at his dinner table, which was large and round and seated about twelve to fourteen. I sat at that table across from Alan Ladd Jr., Guy McElwaine, Stefanie Powers, Dennis Hopper, Tina Sinatra, Johnny Depp, Roddy's partner, of course, whose name I can't remember, but whose caring heart for Roddy I do remember. Everyone became equal and real at his table, everyone had a story. No gossip. Like AA, it never left the table. Roddy was the secret keeper.

This mix of unreachable producers, heads of studios, agents, and talent filtered through Roddy's quiet wisdom and came out simply folks, with stories and problems and pasts, raised and forgotten at Roddy's table. After dinner he would take a Polaroid shot of us all. A reminder, I guess. He practiced kindness and gentility in a town that longed for both.

"I'm calling to say good-bye to everyone I love." If he were calling everyone who loved him, he'd still be here.

We were in our second year at the magnificent Green House when everything suddenly started to fall apart. The roux dissolved in the salad dressing. Everything that had magically come together in California came apart as quickly. In Joey's ever-busy mind, the sale of the new house would give us the money we needed to move back to New York. We'd start a company where I would direct and he could produce, as he had with the commercial company. We would move back to New York and start a new life. My third or fourth.

Couples broke up. Bernardo Segall, the dear friend who composed the theme for *The Stronger*, and his wife split. Bernardo's wife left and took with her their nasty black cat. Bernardo was desperate. He was being fired from his position as professor of music because of his age. I went to downtown L.A. to fight with the head of the university for Bernardo's right to teach music at any age. We lost.

In Beverly Hills, the Yorkins were trying to work it out; Frances Lear was leaving Norman to establish a magazine in New York. Actor Tony Costello, who played the husband in *The Stronger*, died. It was AIDS, though we didn't know the word then. Nancy Chambers left Everett. Mary Beth, my best friend, had split from Peter Yarrow and moved to New York, and the Friedlanders, Len and Jen, were separated. The Friedlanders had adopted James, the little boy brought to us by Dr. Stephen Youngberg in Thailand. Lenny took a small apartment in Venice. James went with him.

Joey was repainting the rooms in the Green House for the rich young tenants who had a year to decide whether or not to buy it. I was an actor butterfly turning into a director moth, neither one nor the other, jobless. Joey was thirty-seven; I was forty-seven.

I had always been the prestigious, sought-after leading lady on TV. Now I was the lawyer, defending the leading lady, or accusing the leading man. Supporting actor.

The magic was gone.

I was almost broke.

Only the Green House stood between me and the poorhouse. Joey knew that. He knew numbers. He had been fighting for the wall around the Green House not for artistic reasons, but for its future sale. He'd understood that from the first minute he'd planted those twigs in the ground, the twigs I'd made fun of, the twigs that were now thirty-foot-tall eucalyptuses.

I was stubborn; he was more stubborn, to the point where I got it.

This was life-and-death. We had a future or we didn't. My instincts for saving myself kicked in. The water flooded in; I held on to the rock, and the rock was Joey. The next rock would be working as a director.

Harry Belafonte owned an apartment in a building on 74th Street and West End in Manhattan and was on the board. The apartments there were vast and comfortable. The Italian professors who leased it to us were going to Italy for a year to study goddesses and muses.

Harry and the board approved us. We had two months or so before we could move to New York, before our new apartment would be empty.

Joey slept in the second floor office while getting the Green House ready, and I asked Jenny Friedlander if I could share her apartment on the beach until Joey, Belinda, and I left for the East Coast. Dinah had a roommate in a small apartment on the Pacific Coast Highway. Belinda stayed with our friends Nanni, Harold, and their kids in Trancas Beach.

While the Green House was being prepared for the tenants, "the girl" went to her family in Wisconsin. But the cold in my belly stayed. I knew nothing would be the same. And the same malady that had struck all of our friends had struck Joey and me. We were in crisis.

It was an uncomfortable time. I was alone with Jenny, a young woman who was doing me a favor in letting me be her guest. We had one thing in common: We were both unhappy. Jenny and I had never been close, so we were awkward with each other.

In the middle of my stay with Jenny, my former stepson Mikey Manoff called. He was in L.A., could he visit?

Mikey had been sixteen or seventeen when Arnie died, still a boy. We'd been in Malibu about twelve years. So a young man knocked on

Jenny's door and entered the apartment. I flashed on the three-year-old Mikey I'd been mother to, then Mikey at fifteen, when I'd left him, and tried to wrap my head around the fact that this tallish stranger was ever my kid.

He stayed about two weeks in L.A., I don't know, with friends. He wanted to be a writer and showed me a screenplay he'd written about a mountaineer-slash-naturalist.

I was between lives.

Mikey needed a mom. His had died ten years before; he was on medication for depression and I don't know what else.

I could feel his need, his yearning, his desperation.

I couldn't recognize him.

Like Peter Pan's mother with her new baby, I couldn't open the window to Peter's tapping.

Mikey was a familiar stranger, a man who looked like him, but shaved and smelled like a man, not a little boy.

J oey left for our New York apartment, 300 West End Avenue on 74th Street.

The Vonzegizers who leased us the apartment went to Greece and Italy for a year to study "seated muses," not standing ones—very specific. Their apartment was huge, comfy, and scholarly. Five bedrooms, ours with a fireplace and a four-poster bed, with windows in the back so there was light. The living room windows faced West End, but it was dark because the apartment was on the fourth floor. The elevator emptied right out into the foyer. No door, no doorbells.

The apartment was perfect. Good things and terrible things were happening within it. Everyone was scratchy. Joey was on edge till the couple in the Green House would decide whether to buy, so we could buy an apartment with that money. Their decision might take a year. Nusski was tearing up mounds of toilet paper in the bathroom, bags of flour in the kitchen, every time we left the house. Belinda was sullen in her room, sneaking in snakes and frogs bought with her allowance, and refusing to do homework.

We had brought Trini to New York City as our housekeeper. Trini, from El Salvador, had been our housekeeper in the Green House in Malibu. She had five grown children she loved and missed, and they her. Trini was the only person Belinda trusted and would talk to. Trini didn't speak a word of English, but that had never mattered. She had a great soul that spoke to me, and Belinda, and she knew and understood everything and everyone.

I was going through the motions, but had a big, cold, empty hole in my stomach and heart. I was unloved. Unloved by daughter Dinah, who was awash with life and love and career in L.A., too busy living for me. Unloved and resented by Belinda, and most sharply, unloved by Joey, still besotted, still reveling at his role in rescuing "the girl."

"The girl" was still in Wisconsin, but calling, loving, a needy young friend. "When we go to work, we'll call you," I said, gritting my teeth.

The apartment came with a housekeeper. Big Erla, so named because her niece Little Erla would come and help her. (Little Erla has been with us for the last thirty years.) Big Erla would complain that Trini, our housekeeper from L.A., did nothing, that she had to do everything. This was true. We had a housekeeper for our housekeeper. Trini was in her late fifties, and we needed her moral support more than a clean bathtub.

This was a time when my father was finding legal avenues to force me to repay the $20,000 of my mother's loan. Incredibly uncomfortable telephone conversations with him in his new adult facility on the sands of Venice Beach: "Hello, dear, how are you?" "Good, Dad, what have you been up to?" No mention of the money ever.

I once saw a play on Broadway when I was a student. The set was a living room; a man and a woman were having a heated argument. Accidentally the actress hit a clay pot filled with earth and a green plant. It fell in the middle of the stage between them. They both ignored it, kept saying their lines. The whole audience was silently begging for the plant to be picked up. It was the best lesson I ever had on wrecking the fragile reality of acting onstage. All they had to do was pick up the damn pot. Use it.

That's what the money my mother gave me was like. A potted plant in the middle of my father's and my life. Ignored and growing into a tree.

Joey had supervised the packing of all our furniture, knickknacks, and paintings and had them put in storage in L.A. All our rentals in New York were completely furnished.

That year, 1981, I'd finished two movies and two TV shows. Then I left to check out the apartment with Joey, leaving Belinda at the Lazy J Ranch Camp, the camp that Dinah had attended most summers.

Belinda loved California; she loved Disneyland. She's like a fish in the ocean, and she loved the freedom of her life in Malibu. On the road outside the Green House there were many children on Zumeriz Drive, children of the pot growers and the old lady with the goat. The goat stood on the old lady's roof. Belinda had made friends for life with the children of *my* friends for life. She refused to leave. Malibu was home, and she was not a city girl. Belinda hated me for prying her once again from the familiar, the known, her home.

That first winter in New York, Belinda was very angry. She was to remain so, in a secret place inside her, for a long time.

My father had moved to a retirement center, an elegant white apartment complex right on the beach. His sister-in-law, Sylvia, the one my mother used to be afraid of, had an apartment there. She was very social. It was a good move for him.

I still had not recognized his right to be paid back for the loan my mother had given me and had specifically forgiven in her will. We left for New York with the subject unresolved.

My father hired a lawyer over the loan. The situation escalated. Caught between guilt and resentment, I couldn't breathe. I felt for him. He'd been an important and respected man in his worlds, first as director of the Bronx Y, then in East Rockaway, where he'd spent two decades on the town council. At the nursery school my mother was Miss Witia and he was Pop Abe. They were both loved and respected. Living with us he had felt rootless, resentful. He was still hurting from my mother's illness and death, and he was lonely, casting around for a position of importance in my life.

Years before, he had lost the fight with Arnie, had been rendered helpless. Now he circled Joey like a lion, repeatedly challenging him, but never winning. Now, from a distance, he could lean on me where it hurt, impose his will, and challenge Joey at the same time. It was animal instinct. I remember when Joey, flush with victory, sat down at our dining room table with Abe, laying his gift at Abe's feet. "I sold the house," he told him, at a huge price that would protect me for life. Abe said to Joey, "Motel management, that's what you should do. Start a little motel." He couldn't stop himself, and my mother wasn't there to reason with him. Indeed, by erasing the debt, she'd betrayed him. He wanted so badly to hold me hostage. To make me beholden to him again. To possess power again. I understood his raw need. But I knew he was comfortable financially. I knew it wasn't about money.

I was fighting him for my mother's right to do what she wanted to do, with her secret savings and her posthumous wiping out of the debt.

She had always sneaked around him to do what she wanted. She enjoyed hiding things from him, small things. When my father said, "Absolutely no cats," she and Fremo sneaked stray cats into the attic in the East Rockaway house. They were excited, giddy with nervous laughter. But he was used to being boss of the house, she accepted that, and it worked.

Our deal on the Green House was complicated. The wealthy young couple who wanted to buy it had a year to make a final decision, which put us in a kind of hold-your-breath position. We couldn't rent or sublet in New York indefinitely. At some point we felt we had to buy something, but only if and when the Green House sold.

A more gracious and mature daughter would have given in, would have just paid off the debt. But I felt my arm was being twisted. I was being tested: Good Daughter, Bad Daughter.

Mark, my father's cousin, called, very sober. "He has a smart lawyer," he said. "Abe can hold up the sale of your house."

My heart sank. We were living in New York, totally dependent on the sale of the Green House for our long-term security. I couldn't sleep. My heart was flip-flopping inside me. Dad was calling, chatting, with never a mention of the house or the loan. We both ignored the dead body in the middle of the room. He had the power now. I felt threatened and airless.

Finally I called Mark. He and my father were close, and he had influence. "Mark, please make him stop. It's making me sick. He scares me." I was becoming more and more frightened of him and his need for power over me, to be the dominant man in my life. We were frozen in a bad play, taking on the roles of father and daughter, totally displacing the real father and daughter we had been to each other all my life. *Maybe,* I thought, *maybe this anger is giving him purpose, a fresh reason to live, strength. Maybe he just needs it—like he needed to be on* 60 Minutes.

Mark called about a week later. "Okay," he said, "he won't go after the house." My father had given me the gift of my own house.

Dad. Daddy. Stalwart, sweet tobacco–smelling Daddy. Daddy of singing in the car, "For I adore, I adore you, Giannina mia." That dad was gone, lost to me. My father took his place.

I think my tunnel vision, my total unawareness of what a woman can or can't take on, was my ticket to doing everything. I'm a very ignorant person in many practical ways—in all practical ways. The only thing I understand about money is in order to get it I have to work; the money goes to wise people who make sure the rent, groceries, and children's school fees are paid. If not for Joey, who has produced every project with our company, I, who was deliberately raised to be the princess who couldn't sleep on the pea, who was so sensitive and protected, would be in a very painful place. I am totally dependent on the kindness of friends. If I were ever really aware of the total responsibility, if I were dollar-wise, reputation-wise, day-, week-, month-, editing-, and especially camera-wise, I would never have pushed so hard to do the work.

A Matter of Sex

I had an idea. Why couldn't *The Willmar 8*, the documentary, be turned into a movie for television? I took the doc and the concept to Joan Barnett and Karen Danaher-Dorr at NBC. They got behind it and they got behind me as the director. It would be my first solo directing job for a wide audience. I loved the idea of casting actors I knew in the parts of the real women I'd met in Minnesota. I loved the idea of bringing the issue to a huge public. Not lecturing about women's issues, but showing the reality of women's place in the banking industry. In those days, 1984, before cable, the three networks supplied everything to the country, so twenty million viewers for an evening's entertainment was average. (Three years later, when we made *Nobody's Child* with Marlo Thomas, we had forty million viewers.)

We were still living in the Green House when I pitched *The Willmar 8* as a TV movie. Joan and Karen gave us the money to go ahead with a script. By the time Joyce Eliason, who'd written the script for *Tell Me a Riddle*, began working on the script, we had moved to New York. The NBC women set up a meeting with their superior, a mild blond guy, very pleasant, who turned the idea down. Sorry, it was not a topic that would interest NBC viewers. I met with him. Again, pleasant; again, no.

I spoke to our NBC supporters. "The only way to get it on is to convince the head of NBC," Joan said.

"Who's that?"

"Grant Tinker."

"How do I reach him?" They gave me his telephone number.

I sat on the bed in New York reaching for the phone, hanging up, walking around the bedroom, breathing deeply. I sat down and dialed. It was Tinker's private number. He picked up. I don't know what I said, or implored, but the essence was, "I know I'm not going through channels and I'm imposing, but I believe this is a good script, and an important one. I'll accept whatever you'll say, but I just ask you to read it. I think it deserves that."

He said, "I'll look into it." He read the script and gave it a go. Thank you, Grant Tinker.

I didn't realize it, I'd moved so quickly, but I was moving on setting the pattern for my next career. The one that not only kept me afloat, but unafraid, fascinated, eager, dazzled, and happy.

I asked Fred Murphy, who shot *Tell Me a Riddle*, to be on camera, and I asked Everett Chambers, an old close friend and an experienced producer, to produce. Everett was a straight-arrow, by-the-book guy. His brother, Dick, had been Joey's first partner in the commercial business.

The cast was led by Jean Stapleton. My daughter Dinah Manoff played the twenty-year-old teller. Jean was a huge star at the time, playing the ditsy wife in Norman Lear's *All in the Family*. In real life, she was deeply aware of women's issues and wanted to be a part of this story.

We found a perfect town for Willmar in rural Canada—perfect

street, perfect real café across from the bank. Perfect cold weather. Except for the snow. It never snowed. We had to import the snow in trucks from the nearest mountain and pack our set with it.

Our first day I shot exteriors: the women walking in front of the bank with their placards, the town kids throwing snowballs trying to provoke them. I'd worked out a dolly shot with Fred Murphy when Everett came running up.

"That's not the way to shoot it!" he barked. I stood there, open-mouthed, while he explained how the shot should be done. "You don't know how to direct it!"

My crew and I were quiet as he walked away. I wondered if I still had a crew. This was the first day, the first shot, and we didn't even know one another. My old friend and mentor Everett, whom I expected to protect me, was going to be an adversary for the whole shoot.

Everett didn't like how I said "Action." As an actress, I never noticed how my directors said it. It depended on the intimacy of the scene or the space they had to yell "A-a-a-action"—or whisper it. It was second nature.

Everett coached me: "AK-shun!" Sharp, decisive, crisp, military, *achtung!*-like. I would say it after him five or six times until he said excitedly, "That's it!" Then I'd go on set and of course do it my way. Same with cut. "Cut!" he'd demonstrate sharply. "Cut, cut!" I regarded him in bafflement. Such strange behavior from a real person. Bewildering.

Toward the end, Everett called NBC and had executives come down and watch me shoot for two days, with a warning from him that I was incompetent. The executive said to me, "You're doing a good job. We were really worried getting Everett's reports about you, that you were a loose cannon." After that, I was a loose cannon for one night. I wanted an extra scene of celebration at the bank. Everett forbade it. All of us, cast and crew, stayed late and filmed it, without his knowledge. It felt great.

Fred Murphy and the crew were brothers to me. They formed a shield, and from that first day on we bonded. After shooting *Willmar 8*, Everett and I became strangers.

NBC changed the title *Willmar 8* to *A Matter of Sex*, a title that might draw or confuse an audience. The finished film was a disappointment to me. It resembled the doc but had little of its charisma and power. I take responsibility for that. And I don't know if it had any great effect. The documentary three years earlier had changed the face of the banking industry. This was *Willmar 8* lite.

From then on we sold scripts based on our documentaries to the networks and made an impact with some remarkable content, to huge audiences. It would be the pattern and the key to my directing movies for television for the next two projects.

Directing Theater
for Joe Papp

I'd returned to Joe Papp, to the Public Theater, at the height of Joe's power and influence. I put my head inside the door, and Joe came to me with open arms like the force of nature he was. "I forgive you, I forgive you," he laughed with his gorgeous face. I was home.

I'd brought him a brilliant anti-Soviet play with a huge cast. Instead, he suggested putting together the short plays of Václav Havel. I'd never heard of him. This was 1983. Havel was a Czech writer. The Communist Czech government cracked down on free speech. Havel, a brilliant satirist, kept writing short plays that infuriated the government. He'd been jailed for about three years when Joe suggested we choose several of his short plays and put them together under one title. I don't know who suggested *A Private View*, but that's what we called it.

Havel's friends and wife had managed to spirit his plays from his cell to living rooms all over the country, where actors performed them for anti-Soviet rebellious Czechs.

It was a great time for me, a great choice from Joe. The plays and the cast were brilliant and caustic; Richard Jordan received an Obie for a star turn in the last play.

I met Havel years later, after the Soviets were thrown out, before he was elected first president of the Czech Republic. Joe Papp set up a meeting in the sacristy of St. John the Divine. I genuflected. He shook my hand. So many heroes in our lives.

And finally, thirty years later, thanks to Joe, I worked on a play expressing my own private views about a regime that imprisoned and killed artists.

When Women Kill

Good things began to happen. An agent had shown both *The Stronger* and *The Willmar 8* to Sheila Nevins at HBO. She headed their documentary department and still does, a quixotic woman, high-strung, dark-haired, attractive. We talked, Joey joked, seduced, opened Sheila's desk drawer. When he found two tampons and stuck them in his ears with the strings hanging down, she was amused, and we got the job. The *Willmar 8* documentary was a great calling card. She gave us a brilliant assignment almost immediately: to go to a prison to find out about women who commit murder. We had our first documentary as a production company in New York.

Ronnie Eldridge was a New York City councilwoman who knew the prison system inside out. (She was also married to Jimmy Breslin, one of my idols—for his brilliant writing, his passion, and for being a bad boy.) Ronnie brought in Prue Glass, a high-ranking social worker who had ties to the prison system. We decided to film at Bedford Hills Correctional Facility for Women in Westchester County, about an hour's drive from the city.

In 1975, my film *The Stronger* and Barbara Kopple's *Harlan County, USA* had been screened alongside each other at the Los Angeles Film Festival, with the two of us seated side by side in the audience. *Harlan County* was a revelation to me. I'd never seen anything like it before. I hadn't known a thing about documentary filmmaking, and it changed my life. It had inspired me to do *The Willmar 8*.

Now her husband, Hart Perry, was set to do camera on our women's prison doc. He told me that Barbara wanted to do the sound. Shocked, I said no, of course not. How could a great filmmaker like Barbara work sound for me, a beginner? I wasn't at her level. Barbara called. "Lee, I do sound. I'm a sound person. This is what I do between making my own films. I'm not going to judge you—really."

So Barbara came on board. Half of the time she carried her six-month-old son, Nicholas, in a carrier and placed him safely out of the way in whatever cell we were shooting in. I never heard a sound out of him. A true soundwoman's baby.

W e became the prisoners' adopted family. The women inmates gathered on the tiers yelling greetings as we made our way across their baseball field from the examining and X-ray house where we were inspected by the police guard each morning. I kept some cocaine in my sneaker, just in case I crashed late in the day. Joey, of course, had it stashed every place he could. We all met in the assistant warden's office. Joey was so nervous about getting caught and sent to prison himself that when the warden entered the office, a huge imposing man, Joey jumped up, held his hand out to shake the warden's, and said, "Hi, I'm Hart Perry." At which point Hart got up and didn't know what to say. Joey said, "I mean *he's* Hart Perry." And Hart said, "And he's Joe Feury!" We all jumped up then, with a jumble of introductions, till the warden, a really nice, smart guy, held up his hands and backed off.

The women on the tier would yell, "Hi, Joey!" They loved him.

One lesbian prisoner would yell, "Hi, Prue! Hey, Prue, c'mon up here!" Prue would duck her head. We were a warm and welcome diversion for these women prisoners.

Violet was Native American. She had two daughters and a little granddaughter. She'd lived upstate, a hardscrabble life, a lot of hard drinking. She was also simpatico, warm, open, tears streaming over her round cheeks as she described, "He came in with a rifle, pushed me out of bed with it. I was begging, running around the room, grabbed the end of the rifle, turned it around, and it went off." Here she broke down completely, sobbing. She loved the fucker.

Did I believe her? Completely. Did she belong in prison? Heartbroken, overweight, and sick?

Her two daughters and four-year-old granddaughter came to visit.

Bedford provided a nice trailer, a little playground for overnight family visits (I guess not conjugal, because most of the husbands were dead). One of Violet's daughters was working to be a lawyer; the other was in a violent relationship with her husband. Violet's pretty granddaughter was on the swing when I asked her what she would do if a man hit her. "Kill 'im," she answered matter-of-factly, in her light, sweet voice.

I'd had an intuition that it was the weak, trapped women who killed to get away from their men. Not the strong women, who could just walk out and slam the door behind them.

My sense of my own "entitlement" was sharply defined by being shut up with the women I filmed, whose stories, one after the other, were so despairing and brutal, filled with so many regrets and losses.

Prue Glass left her job as a social worker and joined our company, Feury/Grant Entertainment (note the billing), for the next twenty years, as did Mary Beth, as did Virginia Cotts, whose cool head has saved my hot one on many an airplane, as did Roberta Morris, who is still working with me transcribing these ink-stained pages onto the computer. All producers with Feury/Grant Entertainment. This new group of friends was a magnet, and I was a magnet for them. Intrepid warriors, swords high, for the many revelations and explorations from one end of the human spectrum to the other. It all started at Bedford Hills.

I was up on my documentary roller skates, downhill racing as I had on 148th Street. This was thrilling, deep inside another world that had opened up for me, to me.

Then "the girl" came to New York. Mary Beth generously offered the couch in her temporary apartment, which was also on the West Side, a few blocks away.

Joey began visiting them first thing in the morning for her fresh-brewed cappuccino, and her neediness, and for the way she laughed at everything he said. She became pink when she laughed, and sometimes even teary. As an actor, she was a great reactor. Who could resist cappuccino and pink cheeks every morning?

Not Joey.

What Sex Am I?

One night I went to the theater and saw *La Cage aux Folles*, a great theatrical success, an extravaganza about gays and cross-dressers and their heightened life. It was funny, poignant, perfect.

I made an appointment with HBO and sold them on doing our next doc on cross-dressers and transvestites, *What Sex Am I?* Without knowing it, I had once more opened the door on an underworld of outsiders and survivors—brave, smart people who'd undergone intense bullying and nonacceptance. The cross-dressers who came out did it with style, but at the bottom, plenty of terrible heartache and confusion. In those days, these people were in the closet for good reason—they might be killed in their hometowns if they came out.

Like Alice, I'd entered Wonderland, and it became curiouser and curiouser.

I knew I was in deep when I was chatting on film with a group of cross-dressing prostitutes in a bar in San Francisco, and one tall, gorgeous, black hooker said to me, "You know, Lee, just because I have a dick doesn't make me any less of a woman!" and I nodded in agreement. "I know," I said, and I meant it.

The middle-class cross-dressers who had adjusted the best, and were most content, were the married younger guys who'd come out to their wives and found acceptance. They were straight men who looked like regular guys. They didn't want to be women, but they found sexual gratification and comfort from dressing, for the most part, in styles from the 1950s. These were big vintage shoppers, the happiest of them husbands who shopped with their wives, members of a closed club where the couples could relax and show off. They were not pretty women: They stuffed themselves into the sleeveless dresses, the pumps, the little hats with veils that were just like what Mama wore. And they gossiped like their mamas did when their mamas played bridge.

Those were the happy, well-adjusted cross-dressers.

The more deeply I explored, the deeper the problems and the pain I discovered, and for many of the beautiful young men, the ends of their lives—through botched operations and medical procedures and AIDS.

One happier story: Two women, a young lesbian couple, working-class, classic New Jersey. He-girl worked in a boiler factory, she-girl a down-to-earth, stocky blonde. Her father whispered to me how he wished they were "normal." The he-girl had his big breasts removed, took male hormones, grew facial hair, and yes, his clitoris was lengthened.

I shot the couple in their backyard having a barbecue with all the guys from the boiler factory. The wife was serving food and drinks. Her mate was joking around the grill with the guys; a real guy.

Her father sneaked up to me, smiling his imp smile. "Normal at last!" he hissed into the camera. "Normal at last!"

. . .

W hat *Sex Am I?* was a knockout. Maybe our best documentary, in terms of depth, revelation about that particular world, one that's just surfacing now as an acceptable lifestyle.

In 1985 I was invited to participate on the jury of the Taormina Film Festival, and *What Sex Am I?* was honored with a showing. The invitation to the Taormina Film Festival opened another uncomfortable door. My passport had expired.

I would have to face "Date of Birth" again.

On my passport was a date of birth that was a lie. I remembered adding a few years to my age on the passport so Arnie would think I was older. Be more comfortable about the sixteen years separating us.

Now I was stuck with it.

Mary Beth, Milton Justice, and I went down to the passport office from our editing rooms on 42nd Street. I was editing *Down and Out in America* with our editor, Milton Ginsberg. *Down and Out in America* was a seminal documentary for me, Joey, and our company; it went on to win the Best Documentary Oscar the next year in 1986.

Never mind—the old "Date of Birth" panic had moved in. Prue Glass researched the situation and provided me with a replica of a lost birth certificate under "Lyova Rosenthal." I had my old driver's license from California under "Lee Grant," a new one from Delaware under "Lee Fioretti," and my "Lee Manoff" passport. Prue contacted a woman at the passport bureau so that I wouldn't have to wait in line for hours. Special treatment. I even had an appointment at three p.m.

We'd worked editing till two p.m., munching popcorn out of a big green plastic garbage bag, all of us, and brought the bag with us on the cab ride downtown to the passport bureau. My intention, of course, was to change the date of birth on the new passport to the five-years-younger one on my driver's licenses from California under Lee Grant and the recent one under Fioretti.

Three of us sat in attached chairs as we waited for the woman behind the counter, who was railing at four cowed Polish men. Beads of sweat rose on my upper lip. They left. Her name was on a plastic holder on the counter.

I took a deep breath.

"Hi, Angela," I said to this strong Hispanic woman, holding out my hand. "Could I talk to you in your office?"

"Why talk in my office?" She frowned.

"Well," I laughed, "it's a delicate matter." I whispered, "I want to change the age on my passport."

"What do you mean, change your birth date?" she boomed.

Heads turned. Milton and Mary Beth filled their mouths with popcorn, hunched in their seats.

"Could we move to this corner? It's a private matter." She moved down the counter toward me, alert, careful.

"Well, you know I lied on my passport, this passport has me older than I am, you see Manoff, I'm not Manoff anymore, my husband, then, was older, so I added a couple of years to my age to make him feel more comfortable, and now I'm not a Manoff anymore."

I was waving the California driver's license Mayor Yorty had given me. We were both tense, wary.

Suddenly I burst out: "I'm an actress, goddammit, I've lied about my age my entire life. Why can't you just do this for me?" The words hung in the air between us. Between me and the rest of the room. Milton and Mary Beth didn't look up from the popcorn bag.

I saw the door slamming shut in the woman's eyes, along with a glint of understanding.

"I can't help you," she said, and handed me back my passport. But she said it quietly.

I took the passport and went through the bubbly glass door, Mary Beth and Milton shuffling behind me. I rang the elevator bell and waited interminably for the old green elevator to come to our floor. We didn't speak. I received a new passport with my old age in time to go to Taormina.

Lina Wertmüller was a member of the jury at the Taormina Film Festival in Italy. *What Sex Am I?* had been invited not as a contestant, but as a film of interest, and I was asked to serve on the jury. To me she was a genius filmmaker, she was the first woman to be nominated as a director for the Academy Award, for her film *Seven Beauties* in 1976. She had a socio-comic view of Italian life, fresh and hilarious.

Taormina is a resort town, and our hotel was on a huge sandy beach, highly organized, long, long rows of beach beds tended by young men with towels, and changing tents. Formal. Not like Malibu. The jury meetings were interesting, but strained for me. I was the only member who spoke nothing but English. Also documentaries, in that period, were not rated as highly as they are now.

Lina saw it, though. Lina got it. Before seeing it, she rattled off in Italian in the jury room, effusive to those she knew, strong in her views, dismissive of those she didn't know. I was happy just to watch her and listen to her great, raspy voice. After she went to a screening of *What Sex Am I?* she turned to me. She said good things; I was watching her face, so alive, gleaming. "I want to make a movie about the first couple. You could play the wife," just like that. I was honored, overwhelmed. Then, *Wait a minute*, I thought, back in my hotel room. *What a great movie that would make, but it's absolutely an American story. I should do it!* Should've, would've, didn't.

In town we ran into Roger and Julie Corman and their brood, one still in a baby stroller. We had lemon ices. Roger and Julie are travelers. Wherever one is, they both are, with kids, doing film business. We've been warm friends forever. Roger directed Joey in his first speaking part in *The St. Valentine's Day Massacre*. The cute guy on the motorcycle who tips off the bad guys on the phone in the gas station? That's Joey.

After Taormina we went to Rome. There "the girl" surprised us. She came to hang out. She'd missed us. She did miss us. She meant it. My heart sank. Joey came to life.

We took a trip to the countryside. They jabbered away, walking together on the narrow streets, with me behind.

I looked at a small whitewashed building made of rocks. In the window was a black cat with a white neck, her paws curled in to her. She looked at me with curiosity. But distant. The way I felt. Distant.

When we returned to Rome, "the girl" wore a transparent embroidered cotton dress. We walked down the street. "The girl" towered over me and was almost but not quite unaware of the effect she had on the men walking by, and the traffic. Her half-unawareness plus her awareness of the effect she was having on men in general, and my man in particular, disarmed and defeated me. Cars honked, Italian men called out to her and whistled.

"How rude," she said.

"Maybe if you weren't naked, they wouldn't be so rude!" I snapped sharply, looking up at her. For the first time I disliked her. We flew home.

There was a curtained compartment on that flight in first class. As I stood in the aisle, I looked through a split in the curtain. A beautiful Italian woman was sitting on a cot-like bed with her eleven-year-old son, also beautiful. She was holding a spoon toward his mouth, a bowl in her hand, murmuring endearments, urging her big boy to eat from her spoon. His pink lips open, her red lips blowing on the spoon to cool the soup before bringing her hand toward his waiting face. Erotic. The image held the same sort of distance for me as the situation with "the girl" and Joey. Separate. Behind a curtain. Me looking in at them. Outside.

Down and Out
in America

T he exploration closest to my head and heart was *Down and Out in America*, which I'd been begging HBO president Michael Fuchs to do for two years. It was my personal comment on the Reagan years.

About Ronald Reagan, all-American Marlboro Man. To me he was all that—a Marlboro smoke screen, the voice of General Electric, his job on television. Like the Wizard of Oz with power, his handsome tan face with the manly, crooked smile, an advertisement for a "just like you" kind of guy.

He was also president of the Screen Actors Guild during the blacklist and quietly did his job of keeping actors' protests unheard at the Guild meetings all the years he presided.

To me Reagan was the scariest kind of opponent, a smooth actor-salesman appeal fronting a ruthless anti-left, anti-union agenda.

Later, after he went from GE TV spokesman to Guild president to California governor to president of the United States, it was the first time I saw real people like me, not just drunks on the Bowery, become homeless. In the eighties. In America. Soon after, his presidency broke the Air Traffic Controllers Union.

By this time I was making documentaries for a living, and everything in me finally felt free and unpressured. I was free to put my thinking, my feeling, my gut, into an art form that allowed me to yell about whatever cause or person I cared about, by examining the true lives, the true plight of people I felt privileged to bring to the screen.

I'm too shy and too afraid of rejection to sell and organize. But Joey filled all those roles as producer—Joey, who's not intimidated by anything, who will pick up a phone, demand a meeting, be crazy, flirt, shock, and is also financially savvy. Because he knocked the doors down at HBO and, later, at Lifetime, it became possible for me to have a long healthy life in the documentary business.

While waiting for permits and backing to do *Down and Out in America*, I went off to Yugoslavia to do *Mussolini: The Untold Story*, a big TV miniseries about the life and death of Benito Mussolini, played by George C. Scott. I was Mrs. Mussolini. My children were Robert Downey Jr., Mary Elizabeth Mastrantonio, Raul Julia, and Gabriel Byrne. George C. Scott's mistress was played by Virginia Madsen. Sarah Jessica Parker was Robert's girlfriend back then, and we were all let loose in Zagreb.

The men in Yugoslavia are the handsomest and most reckless anywhere. Fridays after the last shot, cast and crew danced till dawn; some romanced till dawn. Joey came. He and Raul Julia led us in feasting on oysters and fine wine. We actors thrown together in Zagreb felt this experience was a gift. We had no instinct that we were dancing on the edge of a war that would tear the country to pieces six years later.

I had an emergency call from Joey. HBO was being wooed by another company wanting to do a documentary that was essentially my idea for *Down and Out*. I said, "Oh, give it to them. It has to be done. It's more important that it gets done than for me to do it." "Are you crazy?" he yelled. "You've pitched this for two years and you're gonna let somebody else steal it?" He set the whole thing up with HBO, which turned down our competitor. I would get to explore America—the real America.

D*own and Out in America* was filmed all across the country. In New York, where we brought a hidden camera into a welfare hotel and filmed distressed families newly out of work and down on their luck, and also in the tunnels under Grand Central Terminal, where single men and some women had formed a small city under the railroad to keep warm and survive.

In the Midwest, we filmed the desperation and tears of out-of-work middle-aged factory workers, confused as kindergarten children at suddenly being unwanted. Generations of families who loved their jobs, loved their bosses, their companies. Nothing in their local histories prepared them for being fired forever. They were still loyal, but had nothing more to be loyal to.

We filmed a factory truck driver, sitting high in the driver's seat, trying to figure out how to feed his family and start schooling himself for new upscale jobs in the outside world, which was where his former employer told him to look for work.

We filmed Minnesota farmers, all of whom had voted for Reagan. Two hundred and fifty heartland farms a week were being repossessed during this time. The farmers had been forced into bankruptcy, thanks to a combination of huge corporate farms squeezing them out and their own small banks cooking the books and putting them out of business. The small towns around the farms were like stage sets, full of empty barbershops, groceries, diners. Deserted.

Our last location was filming at a tent city in downtown L.A., "Justiceville." Almost a hundred desperate people, young and old, took over a street, formed a co-op, chose a mayor, and used that block as a base from which to live and try to find work. We were there when the city bulldozed it. In his own charming way, President Reagan had dismantled the country.

It was the most important time in my life, what I felt the sum of all my own experience had led me to. It would win HBO its first Academy Award. And us our first as documentary filmmakers, in 1986, ten years after my first Oscar as an actor.

Directors Accept Me

Mary Beth and I had gone to a Gloria Steinem luncheon where one of the speakers was Marie Balter, a schizophrenic woman who had been raised in a dark Dickensian home in Boston and spent most of her life in mental institutions. She met a fellow patient, fell in love, and battled her demons to get well and to marry him. It became our biggest hit, a TV movie called *Nobody's Child*.

Who was the cinematographer? Only Sven Nykvist, Ingmar Bergman's longtime collaborator. Sven and me, Sven and little Lyova Haskell Rosenthal. Sven made my heart melt. We flew hand in hand like a Chagall painting, my feet off the ground, lovers in heart, art, and soul. Sven told me Bergman had seen *Tell Me a Riddle* and really liked it. My mouth falls open as I write it. Bergman. Of course I tried to copy him in *Riddle*; he must have recognized that.

I was watching a very good play on television. The actress in it was doing very beautiful interior work as a shy, retiring woman. She looked familiar and I waited for the credits. It was an unrecognizable Marlo Thomas.

I called a friend, who gave me her number. I said, "I will never underestimate anyone's talent again," and offered her the part of Marie

Balter. She was superb. She went to Boston to spend time with Marie. She went to the mental institution. With Sandra Seacat, her acting coach, Marlo worked on Marie for months, plunging into the schizophrenic experience. The sound, the movement, the walk. On the morning that Marie is allowed to go out the front doors of this Gothic mental hospital, where we were filming, it started to softly snow. A miracle. Marlo opened the big doors into a wonderland of beautiful whiteness. She put her hands out to receive this blessing on her face, her hair, her mouth. Her joy. And Sven Nykvist, the great Bergman's cinematographer, was there to preserve the moment.

Marlo won the Emmy; I won the Directors Guild Award for TV Director. Directors voted for me! I was a fellow director. I'd earned their respect.

I was directing *Nobody's Child* when my Aunt Fremo was dying. I was in Vancouver; she was in New York. I could have made it. The truth was I didn't want to see Fremo die. I *couldn't* see Fremo die. I didn't want her pain to be my last image of her, to carry always in my head and heart. I didn't fly back for her funeral, either. I didn't want to see her in a coffin. She was buried in the clothes I suggested she would like, her long leopard-print silk pajamas. With a final slash of red lipstick on her lips.

Battered

This is the documentary that changed me and my marriage. There are men who need to control their wives or girlfriends as personal possessions, limiting who they can see and where they can go and how they behave. The threat of punishment, physical and otherwise, is ever present. Sometimes the episode ends with passionate lovemaking and passionate regret, sometimes even tears from the boyfriend or husband—"Sorry, sorry."

A part of me felt very close to these women.

I wondered about my relationship with Arnie. How controllable I was with him. How he'd tried to charm me back when I'd left, and his hatred and rage when I didn't give in to him once again.

But the women we interviewed in halfway houses, running from their lovers, were running for their lives. They were there with their children, unable to contact parents and friends, and living in terror. Other women, because of children or money or sometimes even age, couldn't escape. And how many women have you heard about on the evening news who have been murdered by their husbands as soon as they got an order of protection? The women in the groups we met all knew better than to risk their lives and the lives of their children with an order of protection.

In men's groups, I met some fascinating men, the abusers mostly middle-class men with histories of domestic violence. One, a charismatic, handsome kid, said, "I can spot the woman I can control the minute she steps into the room. Out of hundreds, I can find her."

"Why do you do it? You're so handsome, charming; you could have anyone."

"I don't know," he said. "Because I can."

We were shooting in the Midwest, and "the girl" was working on the film.

I was facing too many truths spoken by women, courageous enough to divulge the hidden torments of their lives with their husbands or boyfriends. Real. Terrible. Protecting the men who were abusing them, years of it. Living with fear and danger. Children growing up with their mothers unable to protect themselves. I realized I'd been permitting this bizarre flirtation between Joey and "the girl" to ruin my sense of myself as a woman. How dare I do that to myself, after all I'd fought through? To turn into a victim myself.

If my relationship with Joey was over, it was over. I'd live. But I would not demean myself by accepting this romance, this flirtation, allowing it to permeate my life and diminish me! I'd never cared if Joey had a girl, I knew it was a one-night or even a one-week stand, but this indulgence, this tease was intolerable. It was over.

I was as bad, as cowardly as the women who wouldn't leave if they could, to tolerate the two people I was closest to wallowing in romanticizing their friendship, each getting out of it what they needed— in her case attention and attraction, in Joey's worship—and fooling themselves into a holy duo by not touching or kissing. A turn-on if ever there was one.

And what was I? A civilized victim. *Battered* lite. Making this film about women who couldn't fight for themselves taught me a lesson. I was so angry with myself. So clear for the first time in more than three years.

We were in Minnesota then. After the work was finished that night, I asked "the girl" to go to the diner with me. I sat across from her in the dark booth. "I want you to stop flirting with Joey," I said.

She looked at me, then down.

"You're wrecking my marriage. Stop it."

The tears started down her cheeks. I watched her cry. "Stop it," I said again, clear, cold. She nodded.

Joey got his cappuccino, but no pink laughs, no wet eyes, no glistening eyes, no appreciative nods, no gales of sighs, approvals, no charm, tickles, sighs, loving concern. Gone.

We rented a house in Westhampton that summer. Joey hated it. We had visitors, but not "the girl." She stayed away. Milton Justice and I played tennis, often. Grim. Joey stared out at the potato fields, at our lawn, at the stream, under a tree. He burrowed down in my lap. "Why?" he cried. "Why can't I have it all?" He was crying.

Joey nearly went crazy that summer. The romance went out of his life. She stopped seducing, the light went out of her eyes, and the light went out in his eyes. "Ahhh-ohhh," he'd cry in my lap in Westhampton.

"Yes, yes." I'd pat his back, bitter at being his comforter. Not really sure if we could make it. Not sure I wanted to. Stunned that I'd lived with it so long. By fall, without the reciprocal flirtation, the air suddenly went out of the balloon and it fell to the ground, limp and airless.

Now in New York City, under stormier skies, we were in the middle of our newest life together.

The Trio

We'd moved from the Harry Belafonte building to the Beresford, a building that faced Central Park on the east, the Museum of Natural History on the south. Another rental till we had the money to buy an apartment and found the one we wanted to buy.

We gave our first big New Year's Eve party in that apartment. The only apartment we ever had whose windows were on the park. So when midnight struck, the fireworks went off in the park and lit up the windows of the living room. We all stood there, our mouths open like children, going, "Ahhhhh, ohhhhh."

Belinda was enrolled in Rodeph Sholom Day School; she could walk to school from the apartment, a little Thai girl singing Hebrew songs in chorus.

One spring night, Joey and I had one of our huge, loud, yelling fights. I slammed the bedroom door on him and went to bed, furious. As I lay there fuming in my white nightgown, eyeshades, and earplugs, it seemed I could hear music through the earplugs. I took them out. It sounded like it came from my living room. I pushed up the eyeshades and opened the door. Loud music, louder still as I walked barefoot down the hall.

There, in the foyer, were three young people: two boys and a girl, a trio. Cello, violin, and clarinet playing Bach, transported from where?

Joey was smiling, watching me watching them.

"Where are you from?" I asked. "Heaven?"

"Juilliard," one said. "We were playing on the street, and he hired us."

"They're a present," Joey said.

Three young strangers, pouring out their hearts, Bach's genius, in my very own foyer.

See, that's why I'm in love with him.

P.S. The thing with "the girl" was over. He was in love with me again.

Months later, in the city once again, I asked "the girl" to come over. Joey was lying down in the bedroom.

When he saw her, he became angry. He didn't want her anymore.

"She's my friend," I told him.

"No!" he said. "She is my friend. That's the way it is."

And so "the girl" has stayed in our lives, and she's our friend now for life.

Staying Together

We found the script for *Staying Together*, written by Monte Merrick, and went to John Daly, a formidable, good-looking Brit who was making big inroads in Hollywood producing independent films. Suddenly he showed up in New York, we had lunch, and the movie was a go—just like that. We cast Sean Astin, Dermot Mulroney, and Tim Quill as the boys. Melinda Dillon played their mom; Jim Haynie was Dad. Levon Helm was in it, and Stockard Channing. Daphne Zuniga played Dermot's love interest. My very own Dinah, as Sean's first sexual encounter, was a waitress in the family's fried chicken restaurant in their small town, in our case Ridgeway, South Carolina. It was a happy set, a happy movie. Happy Joey, happy Lee, happy, cute, sweet adorable actors.

Catherine Keener was Dermot's girlfriend then, hanging around the set in a short skirt, leather jacket, and beautiful long legs. Catherine became a fascinating actress and a leading lady of independent films.

Levon, Melinda's love interest, was and is a music icon. Dermot is a cellist. Music filled our days and nights.

On the last day of shooting, Joey led the mayor of Ridgeway and the businessmen of the community on a drunken golf foray, supplying each golf cart with a beautiful girl serving piña coladas. Joey was a favorite of the Good Old Boys.

John Daly was a generous and easy man to work for. I handed over a cut of the film to him after we worked on it for months in New York. He changed nothing. We were relieved and grateful. The Academy was giving us a big screening, so we hopped to California and stayed with Brenda Vaccaro and her new husband, Guy Hector.

The day of the screening, I put a tape of the film on just to check it. Our musical score had been removed, replaced by a tinny carousel tune, repeating and repeating itself throughout the movie. I burst into tears. My beautiful movie was wrecked. It was shocking. Every film needs the right music to sustain it, particularly a romantic comedy. And the talented composer who wrote our score, Miles Goodman, had written especially charming music, loving and moving.

I phoned John Daly. He was adamant. He loved his carousel sound. I was literally on my knees begging. I'd do anything he wanted if just for tonight, for the industry screening about to take place in a couple of hours, we could restore the music written for the film.

There was a silence. Tears were streaming down my face. "I'll put it back if you bring me five thousand dollars before five this afternoon."

"Five thousand before five?"

I called our business manager, Hersh Panitch. "This is life-and-death," I told him. "Can you deliver the cash to him?"

"It's done!" Hersh said.

I called John. "The five thousand is on its way. Please, John, promise me we'll have our music in it for tonight!"

"I'll see," he said.

So Joey and I went to the Academy screening not knowing what we'd find when the lights went down.

It was our music, thank God. John was given accolades for producing such a charming piece. We smiled and nodded at each other. "I couldn't have done it without John," I said.

"I couldn't have done it without Lee," he said.

But the *Los Angeles Times* review was lukewarm, and John had completely run out of money. With nothing left in the till to promote or distribute our lovely film, the whole charming experience folded in on itself like a big wilting parachute.

No Place Like Home

There is another Christmas, Virginia: We turned our Academy Award–winning documentary *Down and Out in America* into a movie for television. Playing the young couple with children living in a welfare hotel were Jeff Daniels and Christine Lahti. Kathy Bates played the sister-in-law they move in with.

Tony Pierce-Roberts, who shot *A Room with a View* and other Merchant Ivory films, was our cinematographer. He wanted to get away from shooting period films, and when he read this gritty story he figured he could give us a month of his life.

We shot *No Place Like Home* in Pittsburgh. At the time their steel mills had shut down. There were huge mile-long abandoned factories. There were lines of men in suits with briefcases lined up for jobs like fixing cigarette machines. There were broken brick buildings where the walls were down and you could see the blue paint of what had been a bedroom wall, a yellow-painted square of kitchen, with curtains blowing out of a windowless window. It was a perfect environment for *Down and Out in America* and *No Place Like Home*.

Joey produced, I directed. We rented a nice brownstone and took our new poodle, Dude, who came after Nusski. Mary Beth was with us in production. I still love it. Most of it.

I feel the conversion from doc to movie was at its most successful here. The actors were marvelous; Christine won the Golden Globe. Christine and Jeff let the whole out-of-work phenomenon in Pittsburgh seep in. They sank into their parts and into the reality of suddenly losing your job—Jeff fighting with his brother while staying with the brother's family and having no place else to go but a shelter, and then a welfare hotel. True story, folks, and happening today, right outside our windows.

Defending Your Life

D*efending Your Life* was the last good movie I acted in. Albert Brooks wrote it, and starred in it, and directed it, and handled all of us on set like a pro. And Rip Torn, Meryl Streep, and I were not an easy package.

Albert had been interestingly neurotic about showing me the script in the beginning. He had us meet first in the public park across from the Beverly Hills Hotel. He introduced himself and walked me through the small green park for about half an hour. Telling me the story.

He was very intense, very quiet; he'd stop and look at me every once in a while to see if I got it. We walked to his car. He opened the trunk to give me the script. "When are you flying back?" he asked. (I'd been living in New York for almost ten years at that point.)

"Tomorrow."

He thought a minute, then slammed the trunk full of scripts shut. "No, I can't take a chance. Tell you what—I'll mail the script to you express. You read it and mail it back to me the same day."

Me: "Okay."

"You promise? You'll mail it right back? You won't show it to anyone?"

Me: "Promise." After I flew home there were several more calls of caution before the script arrived.

I could do it. I should do it, just to be on set with Meryl, whom I idolized. The problem was almost all my dialogue was courtroom speeches. Long, long pages of just me, talking on and on about Albert's past life on earth and how he blew it.

I get dizzy now as I write this. I was dizzy with fear when I read it that I'd forget my lines. I have to take a deep breath writing about it, the panic is so palpable. The part was simple. Before—before the Neil Simon play, when I went up on my lines, when I was still a free actor—I would have jumped into the water, happy and free. Now I had to hide my self-doubt and fear and this fucking, ever-present tension.

I said yes, of course. Since I was basically in one place at my table in the courtroom, I could write out my lines in my law book and refer to them within the action. That relieved me. It made me more confident, I think that showed, and when I went in for the camera test, the DP, bored at the process, looked at me through the lens and got really interested. He liked what he saw in the camera. I could feel it, and that made me feel more secure.

Well, this cameraman saw something just slightly fuckable in his lens, and I could take a deep breath and relax.

And Meryl Streep. Meryl was "the pretty girl actress." Usually "the pretty girl actress" in most comedy scripts written for the leading man has to be a little ditsy, young, pretty, have a great body, and either worship the leading man or play hard to get, giving him an objective, to try anything to get her to love him through the whole movie.

No, Meryl was brave casting. Her giant talent had to be diverted into a small piece of herself for this comedy.

Still, halfway through filming, Meryl burst into my trailer and leaned back against the door. "They want me sweeter!" she said in a hoarse whisper, and gritting her teeth, she ran back out. She, Meryl, was playing "the pretty girl actress."

Women on Trial

Joey thinks it was around 1991 that we made our last assigned documentary for HBO. Sheila Nevins had given us the assignment on divorce. We called it *Love to Hate*. We headed to Houston, where we stumbled into Family Court to explore bias against women. The film became *Women on Trial*.

Houston, Texas, was where we found America's worst domestic court system. Virginia Cotts was with me in Houston. I needed a strong partner for what we were uncovering there. I filmed four cases of women who'd had their children taken away from them and given to the fathers, in one case a father who hadn't even asked for custody. In another case, a judge removed a five-year-old boy from his school-teacher mother's custody, would not permit her to see him for three years, and then for only a half-hour visit in the offices of a court-appointed psychologist. By the time the child was eight, his habits and manners reflected those of his rather violent cop father.

I interviewed two teenagers, brother and sister, who were given in custody, when they were small, to a father who hadn't asked for custody. The judge ruled no visitation, no contact, between the mother and her son and daughter. The mother erected a large billboard on the side of the road that her children passed on their way to school, telling them she, their grandma, and their grandpa loved them. The boy wrote to the judge many times, begging him to return him and his sister to his mother.

I interviewed this judge. He was pleasant, open, cooperative.

Me: "Why did you give custody to the father?"

Judge: "Any layperson could see she had mental problems."

Me: "How?"

Judge: "She had severe mental problems."

Me: "What about her son? He wrote you many letters asking you to return him and his sister to his mom."

Judge: "Ah—he should be put in a mental institution."

The power of life and death, which I think is what is involved in removing a child from its parent/mother, was in the hands of this judge.

I was appalled at the real lives of the women and children, whose lives were in free fall. There were villains; there were heroes. Rusty Hardin, the famous Texas lawyer, then an assistant district attorney, was helping me on the side. My hero. The fact that we'd caught the Family Court judges on film, that they would be exposed, filled me with a sense of triumph and hope.

The documentary revealing those crimes ran for a few nights on HBO before we were slapped with the first of five lawsuits. We were charged in Texas. The judge and the other people we exposed in the film sued HBO and our company, Joey's and mine, for eighty million dollars. The judge had signed a release before and after we filmed, but that didn't stop him.

Luckily, our personal lawyer, Arthur Jacobs, had persuaded HBO to indemnify me and Joe, our production company, and our crew without a dollar limit, against claims that might be brought in any lawsuits. "Insurance, Arthur, talking about insurance is so boring," I'd tell him. Thank God we had insurance. One case went on for ten years. It was a foregone conclusion that we would lose. HBO decided to never again show the film, and as it was their film, I could never show it again. Yes. That hurts. To have tried to convey the reality of what these women and children suffered, and then to have their one channel to the world outside denied them.

I was to learn from my attorney, Arthur Jacobs, who'd returned to Houston for the case, that the women had banded together for a vigil outside the Family Court building. The women had set up cots and slept on them all night, taking turns from one night to the next for fourteen months, in protest of the Family Court rulings.

Not long after the trial began in one of the lawsuits, the phone rang. It was the wife of one of the court-appointed psychologists. He was divorcing her, she said, and suing for custody of their eight-year-old daughter. Could I help? My heart sank. "I have no more tools, no more weapons, no more power," I told her. "The bad guys won. And my best advice is, don't let anyone know you contacted me."

I kept in touch to give her moral if not active support. She called one evening, crying. Her daughter had gone to her husband, the psychologist. She lost in the same shameful system.

It took me back to when Dinah was two and a half and I left her with her father, with Arnie, while I did a play. I had no money, none. I had no choice but to take this job. My next new life depended on it. But the fear that he wouldn't give her back to me was always there. The fear of losing her washed over me, sickened me, made me dizzy every day and night. Fear of Arnie's power. One of the unwanted thoughts I had when I heard of his death was that he could never take Dinah. So all these years later, when we told the stories of women having their children taken away from them, I found my old fears were still alive in me, and my old pain flared to connect with these utterly powerless mothers from Houston, Texas.

Three Hearts

I directed three TV movies in 1994, not happily. It was a life-changing year. I was directing material that made commercial sense but was not connected to my brain or to my heart in any deep way. When an actor works on an inconsequential job, they do their work and go home. A director is imprisoned within the project for the duration and responsible for everything in front of and behind the scenes. It's an overwhelming job. When I was working on the projects that I was excited to bring to an audience, I couldn't do enough, be enough. I was bathing in the experience. But in this one year, I was to do a very commercial film for our company, which was fine, but on the next two I was working for outside companies. So when I wound up in trouble and disconnected, which I was a lot of the time, I couldn't take it out on Joey. He wasn't there.

I was alone. I was a director for hire. And I wasn't good at it. All of the outlets I had as an actor were gone; the emotion, the highs, the lows, the anger that had a place to go in acting was bottled up inside me as a director. I had to sit and take notes from well-meaning producers and network executives, people who were for the most part really simplistic. As an actor they wouldn't have dared to approach me. As a director, I was their girl, and replaceable. That world really suffocated me. There are people born with a certain kind of resilience, like poker players who hide their hands and play the game and manage to walk away from the table with the winnings. I'm not one of those people.

Seasons of the Heart was the last happy experience I had with a TV movie that year. I was working with Joey producing. I was safe.

Reunion was a stressful shoot for me. The director turned out to be kind of a fifth wheel on this production. It was Marlo's baby, an outlet for pent-up passion, of which she's always had a huge inner reservoir.

I felt frustrated. All the TV movies I'd directed had been conceived by me, or had been dramatizations of a documentary I'd desperately cared about bringing to a wider audience. I had a short fuse. I finished up the second movie and left to take on the third movie of that year, *Following Her Heart*, with Ann-Margret as the star. In Texas.

She is a real angel, eager as a child to explore and to please. I'd recruited a good cast, with good friends: Brenda Vaccaro, Scott Marlowe, and for Ann-Margret's love interest—who else? George Segal, whom I had just finished directing in *Reunion*. Dougie Milson shot it. Everyone, including myself, rose above the material, but I had a big bad thorn in my side the entire time, and as I'm discovering as I write this, I don't take orders easily. Ever since the blacklist and fighting to reestablish myself, I'm bad at being told what to do.

The producer running the show was attached not to the network, but to the Canadian deficit financier. She was young, nasal, ubiquitous, and, in every scene, would stand tapping her foot, looking at the watch on her wrist. "I'm gonna pull the plug," she'd warn. "I'm gonna pull the plug."

I'd get distracted, angry, want to throw her off the set, but it was her company's set. Ann-Margret would ask, "Am I all right? Am I doing something wrong? Is there anything you want to tell me to do?" Roger, her husband, was there protecting her. I couldn't say, "Yeah, get rid of the yenta producer!"

The very last scene of the shoot—it was probably two a.m.—as we set up for the very last shot, the producer showed up. She tapped her foot, looked at her watch. "I'm gonna—" I jumped in, my arms outstretched in joy. "Pull the plug! Please, pull it." I grabbed a plug with the cords attached and held it toward her. The crew picked up on it. "Pull the plug, pull the plug!" They clapped and danced. She stared at us, not amused. We were gasping with laughter and relief. We were tired and crazy, and this was good-bye after a long, tense month together. The producer stood her ground, her arms crossed, till we lit the last scene and shot it, and put our arms around one another, knowing we would never be part of this particular family again.

After directing three TV movies in a row, I was exhausted. Our friend Dyson Lovell offered us his house in L.A. while he was in London, which gave us a chance to see sorely missed close friends.

One night I woke up, had to pee, walked across the bedroom, went up two steps to the bathroom, still half-asleep, started back to bed, and blacked out as I sensed my body hitting the wall on the other side of the bed. I opened my eyes to see Joey and two ambulance attendants looming over me. Our dear Dr. Derwin met us at the hospital. My heartbeat was irregular. Atrial fibrillation.

A very peculiar and frightening feeling. My heart was no longer the heart I had taken for granted and relied on, that had been a really great friend. Now it was literally failing me. Maybe the past year had been too much for both of us. Or maybe all of my life had been too tough on one little organ.

Back in New York, I heard of Marianne Legato, a doctor who specialized in women's heart problems. She became my doctor for everything, and she felt the only way to avoid big complications, since my heart refused to stay in rhythm, was to put in a pacemaker. In 1994 I was booked into Columbia Presbyterian in Washington Heights, where I'd gone to high school. Wires were put into my heart up to the left breastbone. The wires were attached to an oblong silver case, the pacemaker, which was placed in the cavity right below the collarbone.

That first operation hurt. Twenty years ago, pacemakers were man-sized, and mine felt like a big rock in my little shoulder space. I could feel it bang back and forth under my skin (that's why Dr. Legato was so fervent about women's medicine). Joey, who hates, hates hospitals, shaved *LEE* into his hair to make me laugh. I was in the Milstein Pavilion. The Milstein had a big charming room for guests and patients to hang out in. In the afternoon, a pianist played standards and light pop on the big black grand piano. Directly across from the music room, Sunny von Bülow lay in her room. I think she was there for sixteen years altogether. Fed, bathed, changed, never coming out of her coma. I wondered if she could hear the piano playing Cole Porter.

My room faced the Hudson. The window was big and had a window seat. I would sit there all day as I did in the window seat in our apartment on Riverside Drive when I was growing up. Watching the water, looking at the changing Jersey shoreline and traffic crossing the George Washington Bridge.

The year before, I'd gone to two heart doctors at Columbia Presbyterian. One was a South American who'd developed a new system for regulating heartbeat that was too complicated for me to understand. Mary Beth, a doctor's daughter, was with me. "What if it doesn't work?" I asked this charming doctor. "If it doesn't work, eh—you die!" He laughed holding out his hands.

Dr. Mehmet Oz practiced at Columbia Presbyterian. Someone arranged for an appointment for Mary Beth and me. As we all now know,

Dr. Oz is God. He is as good as he is beautiful. He is also a great listener and sensitive to frightened women with scary hearts. He sealed the deal on the pacemaker.

I accept the process of aging by thinking of myself as a "former beauty." But I am old in real years, and kept alive by this little clock inside me, this pacemaker that Dr. Schneller said is doing ninety percent of the beating of my heart, and he's almost ready to put another inside me. That would be my third or fourth pacemaker—what a medical miracle.

Falling Apart at It's My Party

It was the summer of 1996. Randal Kleiser had asked me to join his many friends in the making of his film *It's My Party*. It was a very personal story. Randal had been estranged from his partner of many years who was now dying of AIDS. It was a film about their reconciliation and about his partner's decision to find a way out through a suicide party, with all his loving friends and family around him. Eric Roberts played the boyfriend. I was Eric's Greek mother. In the cast were Randal's friends Margaret Cho, Marlee Matlin, Olivia Newton-John, and Greg Harrison as Randal. We shot it in Randal's house, so the intimacy was distracting.

I was staying in the guest bedroom at our friends Steve and Annie's yellow house on Stone Canyon Drive, up the street from the Hotel Bel-Air. Joey and I had stayed often with Steve Verona; the little room with its four-poster bed and little TV was familiar and comfortable. The veranda overlooked the pool and the gardens.

Joey wasn't with me. I felt isolated in a new way and a very uncomfortable way. I couldn't seem to get inside my own skin. I hated parties with lots of people, and that's what the set was to me. I loved the desperation of my character in the script, but couldn't seem to hang on to it. I developed shingles, blisters on my shoulders and down my back. I was up most of the night putting calamine lotion on the hard-to-reach places. I stayed in my little trailer on set as much as I could.

At Steven's house I sat on an outside dining room chair, staring at the green pool on a cold, gray California day. Something bad was happening to me. I was losing feeling. The last time I felt close to this was at the end of my marriage to Arnie. I felt cold and scared. The migraines were also frequent. The last time I'd stayed in this room, Steve and Annie had given us a party. I'd had an incessant migraine and shot myself full of Imitrex. Suddenly I couldn't move or speak. Joey opened the door to get me downstairs where everyone was waiting. He took one look at me and called our doctor, who told Joey to meet him at the hospital. I thought I'd had a stroke. I was sitting on the edge of the bed. I couldn't speak. I could only look at Joey. Nothing came out of my mouth.

He called an ambulance, threw a blanket over me, and half carried me down the stairs to the car. I smiled at my friends clustered at the bottom. I felt apologetic, silly, dumb. The doctor met us at the hospital. It wasn't a stroke, he said. It was a migraine episode, not uncommon. I had overmedicated myself with the Imitrex, taken three times the normal dose.

That had been a year ago. I'd had shingles, migraines, and now this new bizarre blank feeling.

I felt like I was walking through the film. I didn't feel connected, and most of the time I didn't feel like Eric's mother. I did not feel like a good actress. I didn't feel much of anything but fear.

When it came time for the scene where Eric says good-bye to his friends and to me, I stayed in the living room while he went to his bedroom to take the pills that would give him the death he wanted, before AIDS took over his body.

I had lost Nicky Dante to AIDS. Nicky, who danced with Joey in St. Louis, in the chorus, and co-wrote *A Chorus Line*. Joey, Belinda, and I celebrated the New Year with Nicky in Rome in 1984, the year before his death.

I sat quietly in the living room of the set till the crew returned and the cast was in place and Randal called "Action." As they started moving Eric's body past me—I feel dizzy as I write this—out of me erupted this sound, this roar, this scream, with hot tears washing, falling—of terror, longing, denial.

The last time this sound came out of me was when I ran into my mother's surreal hospital room, looked at her troubled pale face with the frown between her eyes, and it washed over me that I couldn't save her, that she was gone.

There was no holding back that eruption. No saving it for the close-up. I was carried away, and it was gone. It was probably my one true moment. It was probably inappropriate for the scene—too big, too raw, too ugly, too lifelike.

Right after finishing the film, Joey, Mary Beth, and I were invited to the Moscow International Film Festival. Mary Beth was close to Nikita Mikhalkov, the great Russian film director. We flew to gray Moscow. The Russian films were pretty dismal except for Mikhalkov's documentary about his blond daughter, following her each year from her childhood on.

Nikita had a big, big personality, a big, expansive, handsome, vodka-drinking, peasant-song-singing, speechmaking, Russian maleness. He was filling the big hall in the ravenous drinking, dancing party afterward. He was flirting with Mary Beth. She was rosy with pleasure. Joey was pleasantly loaded. I went outside. The air was cold, cold. There was a wooden bridge, a wooden table, and two chairs.

Dark brown. Mary Beth and Joey came out onto the bridge, leaning up against it as they talked. "Mary Beth," I called. She turned, walked over, and sat down. Mary Beth was and is my best friend. "Mary Beth, I'm in trouble," I said. "I'm floating away."

At home on West End Avenue, I went to one haughty psychopharmacologist, then a doughy psychopharmacologist. He gave me a whole Zoloft in his office. Within a few minutes I'd passed out on his carpet. I could feel myself losing consciousness. When I came to, he hurriedly put me in a cab and sent me home. I'm on a regular dose of Zoloft now. I bless it. I have a lot of complex problems, but losing myself isn't one of them. For better or for worse, I'm right here.

Broadway Brawler

Joey's ambitious. He's competitive. He's a player. Joey looks around and sees his friends, who are stars, or big directors, or big players even, and says, "Why not me? Why not me?" Hitting his chest with his fist! Why not? Coming from 6th and Lincoln, a corner of Little Italy in Wilmington, Delaware, Joey and his guy friends all outdid themselves, each in his own field. It's the American way. This is the story of how I, basically, destroyed Joey's dream. He blames it all on Bruce Willis, but I played a major role as director of his film, which starred Bruce and Maura Tierney, in Wilmington, Delaware, Joey's hometown, in 1997.

The script was by a young talented married couple, the story of an over-the-hill pro hockey player, banged up from too many games, who gets so loaded one night that he makes his way back to his old childhood home and passes out in the doghouse in the yard. The house is now occupied by Maura Tierney, a single mother and the sister of his boyhood friend, her nine-year-old daughter, and her seven-year-old son. A love story, of course—how this charming bum wears down the resistance of this tough, smart, but vulnerable lady. Perfect casting, and a charming, fresh story.

Joey sent the script to Bruce in Idaho. The invitation to go to Idaho to talk with Bruce Willis about our movie was the clarion call Joey had waited for. He had a commercial script, ready to go. If he could attach a star like Bruce Willis to it, the money to make it would come through. Joey would join his friends Michael Douglas, Michael Phillips, Danny DeVito—the charmed circle of producers who were one after another getting their films made, and that he, with all his ambitious heart, longed to join.

Bruce was no stranger. We'd known him as a charismatic bartender at Café Central in New York, from charismatic boyfriend to our Dinah for a couple of months, to breakout charismatic TV star. Bruce got the TV show *Moonlighting* and became a big star; the rest is history.

He was now a movie star, with a little dip in his career, but very bankable. He was represented by Arnold Rifkin, an important agent at the time, and the brother of one of our best friends, Ron Rifkin.

Joey and I traveled to Idaho. I felt a little out of my home waters. The Italian kid from 6th and Lincoln and the Jersey boy found common ground.

Out on the sparkling blue, blue lake in Bruce's motorboat, I felt detached. Bruce was a big deal now, a big movie star, looking to raise his actor image a bit. Joey was looking to fulfill his life's dream. I felt conflicted. So much depended on the director with this huge male star.

On the other hand, Joey knew better than to even dream of handing this film to a better-known male director. Our marriage would be over.

When Bruce asked me, sitting in his den, how I saw his character in the movie, I told him, "There is nothing I can tell you that you don't already know better than I do. You've lived this; you're a working-class kid from Jersey. You've charmed and *hondled* your way up from bartender to movie star. Use it. Who better to play this part than you?" I meant it.

He said yes.

Joey put the package together. Andy Vajna, who used to share office space with Joey and was now a big producer, put up the $28 million.

I hadn't thought yet about casting the woman, but Bruce said, "If I do it, I want Maura Tierney." Once I'd seen her TV show *NewsRadio*, I wanted her as much as Bruce did. Maura was funny, real, fresh, very pretty, and sexy in a nice-girl way.

Joey decided to set up the movie in his old neighborhood in Wilmington, Delaware. All the streets had great character. Germantown, the Jewish section, the duPont estates, and of course the Italian section, his family's house at 6th and Lincoln, where Rachel, his mother, was on an oxygen machine, staring all day at the TV. Living in the house with Rachel were his twin sister, Phyllis, and his brother, Ralph, who became a driver on the movie.

All around were Joey's best friends from childhood to today: Peter Pappa, Albert Vietri, Richie Zambanini, Verino Pettinaro. All neighborhood guys who made good, moved into mini mansions, made their working-class families proud—his mob.

Now Joey was showing them all. He was a movie producer, dragging the great carcass of a $28-million-dollar movie into the cave with Bruce riding it.

Joey's last partner in the commercial business, Billy Fraker, a legendary DP, was coming on board as cameraman. Carol Oditz had done costume design on many films I'd directed, and Doug Kraner was a brilliant production designer who had done *No Place Like Home* with us. The editor I longed for, Sam O'Steen, with whom I'd never worked but admired, finally said yes.

We opened production offices in Wilmington. Doug started building the house we were to use as Maura's house, Bruce's old family home. Roberta Morris, who is transcribing these words now, was in production in our offices, as she's been on all my films.

St. Anthony Parish was electrified. The community was welcoming us to use their homes, cast their children, and they catered our meals. All were on board: the priests, the sisters, the Catholic schools that Joey had attended and dropped out of. He was the center of attention, admiration. Joey was the star.

In New York, we had taken over Madison Square Garden and made a deal with the National Hockey League for a five-camera shoot of a hockey game between the New York Rangers and the Pittsburgh Penguins. One of the lead players, who had a build like Bruce's, wore a jersey with Bruce's character's number on it to intercut with the close-ups in our movie.

We'd rented ice-skating rinks in Delaware and Pennsylvania for casting and practice sessions and hired a seasoned skating choreographer who worked for weeks on the young Bruce's skating. He advised us on choosing young athletes from junior teams from New York to Pennsylvania. Tom Bernard of Sony Pictures Classics, a serious hockey player himself, became a great resource for the hockey segments. We hired his entire hockey team to play a rival team in the movie, along with his son, who was a great skater and the right age for some of the childhood scenes.

It was exciting.

We were working with the young Bruce look-alike on a frozen pond we'd built to resemble an ice-covered swimming hole. We'd shot scenes on the ice that had to do with Bruce's character's past with the young skaters—all stuff we could shoot without Bruce.

Finally Bruce arrived. Maura arrived. Her new husband was home in California.

We had a table read, which was delicious, and a day or two of rehearsal for me to get a sense of staging with Billy Fraker. Good. First
day of shooting, our editor, Sam O'Steen, called. He'd decided to take
another job. That was a blow.

I went to the trailer that Bruce's hairdresser was using. I knocked
on the door. The young woman who was doing his hair came down the
stairs. "He doesn't like to be asked about his hair," she said.

"Huh?" I said. We were doing camera tests that day, makeup and
hair. I was sufficiently paranoid about my own looks to understand
another actor's paranoia. But I didn't exactly know how to approach
this. Bruce was a regular-looking guy, not stereotypically handsome,
but a turn-on in most people's books, hair or no hair.

Bruce Willis has something actors die for: authenticity. He's au-
thentic. Comfortable within his own skin, and charming on film. Like
Gable, like Tracy, like Clint Eastwood. But while making our movie
he was going through a transition; he was insecure and bored, a deadly
combination for any actor, in particular the star.

We did the camera tests. Bruce bald. Bruce with close-cropped
hair, a good hairpiece. He asked what I thought. Either was fine with
me, but what would make him most comfortable?

"The hairpiece."

"The one you have on? This one?"

"Yeah. Do you want to see the others?"

"I don't think we need to, Bruce. What do you think, Billy?"

"Either way."

I wish I'd said bald. The hairpiece became such a focus. I should
have been the first to recognize it. During the five weeks we shot, the
hairpiece changed slightly every other day.

In the meantime, I found I could hardly get out of bed. I was sick
with something. We'd rented a charming, many-bedroomed white

house in the suburbs. Mary Beth had a bedroom. So did our chef, Steve, whom we had found in South Carolina while we were shooting *Staying Together.*

I was lying in bed, fully dressed. Joey and Mary Beth were looking down at me. "I can't get up."

The smart young doctor said, "Your thyroid is out of whack." Apparently, the gland that supplies energy was not working. He gave me pills. It helped, but not enough. I felt slightly underwater for the whole film. One thought behind. One blink behind. One step behind.

When you do film, you're up at five a.m., especially if you're directing. You and camera are planning the day's shots. I would have preferred doing them at the end of the day, but Billy Fraker didn't want to. I didn't want a conflict, so I agreed.

Behind the scenes, Dinah was in her eighth month with my first grandchild; Roberta, in the production office, had a miscarriage; and Belinda got into a car accident on a slippery bridge and broke her foot.

Then there began to be other factors, the main one being that the newly married Maura was not flirting with Bruce. He was becoming turned off, taking a private plane after work on weekends to party and play with his band, missing his coaching sessions with the pro skater we had hired. On set, Bruce seemed irritated and disinterested.

The spark between them, the one this film depended on, was definitely dimming. We filmed a less than exciting ice-skating excursion, where he teaches Maura and the kids. I had begun to feel his boredom, and he didn't like the kid we'd hired as Maura's son.

Life for an actor in Wilmington is deadly. It's not Jersey. It's not Hollywood, or New York, or Idaho. Joey was not available for Bruce to play with; the second week Joey checked himself in and out of the hospital with heart pains.

I was not helpful. I was not inspired. I was tired and irritated. In one scene Maura feeds the dog, putting dry food in his dish. Bruce suggested that she have her back to him and bend from the waist to fill the dog dish. Doggy style? Maura looked at me, hard.

"That's tasteless, Bruce . . ." I said.

He argued. He was looking for a way in, the wrong way. He needed a comfortable, Bruce-funny way into the part, an outrageous-Bruce way in, and that's what I was looking for, too. He was critical, not involved. An awful place to be as an actor. I'd like to ask him why. I'd like to ask Maura what she felt happened, or didn't.

The problem when you are a star, when the money rests on you as an actor, is that your freedom to fail is gone. You can't take chances. If you can't take chances anymore, what kind of actor are you?

One morning, as Billy and I were figuring out the shots for the day, Bruce showed up and demanded a shot list, a written list of all the camera moves. This was a bad sign, a sign of distrust of me.

Bruce had brought a pal to hang with, I'll call him Salvio, whom he made a producer on the film. Salvio went off with him on weekends. Every weekend he took off in his plane, ignoring that we had a professional skater standing by to work with him. One weekend, it was to Bali, where he was opening a Planet Hollywood. Bruce saw the dailies each night; now he wanted to see the film cut.

No editor. Right. No editor had been hired to replace Sam O'Steen. Big, big mistake. No argument there.

We hired an available guy and cut a couple of scenes together. Arnold Rifkin and Demi Moore came down to watch them with him.

"Do you think it's sexy?" he asked them. "Do you think I'm sexy?"

"No," Demi said. "I don't."

And that, folks, was that.

. . .

A rnold called a meeting with Joey and me at our house. "Bruce feels you're losing control, Lee. He needs a strong hand."

The next day I went into Bruce's dressing room to talk to him and Arnold. Bruce was happier than I'd seen him in ages. "I love you, Lee, but it just didn't work out."

"Bruce, the scenes are charming. They work." And they did. The tension between Maura and Bruce actually paid off. They were supposed to be wary of each other, of course, before they fall in love. What else do you do in an hour-and-a-half film? There was one scene of Bruce by himself on a balcony. It was snowing. Suddenly he climbed the railing and howled like a wolf into the wind. It was shockingly fresh and original.

B ruce asked another director, Dennis Dugan from *Moonlighting*, to come down to Wilmington to take over as director. Arnold and Bruce had made some behind-the-scenes arrangement with Andy Vajna, who'd put up the money. Bruce took responsibility for the eighteen million. Joey and I were fired.

LOS ANGELES TIMES, MARCH 13, 1997:
The Fight Over 'Broadway Brawler'

———

Bruce Willis' latest film is shut down 20 days into production after director Lee Grant and others are let go.

Scrapping a big star production once filming has begun and millions of dollars are already on the line is rare in Hollywood.

I don't know if this had ever been done before—the star walking out on a picture three weeks into an eight-week shoot. Eighteen million dollars of a $28-million budget already spent. Then firing the producer and director and taking charge himself. Was he desperately insecure and unhappy and frustrated? Or was it the great news that he was offered *Armageddon* and had a three-picture deal with Disney, his future was secure again, so we were disposable? I think maybe both. I think when I walked into his dressing room, both Bruce and his agent were happy men, with a big movie in the bag, maybe, and they were both insecure about our movie—on the one hand, legitimately, not having seen a cut, but on the other hand, without reason. Well, maybe some reason I don't know.

The little boy of about seven and the girl of nine who played Maura's children in the film broke down and sobbed when they heard the news at lunch. There was a terrible, empty, cold fear in the pit of my stomach. It was unreal. Joey was ravaged. He wanted to kill Bruce. He's still ravaged by it. He'd put the whole film together and now he had nothing. His big chance—the gold ring—was gone. Mary Beth remembers riding back to New York with me and my saying, "That was it, I'll never be asked to direct a film again. It's over, that part of my life." I felt it very matter-of-factly. When it was happening in Wilmington it was like a nightmare—falling, falling into an empty, cold, endless black well. I was still waking up in the mornings, going through practical days, but inside I was falling and I was humiliated.

When the heads of each department in the production company quit, the world stopped spinning and began to settle down. Those were the professionals. They all needed this job; they were leaving their paychecks and their own creations. It left Bruce and his new director without a crew.

Everyone but Bruce's friend Salvio quit, from camera to food.

They all walked out. Went home. Left Wilmington, Delaware. Would not work for Bruce. Joey is still devastated. He felt betrayed and humiliated in front of his whole hometown.

I didn't. Bruce was carrying the picture. He needed a hit to stay in the business. He was away from Demi, and I think he really needed a buddy/director, someone he could play with or chase girls with, a guy's guy.

Bruce insisted that every piece of film be given to him, never to be seen. That was cruel for us. I liked the work a lot and wanted to finally edit what we had, to redo it with someone else. To prove how wrong he was—about me, about himself—especially for Joey, who was mortally wounded. We just didn't have the kind of money it would take to fight this in court.

Then he made *Armageddon* and *The Sixth Sense* and became a huge star again.

Arnie Rifkin doesn't represent Bruce anymore. I don't know if Salvio is still a friend. We've all moved on. For Joey, what happens to a dream deferred?

It still hurts.

Lifetime

Joey and I slunk back to New York, I shrunken and vague, he murderous. When we were back in New York, I received an offer from Lifetime, the TV channel for women. Run by women. The assignment was to do a documentary on women with breast cancer: their illness, their lives, their treatment. It was a piece of work that took me to emotional places I'd never been—a place I wanted to go and never wanted to go.

Our relationship with Lifetime marked our coming-of-age as a New York production company. We had arrived. When Joey negotiated the contract with Lifetime for their *Intimate Portrait* series, our company was launched into a multimillion-dollar deal. Before we were through, seven years later, we would have two floors of offices, three production teams running year-round, and more than twenty employees.

I would be interviewing old friends and introducing some of my heroes—Gloria Steinem, Bella Abzug, Betty Friedan—to the Lifetime audience. I was being paid for talking to friends and strangers whom I'd been dying to get to really know and spend time with, and to ask them questions that one never asks in a living room, a good exploration of life, death, and work. We included the people important to them and delivered a well-rounded, unexpected journey into their lives.

It was a great mix of work and family, Joey and I walking the twenty blocks to the office each day with our dog Dude. Joey's sister, Phyllis, was living with us in New York City and working in the production office. Belinda worked as the office manager, bringing her new baby, Rachel, to the office each day. Rachel was a wonderful addition to the office, not bothered by the beehive of activity—we didn't yet realize she was deaf. When we did, Belinda took her to Dr. Louis Cooper, a close family friend and the president of the American Academy of Pediatrics, who recommended cochlear implants. Today with the implants Rachel can choose what and who she cares to hear. Her ambition is to be a rock star.

As Blanche DuBois said, "Suddenly—there's God—so quickly!"

S ome years later I was sitting on the edge of my bed, absorbed in something on television. It was morning. I was still in my nightgown.

The bedroom door suddenly slammed open and Joey burst in.

"You're sixty-five years old!" he yelled at me, barked at me.

I screamed and fell to the floor, covering my ears with my hands. "I am not," I screamed, feeling faint.

"Yes you are!" An assault out of nowhere.

If ever I were to play Blanche DuBois, I had a private moment to draw on that nothing else could have given me.

Apparently my Social Security checks came due, plus the hefty pensions from the Directors Guild and others. The papers were sent to my money manager, Hersh Panitch. In order to receive payment, I had to sign papers acknowledging my age.

Hersh sat in L.A. with the papers for a day. Hersh is a sensitive man. Kind.

He called Dinah, whom he also represented. "Your mother is sixty-five," he said. "Who is going to tell her?"

"Call Joey," said Dinah. "I'm not telling her!"

So Joey, who has great sensitivity except where money is concerned, burst through the door and informed me, "You're sixty-five years old!" The unacceptable was spoken. No year after that has been as hard to swallow or as difficult to accept. I signed the papers he held out to me.

Still, I'm not telling you the number, you can always look it up. I'm not well in that area and, of course, like Blanche DuBois, "I have always depended on the kindness of strangers." The protective magic flies away the minute I say the actual number. Like the Wicked Witch of the West when the pail of water is thrown at her. "Aaaaaaah," she screams, and slowly dissolves as the steam rises from what had been her body.

I know. I can't say it. Don't say it—I could dissolve.

I look up to my big makeup mirror on my dressing table where I write these pages.

I've aged ten years. I've said too much.

Years after my acting life, well into my documentary life, *American Masters* called. Could I get Sidney Poitier to agree to do a documentary on his life? "Please, Sidney," I asked. "For you, Lee," he said. We were old friends after all.

Sidney took us to the Bahamas, to Cat Island, where his father had been a tomato farmer.

Sidney's story is the stuff of legends. From the Bahamas to Miami as a boy, all alone, told to deliver goods to the back doors, to his astonishing breakthrough as a hot, black and brilliant movie star—Oscar winner. When we made *In the Heat of the Night* in 1967 the film couldn't be shown in the South, because Sidney was the star and we were still living in a segregated society.

Leaving Cat Island, I understood where Sidney's intense, proud morality came from. He wasn't burdened as a boy by the horrors of the South or the bleakness of the North. A sense of freedom pervaded him, like a dancer, a romancer. An innocence, almost, that allowed him to react to prejudice and racism in a fresh way.

For Lifetime, I made a documentary about Mia Farrow. I shot her at home with all her children. It was an extraordinary experience. The deaf white cat she'd adopted on *Peyton Place* had morphed into many well-behaved, caring, remarkable children, some with physical disabilities, adopted by Mia.

Mia had polio as a little girl. She was treated as if she had the plague, as were all children with polio at that time. She was isolated for a year in her own home, with her mother and medical help and treasured visits through the window from her girlfriend next door. The experience left her with a calling to be a doctor, a yearning to be there for lonely, sick children like herself. Her passion as an ambassador for the United Nations was yet another extension of her family.

I'd finished the portrait of Mia Farrow's family when we received an invitation to Liza Minnelli's wedding to David Gest. Mia was a bridesmaid, so I figured that accounted for the invitation. I did not know the bride. I was a huge admirer of *The Sterile Cuckoo* and *Cabaret*, both of them milestones, with great performances by Liza.

In the last couple of years, she'd had huge physical problems. I remembered pictures of Liza in a wheelchair. Mia had mentioned how ill she'd been, that she had cared for Liza for a while. Now Liza, well and in love, was marrying her beau. The wedding took place at Marble Collegiate Church downtown. The streets were cordoned off. Crowds pushed in. Joan Collins, in purple, with matching lipstick and hat, pushed by me with her then-new husband. Paparazzi swarmed in, down the red carpets toward the stained glass windows. We took our seats on the side, seven rows from the altar; we could see Anthony Hopkins on the side in the first row. Little by little the huge church filled up. Dina Merrill and her husband sat next to us. The best man was Michael Jackson; the maid of honor was Elizabeth Taylor.

After a while, we realized we'd all been sitting there, waiting for the wedding to begin, for half an hour, maybe three quarters of an hour. Was Liza calling it off? The huge, well-dressed crowd was becoming restless, craning necks.

Suddenly Michael Jackson was onstage. Pale-faced, black-haired, in a dark blue glittering uniform of some kind. Did he sing? I don't remember. A few tuxedoed men joined him. Was there background music? An organ?

The groom appeared onstage through the curtains. A short, flaccid, very pale fifty-something man, patting the dampness on his face and neck with a white handkerchief.

I saw Mia emerging from a door to the side of the stage. She was whispering to celebrities on the aisle. I got up and squeezed past knees and went down to her. She smiled, flapped her hand. "Elizabeth brought the wrong shoes. She's sent her assistant back to the hotel to bring back the right shoes."

"Which hotel?"

"The Plaza."

"The Plaza on 60th and Fifth?" We were on 29th and Fifth.

Mia nodded.

"We're holding the wedding until Elizabeth's assistant makes it up to the Plaza and back in this traffic?"

Mia nodded again and moved on to other guests in other pews.

Well, we all waited in our pews for about an hour. Made best friends with the strangers sitting next to us. I spied Joy Behar and Steve, her boyfriend/partner, in the balcony. We waved and laughed and shrugged. It was a great non-wedding.

Eventually Elizabeth was helped onto the stage by her friend Michael Jackson. She was wearing a long dress, so no one could see her shoes, right or wrong.

The music began.

The bridesmaids, dressed in black net dresses, walked down the aisle, followed by the bride, I think in pale pink. All I remember after that was my stomach turning when Liza's lips met her new husband's, that pale fish head that emerged from the groom's suit, with his full fish lips pursed for a kiss. Uch!

I looked over at Elizabeth. She and Michael were whispering to each other. They broke the mold, folks.

Ryan and Farrah

Ryan. I thought so much about Ryan O'Neal in the weeks after Farrah died.

Farrah's own documentary about her fight to the death with spreading cancer ran on a network twice, and then she was shunted aside by the media because of the sudden death of Michael Jackson. I won't even talk about the nature of celebrity in these times we live in. It only heightens the horror. I did a documentary on Farrah for Lifetime. Actually, a do-over documentary, because Farrah didn't like the way she looked in the first one. And she was right.

Ryan was in it, of course. When I first knew Ryan in *Peyton Place* he was the prettiest, most charming, shining, funny, dearest boy ever made. His whole face said *Love me*, and we all did. At that time he was married to his first wife, who spent most of her time in Mexico, I think. He had a sweet red-haired brother he played with on the beach.

Maybe ten or twelve years ago, I went to a party in L.A. and Ryan was there. It was before I did the doc on Farrah; I hadn't met her. Ryan sat down and chatted. Much time had passed, but it was easy to talk. Then I noticed Farrah was sitting on top of the black grand piano in front of us. She was swinging her golden legs and smiling her red-bathing-suit smile. Her legs were bare. On her feet were white socks and blue Mary Jane shoes. Her dress had puffed sleeves and a Peter Pan collar, and the skirt just cleared her panties. Ryan was quoted later in *Vanity Fair* saying sex with Farrah was the best and craziest of all his women. I flashed on Farrah that night—so crazy, so seductive, so kinky.

What I felt most during the time spent with Farrah was her desperation. You know that look long-distance runners have toward the end of a race, the stride, the push to make it to the finish line? The tendons in the neck, the pulling back of the flesh in the face, the gasping for air. The focus. The fear of not making it in time. The fear. The determination.

She was not sick then. But she was driven. She had an exerciser on her apartment's little Juliet balcony. She wanted me to film her doing push-ups, to show how strong her body was. She was involved in a sculpture project at the Los Angeles County Museum of Art. A sculptor was working on a stone replica of Farrah, which she reciprocated by doing one of him. She was focused, chipping, chipping away on a big piece of stone, an art difficult and fairly new to her. The piece belonged in a sculpture class, not a museum, but the fact that she was performing this concept in the Museum of Art was the triumph for her.

Everybody takes time before they commit to the camera, but especially actresses. We are facing who we are and our changing, aging faces, whether we have a future or only a past. The first time I filmed Farrah, she stayed in the bathroom for an hour before she came out into her apartment. The second time, the redo, we filmed in a private room in the lobby of her building. Everyone was there: all her people—hair, makeup, manager, publicity, all of us from Lifetime, executives, camera crews. Farrah could not leave her bathroom for three hours. She had Lifetime on the hook. Lifetime cannot air a documentary until its subject gives permission, and Farrah would not give permission.

She wouldn't sign the release. So that hot day in the lobby she had us where she wanted us, waiting and wanting.

Privately I always thought there might be cocaine involved. Her little nose was pink and running. My own life in the bathrooms of L.A. was extensive. Everyone, including me, did coke in the bathroom, grass in the living room. As I waited for Farrah, I remembered the cast and crew of *Valley of the Dolls* waiting for Judy Garland to come out of her dressing room. She never did. The studio replaced her with Susan Hayward and the movie went on to become a gay icon.

The point is the mirror. Mirror, mirror, on the wall, who's the fairest of them all? The wicked witch wanted to kill Snow White because she was younger and prettier. Actresses who once saw astonishing beauty reflected back to them, who were petted and imitated and fallen in love with and hunted and paparazzi'ed and offered jobs, jobs, jobs, are suddenly too old, out of fashion, has-beens, not hot. On the outside looking in.

In Europe beautiful women are allowed to grow old. Vanessa Redgrave, a genius actress, was also breathtakingly beautiful. Remember *Isadora*? But there was never any question of her acceptance of her aging beauty. There were no pictures in *Globe* ridiculing her wrinkles or her sagging neckline.

And the real beauties are the ones hurt most of all. The Elizabeth Taylors, the Ava Gardners, the Farrahs—the plastic surgery, the shots, the Michael Jackson syndrome, until the actress is a parody of herself, or can't leave the dressing room to face the camera that once loved her.

Burt Bacharach
to Elizabeth Taylor

In the blacklist days I'd had a swooning romance with Burt Bacharach.

Alan Foshko took me to the Apollo in Harlem. I'd cut my hair short, like a boy, I wore a sweater, a tight skirt, and heeled shoes with a d'Orsay cut. No stockings.

Foshko said, "There's someone I want you to meet."

We walked in the half-light to the side of the theater over the flowered maroon carpet. Foshko knocked on the door to the side of the stage. A young guy came down two carpeted steps. He was half in the dark, the half-light hit him . . .

"This is Burt Bacharach," Foshko said, and my knees went weak.

Burt came toward me and stopped.

"I'm recording tomorrow night; you wanna come?"

Tick-tock.

"Yes."

I showed up at the recording studio. Burt was recording "Walk On By" with Dionne Warwick. Young Dionne, young Burt, young me, the youngest I had ever been.

Burt conducted the orchestra, forcefully, ecstatically; Dionne sang. I was listening to, vibrating to, music that was sensation, holding on to the sides of my chair. Whoosh.

It was the spring of 1963 maybe. I was melting and dizzy and so hot for Burt that I shook. He was to me what Daisy was to Gatsby. He was Pan. Elusive, all music.

He played my old grand piano. All those amazing sounds, new, sexy. Singing in his croaky, cracked voice—the bottom dropped out of me. Talent.

All he ever wanted to do was play the piano, watch basketball on the TV, and go to bed.

I'd go half-faint sitting next to him on the piano bench, half-faint walking back from a party on West End Avenue. Kissing and breathing him in. In constant heat. In the spring air.

We had absolutely nothing in common. I lunched with his folks, his mom and dad, at a nice restaurant. They were lovely. Classy.

I had a clanging realization of the difference in our pasts. How foreign mine was. How privileged his was, compared to mine at that time in my life, with all my baggage. Still blacklisted.

I called my friend Norma Crane. She'd gone with Burt for a while. "Norma," I asked, "is Burt someone who can be there for you?"

"No, Lee, he can't, his life is all about music."

Something in me touched down. My feet landed on the street.

Burt came back from a trip to L.A. "Lee, do you know Angie Dickinson? I really like her."

Burt married Angie. He was in the audience at the opening of *In the Heat of the Night*, my first Hollywood film after the blacklist, with her. He waved. Angie was a warm and steamy woman.

That was 1967. Around 1995, our company, Feury/Grant Entertainment, was working for Lifetime, and I was in L.A. to film Angie for *Intimate Portrait*. Angie and I had acted together in one of my last films, *Charlie Chan and the Curse of the Dragon Queen*, so we knew each other. I remember when I first arrived in L.A. to do *Peyton Place*, I went to a gritty, gangstery restaurant, and Angie was in a booth with a friend and the guys were teasing her: "Hey, Angie, let's see that million-dollar leg." Her great legs had been insured by the studio for a million dollars.

In interviewing her, she talked about the daughter she'd had with Burt. I'd met her daughter on the set of *Curse of the Dragon Queen*. She had Asperger's syndrome and was a handful for Angie. She was older than twenty at that time. Angie also talked about her sister, who was very ill and whom she visited and cared for. Angie's a mensch, and very beloved in the Hollywood community, a great friend, and still steamy.

Anyway, as part of her *Portrait*, I had to interview Burt. Burt had married twice since Angie. When Carole Bayer Sager, the wonderful songwriter, and Burt married, their honeymoon cottage was our Green House on Zumeriz Drive, the Green House that Joey had built. Carole said she was miserable in that house because Burt left her alone and stranded all the way out in Malibu. He was staying in Hollywood or Beverly Hills while Carole stared at the walls and wandered the wonderful terraces we'd built, looking out at the sea, confused and lonely for years.

Been there. Done that.

Burt, she found out, had fallen for another woman. So Carole fled the Green House forever and divorced Burt, who married for the last time, the current Mrs. Bacharach.

It was in the Beverly Hills house of this new family that I interviewed him, as Angie's last husband and father of their child.

His wife, Jane, greeted the film crew, like she'd greeted many film crews. She was blond, pleasant, busy, nice-looking; there were older kids around.

Burt was in his study, his music room, and had an appointment after us. I walked in, curious, wondering if an ember remained, but no, we looked at each other, middle-aged now, both of us. I popped my questions like a professional person; he answered warily. Both looking hard at each other and computing where we stood. There was no strong connection from our past. It was a broken pot on the floor we ignored. We never discussed his and Angie's daughter, who has since committed suicide. But it was odd to go from young, intense lovers for that one spring to basically strangers in a strong wife's home, with things to do and adolescent children to deal with.

Fade out. Fade in: May 2012.

I was lying in bed watching television, and on PBS there was a salute at the White House to the music of Burt Bacharach and Hal David. There, sitting next to President Obama, was someone supposed to be Burt Bacharach.

At the end of the program where every singer you really love sang (and those songs are a big turn-on still), Obama asked Burt to say a few words. The stranger went to the mike and transformed—in his cracked voice he was so damn charming, his smile, disarming; and then he went to the piano and started to sing: "What the world needs now, is love sweet love." I swooned—the guy's still got it. He is the music. Obsession is so attractive. Remember Lenny Bernstein, how in love we all were? He was beautiful, yes, but so are many. He, like Burt, burned for us. Talent.

So many lives we've lived. And the music and man still move me.

Elizabeth Taylor. She died. At seventy-nine. My own sense of mortality comes rushing in. I'm older than she was.

She took on AIDS singlehandedly, when it was still an extremely frightening cause. So much that the president of South Africa who followed Mandela, Thabo Mbeki, declared there was no link between AIDS and HIV, while thousands of young women, children, and men died. Elizabeth took it on when gays were closeted and her good friend Rock Hudson was outed and pilloried by the press. She fought with passion and clarity, legitimizing the plague and, in doing so, may have helped prepare us for gay marriage. I couldn't have done it. I never had her moxie.

I had two encounters with Elizabeth. Once during her marriage to John Warner, the other when I did a documentary on her for Lifetime, maybe twelve years ago.

I was invited by Lynn Redgrave to be her date at a fund-raiser for Republican senator John Warner in 1979. It was an invitation extended to her either by Elizabeth or Elizabeth's close friend, the clothing designer Halston. We had met on the street, Lynn and I.

Me: "Hi, how are you? What are you doing?"

Lynn: "Elizabeth is having an auction fund-raiser for Warner."

Me: "He's a Republican!"

Lynn: "I know, I know." Sheepish smile.

I sat between Lynn and a young plastic surgeon at a luncheon table. There were maybe 350 or 400 people in the room. Celebrity friends were auctioning off oil paintings for the Warner campaign. The paintings were mediocre, and when the bidding was low, Elizabeth would run up front and plead and exhort with all her heart. Lynn auctioned off one, and then suddenly Elizabeth called my name. To auction off a painting. For the Republican senator. I was caught off guard. To a smattering of polite applause I made my way to the front, where an awful little oil painting of two red apples and a brown teapot stood on an easel.

"Who wants to bid on this charming still life?" I started to call out, when the whole situation hit me and I started to laugh.

I couldn't stop, and the people attending did not join in. Lynn scooted down in her seat in embarrassment, and Elizabeth took over. With passion and fervor she talked of her John, what a great man he was, the important work he was doing; please, please buy this wonderful painting. Of course her friend Halston gave a thousand dollars, as he had all afternoon, and I slunk back to my chair. Later, I heard she had contributed one of the diamonds Richard Burton had given her to her new husband's campaign.

Fade out. Fade in. It was twenty years later, and Elizabeth was in New York raising money for AIDS. She was in a wheelchair. She couldn't walk.

My crew was all set up, waiting for her in a room at a ritzy hotel. We'd been waiting about four hours. She was staying in the hotel, about four floors above us. With each opening of the elevator doors, I ran out to the hall to greet her. Finally she appeared. Her face, alive and glowing with color, her body shrunken, her spine collapsing. We moved her to the apricot velvet chair the crew had lit for her.

"Do you remember the last time we were in a room together?" I asked.

"Is this a trick question?" She laughed.

As the camera rolled, I reminded Elizabeth of the auction.

"Omigod," she said, rolling her eyes.

I have this episode on film, so I will only be paraphrasing her description of her marriage to Warner.

First, she committed herself, as only she could, to being a senator's wife, no longer with a career of her own. Day after day, wandering around his estate in Virginia, or wherever, waiting, waiting for her new husband to come home. He was in the Senate working and had no time for his demanding new wife.

And so she ate. And ate. And ate.

Everyone in that period remembers pictures of Elizabeth ballooning into beyond-matronly.

This is a story she told about Warner and herself: Warner kept horses on his estate, and as an experienced horsewoman, she rode as often as she could. One morning riding with John, her horse balked and she fell. Hard. She called to John, "Help me get up."

He, still on his horse, insisted she force herself to get up without help. "You need to toughen up, not baby yourself."

She tried, but she couldn't. He again insisted she force herself to get up.

Elizabeth became a movie star at age twelve in *National Velvet*. She was thrown from her horse during filming and suffered a back injury that haunted her the rest of her life, causing numerous trips to the hospital.

"I really can't get up," she told John.

"You're not trying," he said.

She finally rose to her feet.

"You see?" he said.

The marriage was over.

I don't know how long after that Elizabeth left the Washington scene, lost the pounds, and opened in *The Little Foxes* playing the fierce Regina, directed by Austin Pendleton. Her first foray into theater. Her reviews were great.

"Brilliant," the critics said.

I say, "Brave."

She was a survivor, always.

Divine to the ridiculous, postscript: Carole Bayer Sager, who was Elizabeth's neighbor, good friend, and look-alike, by the way, told me Elizabeth never went to dinner parties without her little dog nestled in her arms. The little guy was not housebroken, a small consideration that Liz never stopped to notice. So nobody else did, either. Everyone just laughed and talked till someone surreptitiously picked up the tiny messes.

I love that image.

A Father . . . A Son . . .
Once Upon a Time
in Hollywood

I filmed a documentary on Michael and Kirk Douglas. An idea Allen Burry, Michael's close advisor, came up with. My first and last film before the blacklist, *Detective Story*, starred Kirk Douglas, who was then in his thirties, I guess. He was a big, big star. Gorgeous. Intense. Amazing. 1951.

Now Joey would produce and I would direct a film about the Douglas men, father and son. Fantastic.

We had attended Michael's very grand wedding to Catherine Zeta-Jones, at the Plaza in New York. Catherine is not only astonishingly beautiful, but swell, and real, and down-to-earth, and fun. She carried their son, three-month-old Dylan, down the aisle, and handed him off to Michael's mother, Diana, during the vows. Catherine comes from a small Welsh village. The most affecting part of the celebration was the blending of voices, the Welsh songs her many relations sang and have been singing all their lives, soaring songs not unlike in *How Green Was My Valley*. Her dad looks like Jon Hamm. Handsome.

Doing a film about a movie star friend with a complicated life and his iconic movie star father was challenging. As anyone who's read Kirk's many memoirs knows, his mother was his angel, and his father an abusive drunk who sold rags from his horse cart, had no education, and was violent with his son. When Kirk became a well-known and respected actor and movie star, he went home to upstate New York, found his father in a bar, and still could never get any acknowledgment from him that his son was successful, talented, rich. Nothing. Ever.

The rawness Kirk showed on film, the intensity and need and sexuality, he also had in life. Which made him a very complex dad to be around for Michael and his brother Joel. When they were very young, Kirk and Michael's mother, Diana, divorced. Michael and Joel wound up living with their mother on the East Coast, visiting Kirk and his new French wife, Anne, and eventually two new half brothers, Peter and Eric, in California.

The incident that stuck in Kirk's craw was *One Flew Over the Cuckoo's Nest*. Michael's first film as a producer, which was wildly popular, brilliantly acted, directed by Milos Forman, and earned Michael an Oscar as producer his first time out. Kirk had bought the book and the play of *Cuckoo's Nest* for himself. To star in and to revive his career. He acted in it on Broadway to lukewarm reviews. He turned the play over to Michael. The play was pretty much dead in the water. Michael developed the script. His partner was Saul Zaentz. He got Milos Forman on board, who cast Jack Nicholson in the part that would make Jack a big star—the part Kirk played on Broadway and was on fire to play in the film. Michael could not convince Milos to give Kirk the part. "You're the producer." Kirk banged his fist on the table. "You could have demanded I do the part." This is an old bitter fight, still alive and deep and contentious. "I gave you *Cuckoo's Nest*, I gave it to you to produce a movie for me." Kirk thumped his chest, still a contender. And so the two men, both of them producers and actors, have this deep-seated raw wound between them still. They are open about it in the documentary, never covering up their differences or their anger, but not crossing the line.

During the making of the documentary, the week we were to film Eric Douglas, who had been in drug rehab, he died of an overdose. Kirk and Anne were devastated. They'd been living in fear of this since Eric was an adolescent.

Eric was a story in himself, always struggling for recognition, needy, hungering for attention and for the stardom of his father and brother. So Michael's son Cameron was not the first in the family to struggle with the need for life-altering substances. Cameron had an easy reality in front of the camera. He was an in-demand disc jockey, well-paid and popular, and charming. He's now serving time in prison on a drug charge. Cameron and Michael are deeply connected as father and son.

Kirk losing his youngest son, Eric, to drugs; Michael bearing the burden of his oldest son, Cameron, imprisoned for selling drugs. A heavy bond between them. Kirk forever contentious, passionate, competitive; Michael forever cautious, with a demanding father, both striving to expand their lives through their art, Kirk discovering and rediscovering himself through writing his books, Michael taking chances as an actor, building his own legendary career.

Baghdad ER

Suddenly, Sheila Nevins asked Joey to produce a documentary directed by Jon Alpert and Matt O'Neill. I was kicked upstairs to executive producer.

It was called *Baghdad ER*, an unsparing, groundbreaking exploration of the 86th Combat Support Hospital in Iraq. Jon and Matt filmed American servicemen and Iraqi men who had been devastatingly wounded, from the point of impact, by bomb or bullet, through the attempts our medics made to save these young men. The heroes included Jon Alpert and Matt O'Neill, who placed themselves alongside the doctors and the medics in the helicopters that transported the wounded to hospitals in Germany and the States and stationed themselves in the emergency rooms at the operating tables.

Sheila asked me to take on one role.

One of the soldiers Matt and Jon filmed breathed his last breath surrounded by three fellow Marines from his company and a loving young priest. Sheila asked Matt and me to travel to Poughkeepsie, where the soldier's parents still lived in a small house. The mother had been an operating room nurse. Matt and I were to tell her we had footage of her son when he was wounded, during the operation, and of his last breath in the company of the priest.

She and her husband said they wanted to view the film and make up their minds about its inclusion in the documentary.

Sheila was at her best. As a mother herself, she was totally sensitive to this woman.

The parents, Sheila, Matt, and I watched the footage together at a screening room at HBO.

It was too damn real. They said, "Yes, put it in the film."

I am a Chekhov person. The human condition is what I know, the surprises, the pain, the small sweetnesses, an occasional triumph.

A "stranger in my own time" was Thomas Benton Reed's quote as he watched the first plane fly in the air. I was a stranger in my own time in that film. Matt and Jon could take the assault of blood and bone, horror, helplessness, but that's not a world I have the heart or bravery to enter. Patrick McMahon was the editor of the film. He edited out the unwatchable. But he watched the unwatchable before he edited it. The burden he carried watching hour after hour of carnage five days a week, for months, wore on him. The documentary was screened at the Pentagon and went on to win four Emmys. What is it Conrad wrote? The horror, the horror.

Children of
the Blacklist

An odd postscript to the blacklist period.

I'd cut out an item from *Daily Variety* on December 20, 2011. **WGA ADDS BLACKLISTED SCRIBE TO *ROMAN HOLIDAY*.** Translation: Blacklisted writer Dalton Trumbo was given credit for cowriting a hit movie script sixty years after the fact. The item mentions that this credit was accomplished due to the efforts of Dalton's son, Chris Trumbo.

Chris was a very beautiful young man, who died two years ago in Ojai, California, after bringing a play using his father's letters to him as a boy to the off-Broadway scene. Very successfully. Chris made his father a big hit after Dalton's too-early death, and as is mentioned in *Variety*, he sought and achieved acknowledgment of Dalton's credits. Six of the films that never carried Dalton's name, including *He Ran All the Way* and *The Brave One*, titles strangely appropriate to a blacklisted writer's life and history.

The Writers Guild, the article said, had revised writers' credits on ninety-five films, which says something about artists' fights for survival, producers getting great writers cheaply, but having their hearts in the right place, too.

Also credited with writing *Roman Holiday* was Ian McLellan Hunter.

Ian's son, Tim, and Dalton's son, Chris, met when their families fled to Mexico in the fifties. They were children who bonded over the persecution of their fathers, became fast friends, and took it as their mission to redeem their fathers' work, worth, and reputation.

All of those children had their lives blasted, in a way. Still fighting their fathers', and some mothers', wars.

There were war wounds for families like ours, boys who were raised to be silent about their parents' politics outside the 444 Central Park West fortress. Tommy retreated inside to his music for relief and consolation.

We were all damaged. We were pariahs in our land for more than a decade, a lifetime for children.

So, last night I was working on this piece and watching *Jeopardy!*, Monday, January 2, 2012. I asked Roberta, my friend, to find the *Variety* item on Dalton. As she was looking for it, the last question was asked by Alex Trebek.

"What writer refused to answer questions in front of HUAC, was accused of being Communist, and wrote an antiwar book?"

Of course none of the contestants knew it was Dalton Trumbo. Alex intoned in his deep voice, "Dalton Trumbo, and the book was *Johnny Got His Gun*." Spooky, huh?

I think I may have been the only blacklisted actor to climb back up to the position I'd had when I'd started out and become even more visible on television and film, if not in theater. Just young enough to absorb those twelve years and start over. But my stepsons, Tommy and Mikey, were affected.

When I walked out that apartment door, for the boys it was abandonment. Their father fell into their protective arms, apoplectic and purple with a rage I'd never seen before, inchoate, weak-kneed with the rage I'd always felt afraid I'd see if I said or did the wrong thing.

Three years later, they lost their father. Ten years later, their mother, Margie, died when influenza hit New York one summer. Meanwhile, I was sailing into the blue seas of L.A., walking on red carpets, visible to anyone who had a TV or went to a movie. The only blacklisted woman to shoot to the sky with a big, visible career. That's suspicious. Arnie must have shown the boys the telegram he sent me accusing me of naming him to get work.

I went to New York from California and stayed in a hotel on Central Park South. Tommy came into the room with great urgency. He couldn't have been more than eighteen or nineteen. I don't remember the words, but the gist of the warning was that Dinah was doomed to mental illness: he and Mikey were being given medication for depression, Daddy's sisters were affected, one permanently in an institution, and Tommy warned me that Dinah had inherited the same genes, future diagnosis, and dysfunction. He was insistent; I was resistant and protective of my small daughter, who was being handed a legacy of mental illness. I pushed Tommy out of the hotel room.

"Not one more word," I said. "No."

"But I'm telling you for her own good."

"No, no, no, Dinah is fine! Dinah will always be fine forever!" I shouted.

The alternative was unacceptable. But there was a divide between Tommy and me. He was a threat. I felt there was an almost vampirish pleasure, an excitement in Tommy pulling Dinah over to the Manoff dark side.

Tommy, in 2000, accused me of naming his father so I could work again. Walter Bernstein, Arnie's best friend, telephoned me. We met at the diner at 90th and Broadway. He wanted to warn me that Tommy had been in touch with him and was intent on exposing me.

One of my employers was sent several e-mails from Tommy threatening to expose me. He was a music critic on NPR, and warned that he had the means to tell on-air what I'd done.

I waited for the accusations to come. Both Dinah and Walter felt it would be fuel on the fire for me to confront Tommy. "Don't take the bait," they said. My chest burned with resentment, with things unsaid, with how-could-yous.

A week passed, a month, a year went by, the threat dissolved, went out of my consciousness altogether.

Mikey, at that time, lived a quiet life with his wife, both librarians in a Southern college town.

On February 3, 2012, Dinah called, very late. Mikey Manoff had killed himself. Put a bullet through his troubled head.

He'd tried downing pills three weeks before, but his wife, Mary, had rushed him to the hospital and his stomach was pumped.

From the time he'd hit adolescence, Mikey was battling demons. Tommy had rage; Mikey had anger, confusion, and desperation. He had been a needy sweet baby at four when Arnie had us all spend our first afternoon together on Riverside Drive near the docks overlooking the water.

Tommy furiously rode his tricycle, ignoring me. Mikey climbed in my lap, me sitting cross-legged on the sweet grass, overlooking the Hudson, pointing out the boats to him. His hard, tiny boy's body fit right in my lap. I was nineteen years older than Mikey, eighteen years older than Tommy. Fourteen years older than Eva, Arnie's daughter from his second marriage, to Ruthie.

After we married, Arnie and I raised the boys. They were the lure, a family of my own. No longer the lengthened childhood in my parents' home. I was instant head of my own home. Instant mother, cook, and dishwasher. A new and fascinating world to enter. With one big man, the Director-slash-Teacher-slash-Husband, and two little men who really needed me, as a mom, and their new maid, and housekeeper, learning how to live in this new life as it quickly replaced my old one and blocked it out.

When it came time to tell eight-year-old boys how babies were made, I couldn't sidestep or avoid the subject any longer. I remembered my disgust with the Mae West and Hitler cartoon I'd found at their age, and my horror at my parents for doing exactly the same thing to each other. Tommy and Mikey, on the other hand, fell off the bed laughing, each one surfacing to gasp, "The penis goes in the vagina . . ." It started to sound pretty ridiculous to me, too. One night when Mikey got up to pee, half-asleep, he whispered, "A girl in my class has two baginas."

In Lake Mohegan they went to day camp with the Kaplan kids, the Salt kids: "This land is your land, this land is my land."

We all went to Mikey's wedding in 1982, in the South somewhere. Tommy. Dinah. Eva and me. It was our first time all together since I'd left. Tommy showed up for the wedding, stout, bearded, overwhelming. He was a man I really didn't recognize.

Mikey, now in his forties, and Mary, both librarians, and deeply, sweetly in love. They spun a web around themselves. Mikey was fragile; with Mary he was secure and safe. She was everything to him, everything that had been taken away and more.

When I spoke to Mary there were no tears, no sadness in her voice. He is her private Mikey.

One day she will take his ashes to her brothers' farm in upstate New York. Her father's ashes are buried there. "I'll go with you if you want," I told her. There was a silence. She didn't want to hurt my feelings.

I hadn't seen Mikey since the wedding twenty years ago, and we'd stopped calling each other.

I have a right to my memories of Mikey, that's all.

They had been so close as children, inseparable. Tommy and Mikey.

Then so was I, close to them as children, I was their mother in another life.

As a grown man, Mikey's neediness overwhelmed me. And Tommy's accusations and threats frightened and alienated me. He was Margie's boy. Her son.

Yes, the demons still abound, affecting our children, who are still protecting their parents, still fighting for their lives and reputations.

So, as Chris Trumbo fought to keep his father, Dalton, alive, so in his own way was Tommy Manoff, in focusing on me, in threatening to expose me, protecting Arnie forever.

The Night of Apology

It started out as a great night in October 1997. All of the unions and guilds gathered for a Night of Apology, televised for all of America to see. AFTRA joined with the Directors Guild, the Screen Actors Guild, and the Writers Guild in a groundbreaking and stunning revelation. The union heads offered deep apologies for the actions of their predecessors who led the unions in the fifties. For not protecting their actors, writers, and directors, and in AFTRA's case, for actively blacklisting members themselves.

Well-known actors David Hyde Pierce, Kevin Spacey, John Lithgow, Alfre Woodard, and Kathy Baker read statements of testimony made by the blacklisted who stood up to McCarthy and the Un-American Activities Committee while fighting for their careers in the fifties.

Three of the honorees in attendance were Marsha Hunt, Ring Lardner Jr., and Paul Jarrico.

Billy Crystal spoke the words of Larry Parks, who was the very first Hollywood actor called to testify in front of the House Un-American Activities Committee.

Larry was a big musical comedy star in Hollywood in the 1950s when musical comedy was huge—Fred Astaire, Gene Kelly, Judy Garland. They asked him to name his friends in the Party. Larry Parks answered:

I will answer any question that you would like to put to me about myself. I would prefer, if you will allow me, not to mention other people's names. . . . The people at that time as I knew them—this is my opinion of them. This is my honest opinion: That these are people who did nothing wrong, people like myself. . . . And it seems to me that this is not the American way of doing things to force a man who is under oath and who has opened himself as wide as possible to this committee—and it hasn't been easy to do this—to force a man to do this is not American justice.

The studio threatened him. He caved in and gave the committee his friends' names. One of them was Joe Bromberg. Larry Parks's career was over.

His studio, Columbia Pictures, dropped him.

I met him and his wife, Betty Garrett, at somebody's house in L.A. His eyes, when they met mine, were so full of pain as we shook hands that I yearned to comfort him. I still do.

Larry died of a heart attack in 1975 at sixty.

Arnie's heart failed at fifty.

Joe Bromberg had a heart attack at forty-seven in London in 1951.

In 1952 Canada Lee, the esteemed black actor, suffered a heart attack just before his appearance in front of the committee. He was forty-five.

Phil Loeb, at sixty-four, committed suicide in a midtown hotel after being fired from his hit TV show *The Goldbergs*.

Don Hollenbeck, newscaster with Edward R. Murrow, succumbed to gas fumes at forty-nine in 1954.

John Garfield had his fatal heart attack at thirty-nine, in 1952.

I wish all of them had lived long enough to attend the Night of Apology. Paul Jarrico was eighty-two that night. He, Ring Lardner Jr., and Marsha Hunt, all in their eighties, received a standing ovation as survivors of the witch hunt and heroes to their peers. After the ceremony, while driving home in his car on the Pacific Coast Highway, Paul Jarrico hit a tree head-on and died that same night, October 28, 1997.

NEWS

Writer Dies After Long-Awaited Triumph

———

October 30, 1997 | Patrick Goldstein and Fred Alvarez, Special to the Times
For Paul Jarrico, Monday night was the culmination of a five-decade crusade to gain justice for screenwriters like himself who were blacklisted during Hollywood's "Red Scare" era.

On both sides, the children of the blacklist still mourn.

. . .

I write not anticipating what I'll say. Sandy Meisner said, "Don't anticipate, surprise yourself."

I've just reread for the first time what I wrote about the documentaries I made with Kirk Douglas, with Sidney Poitier, with Mia. I realized that I had gone back to my first movie, *Detective Story* with Kirk, my first television hit after the Blacklist, *Peyton Place* with Mia, and my first post-blacklist film, *In the Heat of the Night* with Sidney Poitier. Back to the beginning.

I seem to have gone back to the good places, to the people who made an imprint, in a new way, starting out, and making a comeback. When I make a doc, I tell their story, not mine.

When I began acting, when I was sixteen, I found my family. I was safe. Safe to do the most dangerous things. My dream was never to be famous, a star; I don't think any real actor's dream is. My dream was to be in a repertory company for life, like the Group Theatre, and play different parts, week after week, grow with friends I loved and admired growing with me. Play the small part one week, the lead the next.

I realize that I morphed that dream and accomplished it, actually, when I began making documentaries. I created a family to make films, or Joey did; the films worked or didn't, but the repertory family moved on to the next project. And the next, and the next.

Not so different from moving our friends and family to Italy or to Spain or to Hollywood. Joining or creating new family and hanging on to the old. Look at the Actors Studio, grown out of the Group Theatre. I've felt lucky always, but not been able to put my finger on why. Now I know.

Queen of Denial

When it comes to end-of-life experiences, or serious, debilitating illness, or plain old facing the end, or death, if you must, I am the queen of denial.

The ashes of my mother-in-law Rachel, who was such a strong friend and who was with Fremo when Fremo died, are on the shelf above the TV she watched all the time, in the sunroom. Next to her are the ashes of Dude, our last dog.

Belinda and Phyllis went to the hospice on Rachel's last day to kiss her and say good-bye. Phyllis said, "Go, Ma, we're all right." Rachel went before the door closed. She had told her children, Joey, Phyllis, and younger son Ralph, that she wanted her ashes spread on 6th and Lincoln, the street in front of her home, where she had raised her children.

Lincoln Street is a heavily trafficked street. We'd feel as if we were throwing Rachel under the wheels of a speeding car. So we Scotch-taped a picture of Rachel on the gold-colored can containing her ashes and put it high on the shelf over the flat-screen TV. It feels comfortable.

· · ·

When my father died, his ashes were given to me by the people who burned him up, set his body on fire. He had raised the issue—"Take my ashes to Israel"—when he briefly visited us here in New York.

"And if I don't go to Israel?"

"Pour my ashes over your mother's grave."

I took a cab to Mount Hebron Cemetery in Flushing, New York— it was a cold autumn day. I was led to and left at my mothers' family gravesite. There they were. Grandma, Mother, Fremo.

Big, tall, gray stone markers loomed over them, close together in the crowded cemetery. I tried to make it real that these crucial women in my life were under there. Bones, yes. I give you the bones crumbling in boxes. But the spirits of my women were not in the cold Mount Hebron earth. I placed the respectful stones on top of the markers. To say *I was here. I visited you.* The endless whoosh and dust of the traffic on the highway was distracting. Tires, brakes, engines. This was not a quiet resting place. I carried the vessel of my father's ashes. The remains of Abraham Rosenthal. Dad. The wind whipped. I looked at the highway. I couldn't allow bits of my dad to be carried by the wind to the endless, zooming, anonymous, loud cars, under the wheels, ground into the road. No.

The grass in front of my mother's gravestone had all but gone. The soil was hard blackish-brown. I tried to dig with my hands, then with a brush handle from my bag. I asked a cemetery man for a spade, but though I tried and tried, I couldn't bury the vessel deep enough to be absolutely safe. The soil was unyielding, frozen. I had told the cemetery man it was a plant I was putting there. I didn't know if the whole vessel was allowed. It was Mount Hebron; the last thing I wanted was a confrontation with cemetery Jews and their rules. This was a mean, cold corner for my family to come to rest in. Their choice of burial, not mine. What would mine have been? *You're not going to die. Don't even think about it!*

How could I watch them die, when they depended on me, with my magical power, to save them? How could I let them down, when they would have given their lives for me? Their crazy, quixotic, amazing, beautiful, beautiful lives. For me.

I am so filled with longing and regret, my throat closes, constricted, eyes wet as I write, everything a blur. I want them back, laughing around the dining room table, whispering in the living room.

I do spend time thinking about the best, most palatable place for my ashes to rest, or be sprinkled, or hidden (Central Park, mixed with Joey's, on Dinah's property, not mixed with water, etc.).

The work is gone now. In this overly competitive world, everyone's next-door neighbor is making documentaries, or documenting themselves online. And the truth is, I'm relieved. Now "We Are the World" has opened up the consciousness of the musical and theatrical communities. There are good activists everywhere, and the issues in these years are too horrendous to contemplate. I'm not opening that door.

And so our family lives each juicy day, by day, by day. Phyllis, my sister-in-law, has been a minor character in these pages, but she's a major character in my life. She is a constant, by my side in the house and in the emergency room. Her Italian name is Philomena Rose Fioretti, my grandchildren call her Zia, Italian for "aunt," and she is the heart of our house. Quirky like Fremo, passionate like her twin brother, Joey. Strong and fragile, too. We both wanted a sister and have each other, working through our heightened nerves and tempers over the years together. She shops every day in the markets and makes beautiful food every night. Drowning out fear with food and friends.

In these last two years, Joey, now seventy-four, wakes up and takes my hand. He doesn't want to lose me. I worry about his hip. We both run from the inevitable. We're so, well, alive, we're so young, we are both so young, and Joey, since he was a boy, practically when we met, has always had a mythical view of my talents, not unlike my mother. The more we run, the more puzzling and mystifying the reality. How can we die?

I miss my friends. I have a shelf on my bookcase where I keep pictures of all my dead friends. Gladys and Waldo in a frame together on top, that she drew on in pen, with their faces growing like flowers. Bob Altman, Spalding Gray, Bruce Paltrow, Larry Hauben, Nick Dante. Pictures of my living family and living friends surround them. I won't let them die.

A year and a half ago I adopted two black kittens. I named them Fremo and Gladys. They were born in a cellar, permanently spooked by everything. But I get to say their names all day.

Russian Easter Egg

And here I am on the Upper West Side again, living in an apartment as beautiful as a Russian Easter egg, surrounded by the things my mother bought at auction when I was growing up on the Drive, with Fremo's painting on one wall, the markets and shops on Broadway beckoning, and especially the people, the parade I join daily, melting into the stream. A sea of baby strollers and old people with walkers and electric wheelchairs and schoolchildren, protected as I never needed to be, the beautiful men and women, white, Asian, black, with their strong gym bodies, creating a parade of life as I walk down to Zabar's and back. I look down the wide streets. There are no children sitting on the steps, playing in the streets, not anymore. Not like 148th Street.

The daughter Joey and I adopted from Thailand, Belinda, and her husband, Jay Jones, have two girls, Rachel, eleven, and Leah (named for me), eight, half African American, half Thai. They live in New Jersey.

Dinah left Hollywood with her husband, Arthur Mortell, and three sons—twins, Oliver and Desi, nine, and sixteen-year-old Dashiell. They live happily ever after on Bainbridge Island, Washington. When I need advice, Dinah is my go-to girl.

Dinah flew here to New York City from Bainbridge Island this past Christmas, Dinah's family and Belinda's camping out on our living room floor. Sunday morning, I woke and padded to the kitchen in my white cotton nightgown. It was eleven a.m.; Dinah was to leave for the airport at two p.m. For two hours we talked in the kitchen. The heart of our house, the kitchen. We nodded across the generations, across the years. Belinda, Dinah, and me, with the grand-girls and -boys in and out. And the sweet sound of nine-year-old Desi playing his violin floated in. Phyllis making prosciutto sandwiches for Belinda, Dinah picking up lox and cream cheese on bagels from Murray's deli around the corner on Broadway for the plane ride home. Busy—leaving.

We sat across the dining room table—looked at each other, the tomato and me.

"Joey," I said, "look what we did!"

The family we created surrounded us.

Joey and me.

Acknowledgments

First, to Roberta Morris Purdee, for her calm smarts and her ability to translate and arrange my handwritten ink-stained pages into this book, for producing me.

Then my heart doctors, the great Dr. Marianne Legato and Dr. Schneller, also Dr. Livoti, Laurie Hurt for many years of Pilates and good gossip, and Dr. Slatken, for saving my eyesight just in time.

To Letty Pogrebin, for giving me her agents, David Kuhn and Becky Sweren, who led me to Penguin's wonderful David Rosenthal and Sarah Hochman.

—and to all my girlfriends, who will be in the next book; also Julian Schlossberg, David Bruson, and Dinah Manoff Mortell, for their painstaking editing, and Walter Bernstein, for his wise encouragement.

And last—to Jimmy Breslin, who said, "Just write it!"

Index

Note: "LG" refers to Lee Grant.

Photo Credits